D0334894

MY CHEQUERED CAREER

STEVE RIDER

© Steve Rider 2012

All rights reserved. No part of this publication may be reproduced, stored in a retrieval system or transmitted, in any form or by any means, electronic, mechanical, photocopying, recording or otherwise, without prior permission in writing from the publisher.

Published in October 2012

A catalogue record for this book is available from the British Library

ISBN 978 0 85733 273 8

Library of Congress control card no 2012938594

Published by Haynes Publishing,
Sparkford, Yeovil, Somerset BA22 7JJ, UK
Tel: 01963 442030 Fax: 01963 440001
Int. tel: +44 1963 442030 Int. fax: +44 1963 440001
E-mail: sales@haynes.co.uk
Website: www.haynes.co.uk

Haynes North America Inc.,
861 Lawrence Drive, Newbury Park, California 91320, USA

Designed and typeset by Dominic Stickland

Printed and bound in the USA by Odcombe Press LP,
1299 Bridgestone Parkway, La Vergne, TN 37086

Jacket illustrations
Front: Brazilian Grand Prix, 2006. (Sutton Motorsport Images)
Back: Australian Grand Prix, 2008, with Lewis Hamilton. (Getty Images)

MY CHEQUERED CAREER

STEVE RIDER

THIRTY-FIVE YEARS
OF TELEVISING
MOTORSPORT

FOREWORD BY
DES LYNAM OBE

Haynes Publishing

CONTENTS

FOREWORD

BY DES LYNAM OBE

'Right Des. I'm getting bored with this procession, link over to the cricket.' It was the editor's voice in my earpiece half an hour into a Sunday *Grandstand* programme.

'Are you serious?' I said.

'Oh yes, this is supposed to be a programme dealing with all the afternoon's sport, not just the Grand Prix,' he replied.

And so I found myself saying, 'Well, for the moment we're leaving the French Grand Prix and it's over to our commentators at Buxton for the John Player match between Derbyshire and Gloucestershire.' I could feel the viewers' venom coming back down the camera lens.

Those days didn't last too long and eventually Grand Prix motor racing was given its due status on BBC television and later ITV before reverting to the Beeb.

For me the best presenter of the sport for either channel was Steve Rider – a consummate professional whatever sport he introduced but Grand Prix motor racing was his first love. His knowledge was extensive but he never fell into the mistake of sounding like a petrolhead. As an occasional viewer of the sport, nowadays I rarely know what they are talking about, whether it's KERS or tyre compounds. Steve, as always, had the viewer in mind and kept it understandable.

In truth, when we both worked for BBC television there were a couple of things about him that annoyed me: he never made a mistake and he had world-class hair. Now I've joined the envy club again because Steve has produced this superb book, which goes inside the worlds of Grand Prix motor racing and television and is written with considerable knowledge and flair. It's a great read.

Oh, and by the way, the hair still annoys me.

Leabharlanna Poiblí Chathair Bhaile Átha Cliath
Dublin City Public Libraries

Introduction

The last thing I want to do is come across as cocky, but I don't think there will ever again be a sports presenter quite like me. It has nothing to do with ability; in an era of Lynam and Coleman I was firmly back in the pack. Instead it has everything to do with opportunity. I cannot imagine that in this age of multiple broadcast outlets and fragmented rights any presenter will have the chance to work on the range of major sport that I was lucky enough to be offered.

The key was the BBC *Grandstand* chair. With your backside parked in that, especially through the '80s and '90s, the treasures of the sporting world were paraded in front of you. How deeply you got involved would be entirely up to you. For me it unlocked a strong involvement in golf and rugby and helped to take me to 12 Olympic Games; the BBC, and in particular *Grandstand*, had also become the established home of Formula One at that time.

In 1992 I was on the road throughout the summer, presenting Wimbledon in place of an absent Des Lynam, then down to Silverstone for the grand prix, after which I was straight up to Birkdale for the Open before flying to Barcelona for the Olympics and a linking position above the finish line as Linford Christie won the 100 metres. As has been said so many times… the best job in the world.

It did have its drawbacks, however. When I had lunch with a publisher who was keen to do some sort of autobiographical book, he reached the conclusion that with my small involvement across such a vast array of events and occasions he would not know where to place the book and which section of the sporting audience to target. That got me thinking of which sport had given me the greatest depth of involvement and excitement. The answer, clearly, was motorsport.

Hence this attempt to compile everything that I have seen happen in motorsport over the course of the past 35 years, especially from the perspective of the growing influence of television. Sometimes I have been at the fringe of things, sometimes right at the heart, but motorsport provides such a rich mix of competition, personality and politics that it is impossible to emerge unaffected by everything that has been experienced.

Since the mid-'70s I had been in a unique position to see a sport completely transform itself, especially at the highest level. I had seen grand prix motor racing move out of those dark and dangerous years when drivers took to the track with the same courage and life expectancy as Battle of Britain pilots. I had also seen television as a fundamental part of this transformation.

You would have expected Formula One, at the cutting edge of technology, to embrace television more enthusiastically than any other sport; but it took a while. When I became involved a lot of the coverage was still on film, live coverage was far from guaranteed and there was no such thing as a contest for rights. Even into the late '80s and early '90s, Formula One was one of the last categories of motorsport to embrace on-board camera technology, or even see the need for it.

What a contrast with 2012, where we have two broadcasting giants going head-to-head with Formula One coverage and the viewer is spoiled with a wide choice of viewing platforms and viewing options, including dedicated camera angles and rolling race data, and all of this after ten years in which the rights had become eagerly sought but overvalued by both ITV and BBC. I was in a position to experience all the good and bad things that were happening in this period, greeting three British World Champions, losing the rights twice, standing in the Monza pits with Lotus when Ronnie Peterson was fatally injured, and standing on the Imola pit wall for *Grandstand* when Ayrton Senna lost his life.

Aside from Formula One and television presenting, I found myself as a fixer and fundraiser as the British Touring Car Championship struggled to establish itself on the TV stage. However, my efforts were less productive on behalf of rallying, both from the producer's chair and the co-driver's seat, and there were also the regular invitations to stick on a black tie and act as host at some of the sport's more significant celebrations and announcements.

Golf takes place on a golf course and rugby players take chunks out of each other on a rugby pitch, but motorsport operates on many different levels and in many different environments – and I got the invitation to be involved in the full catalogue of events and activity. If you form the impression that I have emerged as not totally obsessed with the great god of Formula One, I would not disagree. It is the pinnacle of the sport, and always will be, but I have been able to see it in the context of all the endeavour and sacrifices made further down the motorsport pyramid.

I have also been able to view it in the context of other sport, and although my publisher is delighted to aim this book at the motorsport market, you will forgive, I am sure, the occasional reference to what was happening in the rest of the sporting world, and also what was happening in the rest of my career in televised sport.

I have had enormous fun and am more than happy to step aside for the next generation of more talented and more energetic presenters who will set about feeding the monster that has been created in this astonishing age of television technology. In the meantime I will have gone from the *Grandstand* chair to the rocking chair, and a role on behalf of Sky, sitting back and reminiscing at length with the greatest drivers in history, reliving the astonishing stories and achievements of the post-war years.

It has been a privilege to be a spectator behind the scenes for at least part of that and I hope you enjoy my small insight into some of the events as they happened – or at least, as I remember them.

Chapter 1

THE END AND THE BEGINNING

The moment had been a long time coming for ITV Sport, and arguably when it finally arrived they didn't deserve it. Football had long since engulfed the schedules and ITV's prestigious Formula One contract, with close on three years left to run, had been sold off to pay for the Champions League rights.

Now, in 2008, as the first raindrops of a São Paulo downpour started to hit the Brazilian Grand Prix paddock, we had entered the last lap of the last race of the last season. For one final time Mark Blundell, myself and the rest of the ITV crew checked batteries and talkback communication, and prepared for whatever lay in store once the last chequered flag had fallen. We were preparing seemingly to give the last rites to ITV's Formula One commitment and not for the exultant celebration of a Lewis Hamilton world title.

There had been no shortage of commitment from the production team. Over the previous 12 years they had set the template for a new, dynamic approach to the broadcasting of the sport, and in Martin Brundle they had developed an analyst of great authority. They had struggled through the Schumacher-dominated years, and now it was obvious that Hamilton and other supremely talented young drivers were poised to take the sport to a new competitive level.

The ITV accountants certainly didn't see it that way. Just as they had done with the ITV golf commitment 25 years earlier, they were panicked into allowing the BBC to expertly reap the rewards that came with a sport ready to deliver a big new audience.

It all left the broadcast team bemused rather than bitter, but my mood certainly wasn't helped by having to take shelter under the awning of the Ferrari engineers' cabin as the downpour got heavier. Inside, the attention had moved from the computer screens to the television monitors.

The Ferrari of Felipe Massa was approaching the last corner with victory assured. Inside the garage his tearful father was already receiving congratulations on behalf of his son, who was seconds away from becoming World Champion. The engineers had also started their celebrations, and they were happy to aim their singing and finger-pointing at the hapless British TV crew glumly hunched around their small mobile monitor.

It was Martin Brundle who spotted it first, swiftly confirmed by James Allen in what was a career-defining final moment for an outstanding commentator. In the increasingly heavy rain, Timo Glock had gambled on completing the race on slick tyres and was struggling for any kind of grip on the soaking-wet track. Now Hamilton was bearing down on the Toyota and the fifth place that would give the British driver the title. In an error-strewn drive it was a fifth place that we had long since given up on, but now it seemed that a miracle was unfolding.

Mark Blundell grabbed the monitor that was mounted on a pole and waved it at the uncomprehending Italians, jabbing his finger at the screen. Hamilton went past Glock: the Italian celebration didn't stop, but ours had now begun. Other broadcasters were still applauding Massa, but we were convinced that the new World Champion was British, and now the celebrations had also begun among the disbelieving McLaren ranks. It was left to Mark Blundell to quell the Ferrari euphoria by explaining the World Championship outcome in his most succinct Essex-Italian.

The last corner of the last lap of the last race of the last season. Astonishing. My frustration was replaced by a sense of completion, and a story that now had a beginning, a middle and an end. We could sign off with no unfinished business, and the

BBC could move the coverage on to their new ultra-professional level. That night in São Paulo a new era had dawned although, it has to be said, no one was predicting Jenson Button as the next World Champion.

For me, though, this was enough, and I was more preoccupied with the era I had just passed through instead of the one that lay ahead. With the help of a press pass and a microphone, I had been given a front-row seat to observe the talents of Ayrton Senna and Nigel Mansell, the eccentricities of Bernie Ecclestone, and the inspirational qualities of Colin Chapman and Frank Williams. There had been the diversions to admire the genuine driving talent in the World Rally Championship and the box office appeal of Touring Cars. Along with all that there had been the glamour and egos encountered in hosting Formula One new car launches and 22 years of presenting the annual Autosport Awards.

The last corner of the last lap of the last race of the last season. It seemed to encapsulate the pantomime qualities of Formula One and the madness of motorsport. The last corner of my first season with ITV had also emphasised these qualities.

The scene was Foxhall Heath in Ipswich, and the climax of the British Caravan and Camping Trailer Destruction Grand Prix (its absence still leaves a large hole in the motorsport calendar). The leading Ford Cortina had rolled in front of me and had settled on its roof. The driver hung from his straps awaiting the arrival of the marshals. His obligatory caravan had long since been dislodged but he still had a chemical toilet hanging from his towing hook.

I was the first to arrive at this dramatic scene. 'Hold that position for a minute,' I yelled, 'and then you'll be live on *World of Sport*.'

'Right you are,' he replied nonchalantly in a Norfolk accent, seemingly oblivious to the steaming liquid dripping from under the dashboard and on to his chin.

'Tell me if that radiator fluid is a problem, but it really is a great shot,' I said, waiting for the crew. 'No problem,' he replied cheerily, 'it's battery acid.'

At its absolute grass roots motorsport is full of enthusiastic, good-natured amateurs living the sort of dreams that will always be distant. But point a television camera in their direction and it all becomes a kind of bonfire of vanities in which realism is forgotten. Television equals exposure, which equals sponsorship, which equals the opportunity to pump up the budget, extend the motorhome and start dreaming of Monaco. Television equals politics, marketing opportunities, global audience figures and 'broadcasting rights at any price'. The camera pointing in the window of that Ford Cortina had a long lens that would eventually take in Senna, Mansell and Hamilton, and the very different kind of madness of Formula One; and at times it would all be just as silly as that afternoon by the cinder track in Ipswich.

Chapter 2

ANDRETTI, PETERSON, CHAPMAN AND LOTUS

M otorsport was not part of my expertise, interest or experience when I left school in 1968 to join my local newspaper in south-east London. In my role as a junior sports reporter I was aware of a correspondent who sent us occasional, baffling accounts of events at Brands Hatch, but I had never actually been to a race meeting myself. You could hear the distant drone of racing engines at Crystal Palace from the back garden of our family home in Bromley, but on the local paper we were too preoccupied with events at Millwall and Charlton Athletic to concern ourselves with such a lofty and seemingly sophisticated world. How wrong I was, and what excitement I must have missed. I would learn later that the distant sound was quite possibly Jackie Stewart, Jack Brabham and maybe Graham Hill challenging Bruce McLaren.

Modern grand prix motor racing is a world of privileged access, stifling security and multi-million-pound television rights, not to mention sky-high ticket prices. But 30 years ago it was a very different environment – not quite the people's sport, but certainly, as we slowly found out, more welcoming to the casual observer.

In the mid-'70s I was sports editor to the newly launched London Broadcasting Company, LBC, home to every wannabe radio journalist around. Some were talented – like Jon Snow and Peter Allen – and setting out on great careers, but others, desperate for any kind of experience in the glamorous, growing world of broadcasting, were merely persistent and irritating.

Among the last category was a young South African who, on this particular Saturday morning, planted himself on the sports desk with his newly purchased tape recorder and insisted that we could send him anywhere and he would deliver a decent story. Smugly we dispatched him to the British Grand Prix. At 9:00am he was still poring over a road atlas trying to work out where Silverstone was. We were confident that we had got rid of him for the day, maybe forever, but at 1:00pm the phone in the studio rang. Not only had he got to the circuit, he had blagged himself a pass, got into the press centre, found a phone and was now alongside a nice Mr Fittipaldi who had happily agreed to be interviewed live on air.

Even in the early '80s, working with an Anglia Television news crew, we were able to head off to the British Grand Prix, or any other major motor race, and pick our spot around the circuit. Our favourite places were the Bomb Hole at Snetterton and the outside of the then high-speed Woodcote chicane at Silverstone. I can still remember the violent machine-gun snapping sound of the catch-fencing supports as Alan Jones and Andrea de Cesaris crashed heavily at Woodcote just a few feet in front of our camera position. This was the kind of access that these days would be denied by health and safety, let alone by the impenetrable accreditation requirements of Bernie Ecclestone.

But at this time the sport still had glamour and mystique in abundance. James Hunt had taken the Formula One World Championship of 1976 in *Boy's Own Paper* style, holding off the heroic challenge of a dreadfully injured Niki Lauda. It all followed the era of Jim Clark, Jackie Stewart and Graham Hill, any of whom could have sparked my enthusiasm for the sport. But instead it was a charismatic designer and team owner who captured my imagination and turned me from a detached broadcaster into a fan.

Colin Chapman was the great innovator of modern motorsport, the pioneer of the monocoque chassis and ground-effect aerodynamics, none of which was particularly impressive to a television reporter who didn't know a turbo from a wind tunnel. But Chapman was the man whose Lotus cars would eventually win seven Constructors' and six Drivers' World Championship titles. He had also formed an inspirational relationship with Jim Clark in the '60s and now, in 1978, he was clearly doing the same with the American superstar Mario Andretti.

Lotus Cars was based at Hethel, near Norwich, and the Formula One team was housed in a converted stable block at nearby Ketteringham Hall. It was from here that Chapman exerted a sometimes mischievous hold on Formula One, and as a man of style and charisma he also seemed to have a pretty powerful effect on Norfolk society. His untimely death in December 1982 robbed the sport of a delicious element of unpredictability, but he exists today in the brilliance of Adrian Newey and Ross Brawn, the obsessive nature of Ron Dennis and the negotiating skills of Bernie Ecclestone.

Back in 1978 he also came at you with the charm of David Niven. I was in no doubt that he was using my very modest outlet at Anglia Television to further his own agenda and we were very happy to oblige. We were invited to film at test sessions and key moments of development, although on one occasion, having been summoned to Ketteringham Hall for an urgent exclusive announcement, we were sent away because he preferred to make the announcement the following week when he had returned from his Florida holiday with a sun tan.

Mario Andretti had the same sort of style but none of the ego. During his Championship-winning 1978 season he became familiar with the Anglia studios, and on one occasion – for reasons too complicated to relate – he got there as a passenger in my 12-year-old DAF Variomatic van that I used mainly for carting straw bales around in Suffolk. During the five-mile journey he was too polite to ask why the passenger door no longer opened but wanted to know all about the advanced technology of the decrepit old car's rubber-band transmission.

It was the glamour and glory of Formula One, however,

that we wanted to capture when we reached agreement with Lotus to do a 'behind-the-scenes' documentary on the team's trip to the Italian Grand Prix at Monza, where the 1978 World Championship title was within their grasp after a season of total domination. Mario Andretti, who had spent the bulk of his formative years in a post-war displaced persons camp in Northern Italy, would be heading back to his homeland with a 12-point lead over his teammate Ronnie Peterson. With just three races left the new World Champion was certain to be a Team Lotus driver, probably Andretti, so Monza could be a weekend of history and celebration.

Ronnie Peterson was clearly an overqualified number two driver. He had won seven races with Lotus in his first spell with the team in 1973 and 1974. Now in this current season he had won in South Africa and Austria, but had five other podium finishes in support of Andretti's challenge. Peterson was quiet, unassuming and utterly charming. He had an agreement to support his teammate that fell just short of formal team orders, and as the season progressed it seemed he was not going to break it, even though there had been times in the season when he could have battled Andretti and probably beaten him.

But now, in September 1978, there was a feeling that things might be changing. Many found him distracted and aloof in the days before Monza. For the 1979 season it seemed he had confirmed a deal to drive for McLaren. Would he still feel as committed to his agreement with Andretti? After all, Peterson still had a chance of taking the World Champion's car number '1' to his new team.

There were few signs of tension as the team went about their business on the Saturday of the Italian Grand Prix. Andretti took pole position with consummate ease, but Peterson had suffered a blown engine and brake problems and was back on row three. If there were tensions they came from the suffocating atmosphere of the Monza paddock with Andretti constantly besieged by the Italian fans, and trying without success to arrange tickets and passes for a host of long-lost relatives who had emerged from the Milan suburbs. Everyone else was wanting to grill Peterson on his 1979 plans and his potential race tactics. Only Colin Chapman seemed to be enjoying it – the master of intrigue was also the centre of attention as the man behind a glorious World Championship season.

The one contrast with the current Italian Grand Prix was that there were few sponsors' commitments and no press officers with a shopping list of interviews and duties for the drivers. So it was still a glorious sunlit Saturday evening when we met up with Ronnie on the verandah of one of the world's great hotels, the Villa d'Este overlooking Lake Como.

Ronnie's wife Barbro was ill and had stayed back in Monte Carlo, and despite the problems at the track he had time and was happy to talk.

He reflected on his traditional start in karting and his progress through Formula Three that earned him the nickname 'Superswede'. He talked of his friendship with Andretti and his respect for the man he knew was going to be the new World Champion. He was pessimistic about the next day's race prospects but happy to finally confirm his 1979 plans and was clearly excited by the future with McLaren.

And when all that was done his concern was for myself and the well-being of our crew. 'How much more for you to do? When are you guys going to eat?' We explained we would be here at least until we had a decent interview with Colin Chapman and Mario Andretti. 'I can help with that,' he said enthusiastically and off he went to drag the Lotus boss out of what seemed like a pretty high-powered meeting. When that was done he re-emerged to tell us that Mario was in the shower but Ronnie got him to guarantee he'd be down in no more than ten minutes and he duly arrived. Rivalries? Tensions? We had just spent a couple of hours with clearly one of the nicest men in the sport and a pretty effective Formula One press officer as well.

The next morning, as Andretti swept into the circuit in a borrowed Rolls-Royce, I recall there being a far more upbeat mood around the team, but the optimism didn't last long for Peterson. After all the problems that had plagued his Lotus 79 the previous day the crew had worked hard, but the yellow helmet of the Swedish driver went missing minutes after the start of the morning warm-up. Peterson had apparently suffered brake failure and gone off at high speed at the second chicane.

We waited with mechanic Rex Hart as the car was brought back on a flat-bed truck: it had mown down several rows of catch fencing and was a wreck. But thankfully, and what was to prove ironically, the strengthened tub of the 79 had prevented any serious damage to Peterson's legs.

The team had brought only three 79s to Monza. Andretti's car had not yet been repaired from his crash in Austria a month earlier, so Peterson's spare was last year's 78. In the motorhome he reflected that 'someone had messed up on the brakes, there was a split-pin missing', but there were to be no interviews, no recriminations, even though it seemed any plans to challenge for the title were now out of the question.

It was the days before broadcast grid-walks, and the Monza grid was businesslike and far from celebrity laden; but the atmosphere was still extraordinary. With our television crew we patrolled the front three rows with Colin Chapman, first of all to Andretti on pole, and there was a kind of formality in his last words of encouragement to the man who was clearly about to become the next World Champion. Then to Peterson on row three, and any kind of a rehearsed speech was soon abandoned as the Swede launched into a catalogue of everything that was wrong with the outdated 78. The car wasn't pulling any revs, the cockpit was cramped, the car just wasn't set up for the chunky frame of Ronnie Peterson. All Chapman could do was shrug, put his hand on Peterson's shoulder, and half-apologise. Then we headed off to the pit-lane to watch the start of the race with the Lotus boss.

We were on the pit wall as soon as the cars had blasted away, all set for precisely the kind of footage we had come for. The master team boss at work. In the days before computer screens and cockpit communication, Colin Chapman was defined by a clipboard, a stopwatch, and a black cap that we knew he would hurl into the air when his American driver was crowned World Champion.

Instead, the first thing we saw as the grid thundered into the distance was a column of grey smoke at roughly the entrance to the first chicane. Peterson, certainly, had been slow off the line, maybe the back of the grid had been still moving when the start came. But the result was that the midfield was four or five abreast as they approached the compression at the end of the main straight. The hard-charging Riccardo Patrese was in the thick of the traffic jam, but it was James Hunt who nudged Peterson into a violent impact with the barrier. The smoke we saw was the Lotus erupting into flames.

There was no way of knowing precisely who was involved from our position in the pit lane. The reaction from Colin Chapman seemed to be one of resignation, there was a kind of world-weary sigh as he extricated himself from his position on the pit wall and dropped down on to the track, first walking towards the scene some 600 yards away, then running.

For us it was a choice between hard-bitten intrusive journalism or discretion. I'm glad we held back, not least because suddenly the paddock area had become populated by heavy-handed security, Italian police and barking dogs. After about ten minutes we met James Hunt returning helmet in hand from the scene. He was being pursued by photographers but gestured us into the motorhome. He was shocked and close to tears. He was also flushed and pouring with sweat, as you would expect a Formula One driver to be when he climbs out of a grand prix car. But around the eyes in particular there was a deeper red. He was at least scorched, if not burnt. Hunt and Patrick Depailler and Clay Regazzoni had been incredibly brave in diving into the flames to release the stricken Peterson from his car.

Peterson was certainly seriously hurt, but the reports of two badly broken legs at least didn't suggest life-threatening injuries, and as Peterson was helicoptered away the paddock regained a kind of sombre composure. It meant, of course, that Andretti was now World Champion, although that seemed of less importance. When the race took place Villeneuve would win from Andretti, but both would be relegated down the order for jumping the start; it sort of summed up the day.

We were hardly returning with the film we expected, but as Ronnie Peterson was prepared for complicated surgery to repair his damaged legs there came the encouraging prognosis from Formula One medical guru Professor Sid Watkins that Peterson would drive again, and would probably be fit to take his place in the McLaren line-up the next season.

This was before the days of Internet and super-fast communications, and it wasn't until we arrived at Liverpool Street Station the following afternoon that we saw the headline on the *London Evening Standard*: GRAND PRIX STAR IS DEAD.

The recriminations began. Peterson had died from an embolism (bone marrow in the bloodstream), and the Italian hospital was roundly condemned as being filthy and not up to the task. James Hunt, very unfairly, had his critics, but most were saying that it was the poor driving standards of the aggressive Riccardo Patrese that caused the crash; indeed, the drivers' opposition prevented Patrese taking part in the next grand prix at Watkins Glen. Then there were those who were blaming the starter, the track layout and the marshals. Back at Ketteringham Hall, the atmosphere was not helped by Colin Chapman wondering why his workforce couldn't have got the Austrian Grand Prix 79 ready for Monza – the stronger car would surely have prevented such fearful injuries.

For me any wide-eyed innocence I had about the magic of Formula One was lost that weekend. For Team Lotus and

Chapman it was also the end of an era. Andretti would not score a point in either of the two remaining races in 1978; it would be three years before Lotus would win another grand prix and they would never again threaten a Championship victory.

Chapman himself was seduced by the big money sponsorship of the discredited David Thieme at Essex Petroleum, and despite the uncompetitive nature of the team they still managed high-profile grand prix car launches at the Royal Albert Hall, with the likes of Ray Charles and Shirley Bassey providing the entertainment. In the future lay Chapman's unfortunate association with John DeLorean, before the sudden death of the charismatic Lotus boss from a heart attack in December 1982.

He was a fabulous character, and a fabulous talent who would have prospered in the modern Formula One environment. Halfway through that 1978 season, the Brabham team had tried to halt the Lotus dominance by introducing their outrageous fan-car, which won on its debut in Sweden and was angrily condemned by all its rivals, especially Chapman. The assumption was it would be swiftly outlawed, but as Mario Andretti told us years later, Chapman had his own design with two rear-mounted fans just in case it was declared legal.

He relished playing the politics of Formula One and coming out on top, but at the same time he never seemed to take it too seriously. In the midst of all the excess of the early '80s, our Anglia TV crew were flown by Lotus to Le Bourget in Paris for the launch of the Lotus 81 in the Paris-Latin night club. It didn't seem to matter at all to Chapman that the music was so loud and the atmosphere so vibrant that we couldn't record a single meaningful interview. The one thing I do remember is almost yelling a question at Chapman: 'Who do you think could be the next British Formula One World Champion?' He leaned toward the camera and yelled back with mistaken emphasis on the final syllable. 'Man*sell*, put your money on Nigel Man*sell*.'

Chapter 3

IL LEONE: LIFE WITH THE LION

Early one Monday evening in January 1986, I was in the passenger seat of a hire car alongside *Sportsnight* producer Roger Moody He pulled up at a set of security gates at the foot of a long drive just outside the Isle of Man village of Port Erin, and pressed the intercom on the wall. An unmistakeable Birmingham accent welcomed us and as the gates eased open informed us there was another set of gates about half a mile up the drive, and they would be closing in exactly 38 seconds from now.

The challenge was clear, and it was also impossible. Despite much tyre squealing and a brief excursion on to the manicured grass, by the time we arrived at the top of the hill the gates were slowly closing 100 yards in front of us and Nigel Mansell was leaning on the gatepost with a big grin on his face.

He explained that he was the only driver who could 'beat the gates', thanks to his unique combination of technique and talent; for us it was the start of an exhausting 48 hours of competitions and contests and the chance to reluctantly 'prove ourselves' against the great new talent of British motorsport.

By 1986 Nigel Mansell had already been racing for 23 years and had endured and survived everything that an ambitious young driver could possibly be faced with: big crashes, a broken neck and near bankruptcy. But he had earned his chance in Formula One and towards the end of the 1985 season with Williams he became a grand prix winner with back-to-back victories at Brands Hatch and Kyalami.

Now with just a few weeks to go to the start of the 1986 season in Brazil we had come to the Isle of Man to film a *Sportsnight* feature explaining what Mansell was all about. It wasn't a difficult task. From our social call on the Tuesday evening through the following day's filming we had to get through six deadly serious frames of snooker; in the swimming pool the challenge was who could hold their breath under water longer than him; in the gym (with temperature set to match Brazilian humidity), could anyone possibly outperform him on the exercise bike – and that was before we even got to the golf course.

We came away exhausted, but with a very accurate film portrait of a dedicated if slightly obsessive racing driver. Nigel Mansell was not a man you would go to for the romance and mystique of motorsport. He was sheer blood and guts. His motorsport had been funded by remortgaging the family home, not by being the poster boy for a global corporation. As a result he came across as being unsophisticated, naive, boyishly enthusiastic and self-absorbed, a nightmare to deal with but a privilege to be associated with. Clearly, for the next decade British motorsport fans felt the same, thrilling to the exploits of this combination of Fangio, Moss and bloke down the pub.

It didn't surprise us that 24 hours after leaving the Isle of Man we were engrossed with the material in an edit suite at BBC Television Centre when the door opened behind us and there was Nigel. He had strolled through the different layers of security that were in force at the White City complex and just wanted to check on the rushes and the quotes we were using, and needed to make sure that the exterior shots in the film did not compromise the security of his house in the Isle of Man. At the time we were irritated, but with hindsight, how refreshing it was that through the last (rather trying) few days, no public relations or marketing man had been involved, no sponsors, just Nigel himself.

We were to meet again a few days later, for a hasty interview in a Heathrow airport car park. Nigel had gone testing with his Williams team at Paul Ricard in the South of France. On his way back to the airport in Marseilles, team boss Frank Williams had crashed his hire car and was dreadfully injured. He would survive, but would spend the rest of his life wheelchair-bound as a quadriplegic. The fact that he remains at the helm of Williams F1 to this day is one of the great courageous stories of modern Formula One.

But in that Heathrow car park in 1986 it would seem a desolate way to start a season that would actually turn into a Mansell epic.

Williams F1 reorganised internally to cope with Frank Williams' absence and, for Mansell, the momentum from the previous season was maintained. It was a season that saw the start of the intense rivalry with Piquet, Senna and Prost and included a fantastic Mansell victory in Spain, beating Senna by the narrowest margin the sport had ever seen. When Mansell claimed another electrifying victory at Brands Hatch, with a wheelchair-bound Frank Williams returning to the pit lane for the first time, the British driver found himself heading the World Championship.

He was still leading into the final race of the season, the Australian Grand Prix at Adelaide. His six-point lead over Alain Prost meant that a finish anywhere in the top three would make him World Champion.

Historically there was no great enthusiasm at the BBC for scheduling live coverage of Formula One from the other side of the world in the small hours of the morning, let alone firing up a Television Centre studio to add some glossy presentation; but this was different. Not only was it odds-on that we would be celebrating a British World Champion, but Frank Williams, despite his incapacity, had agreed to join us in the studio, his first live television appearance since his accident.

However, nothing was going to stand in the way of the BBC doing it on the cheap, and instead of linking the coverage from a corner of the large and accessible *Grandstand* studio we were shoehorned into the first-floor weather forecasters' room, which was great for standing up in front of a chart but had barely enough room for two chairs and a desk, let alone all the extra equipment that Frank Williams required.

By the time that Frank and his assistants and minders had negotiated the labyrinth of stairs and corridors that got them to the studio door, we were seconds from going on air. Although his wheelchair was then put in position, a breathing problem limited the contribution he was able to make at the start of the programme. It was an embarrassing way to treat a distinguished, wheelchair guest for a routine programme, let alone at four o'clock in the morning with all the nerve-wracking tension that lay ahead.

He was calm as he watched the race unfold, Mansell seemingly secure in the title-clinching third place. Maybe there was a chance to bring him in for a fresh set of tyres to provide a bit of extra insurance; off-camera Frank felt that might be the right thing to do.

On lap 64 we watched together as Nigel's left rear tyre exploded at nearly 200 miles an hour. Frank's expression hardly changed, a wan smile and a small philosophical shrug was the only reaction he was physically capable of. Just like Mansell on the other side of the world, minutes earlier he was preparing to celebrate the World Championship title; now in a first-floor weather studio in front of a dodgy monitor he was having to come to terms with the biggest disappointment of his Formula One career.

It would be six years before that anticipated celebration could finally take place, Nigel taking the 1992 title for Williams in record-breaking style. But that early October morning, as his nursing staff wheeled him out of the deepest recesses of Television Centre, there would be an awful lot for Frank Williams to come to terms with.

Seven weeks later Nigel would be with us at the White City, not in that claustrophobic little room but in the glitzy surroundings of the BBC Sports Personality of the Year studio on the ground floor, collecting the top award in front of a star-studded audience.

There were some in the audience who could be seen shaking their heads as Nigel received the trophy ahead of javelin world record holder Fatima Whitbread – after all, he hadn't even won the world title. But 1986 was the year that Nigel established himself as 'The People's Champion', and in terms of racing, and also in terms of broadcasting his exploits, many adventures and frustrations lay ahead.

The best way of describing Nigel at that time would be 'unsophisticated and uncomplicated', and both those terms are meant as a compliment. James Hunt had a roguish charm and a dismissive nature; there was none of that about Nigel. Senna, Prost and Piquet could be devious and conspiratorial; there was none of that about Nigel, who assumed the best in people and often got the worst.

He was also devoid of any sense of irony. In the summer of 1991, when Alain Prost was plotting and scheming to replace him at Williams, we did an interview with Nigel at the British Grand Prix at Silverstone. We struggled to get the interview started because Nigel insisted on wearing a heavily branded Canon hat pulled down to a ludicrous extent over his forehead.

We tried to negotiate. Could he just lift the peak of the cap a fraction above his eyes so the cameraman could, at least, frame the shot while avoiding the sponsor's logo? 'I'd love to help,' explained Nigel, 'but you have to understand that I've just done a big deal for the sponsor's name to be on the cap like this and I am contractually obliged to wear it, in this manner, for all television interviews; so I won't be changing.'

In the end we cut our losses and got the interview under way. 'What is your reaction,' I asked, 'to what seems to be Alain Prost's attempts to undermine your position at Williams?'

'What depresses me sometimes about Formula One,' replied Nigel in a solemn tone, 'is that everything seems to be commercially motivated.'

We had to stop the interview because the cameraman and sound assistant were laughing so much, but Nigel, with his Canon hat pulled low over his bushy eyebrows, never saw the joke.

Nothing ever quite went to plan with Nigel, although on occasions this was clearly my fault. At the 1989 British Grand Prix at Silverstone, when he was driving for Ferrari, we invented the first grid-walk. I would put *Grandstand* on the air from the front of the grid, we might get the odd shot of the Home Secretary or Prince Michael of Kent, but the drivers would stay in their cars and it was nothing like the sexy, celebrity-laden extravaganza that Martin Brundle presides over these days.

In 1989 we attempted to change this and I suggested to Nigel the revolutionary idea of a live interview after he had brought his Ferrari on to the grid. He agreed, even though this had never been proposed before, and said he would catch my eye and indicate if the moment was right. The Ferrari nosed its way to the front of the grid to a fantastic reception from all those packed around Woodcote and the start–finish straight. Immediately Nigel caught my eye, winked and nodded, even though he was still wearing a full-face helmet.

At exactly the same moment the floor manager indicated that Murray Walker had handed down to me with Nigel Mansell. I had to go for it. I asked him a question, although he had no apparent means of hearing what I said. I shoved the mike into his helmet and he seemed to be giving me a lucid, animated reply, although with no off-air sound I had no idea what he was saying. But, suitably encouraged when he stopped talking I asked another question. It went on like this for a few minutes, and it was only later that I was told that Nigel, in fact, was talking to his pit-crew and was desperately trying to get me to shut up. It all hastened the arrival of the Martin Brundle era.

There was so much to admire about the record-breaking manner in which Nigel finally nailed the World Championship title in 1992. Five straight wins from the start of the season, all from pole position in the Williams Renault, effectively ended the contest by mid-May; but then a mixture of pride and the superior political machinations of Alain Prost prevented him defending the title in 1993.

But without all of that we would not have seen the mixture of determination and self-belief that took him to America to claim the IndyCar World Series title at his first attempt. He didn't need Formula One to demonstrate that he was the most competitive and exciting driver in the sport.

It was something he demonstrated again, to a perhaps smaller degree, at Donington Park toward the end of his triumphant 1993 season. With the aid of Ford and a few other connections in the British sport we had persuaded Nigel to join the Touring Car drivers in the end-of-season TOCA shoot-out. He didn't have to come, and he certainly didn't have to take it especially seriously. However, the anticipated 25,000 Donington crowd swelled to over 70,000 in the confident expectation that Nigel was going to put on a show.

He certainly did that. Midway through the main Touring Car race, Mansell, charging through the field, got a subtle tap from Tiff Needell, went spearing off the track and hit the Donington bridge in one of the most violent Touring Car accidents ever seen. Not to be deterred, he was back behind the wheel of a Touring Car in subsequent years, including 1998 when, with huge crowds at the circuit once again, he fought his way from 19th to lead the race in torrential conditions. In the commentary box Charlie Cox and John Watson struggled for superlatives, Watson describing it as one of the greatest drives he had ever seen, in any category. Mansell would not win the race, but in parc ferme afterwards Mansell, John Cleland and Derek Warwick were hugging each other and almost in tears as they reflected on taking part in such a classic conquest, of which Mansell had been the main ingredient.

To the tens of thousands of extra fans who came to race meetings just to see Mansell in action he must have seemed like a man of towering confidence and unshakeable self-belief; but those who worked closely with him saw a different character. In time he became someone who saw plots and conspiracies around every corner and, on occasions, showed an insecurity and a caution that was never in evidence on the track.

At the end of his World Championship season in 1992 he was the obvious prime candidate to be named BBC Sports Personality of the Year once again. I was given the job of making sure that Nigel, who had now headed off on his American adventure, would definitely be with us in the London studio. It wasn't easy.

Slowly the messages started coming back from his assistant Annie Bradshaw that he wasn't sure he was going to come. He only wanted to make the trip if he was certain he'd won the award. He wasn't being precious or arrogant – by his logic, if he'd won the award when he came second in the Championship, and didn't win it when he was World Champion, then the rejection by the British public would reflect badly on the IndyCar Championship and would really upset his new bosses at Newman Haas.

My problem was that a month out we had no way of knowing if he had won it, and wouldn't be able to tell him anyway; after all, the voting was highly confidential and didn't even close until 24 hours before the programme. We could tell, however, by the votes that had already come in that he was seemingly polling twice as many as everyone else combined. The date drew nearer and without actually telling Annie Bradshaw of the voting position all I could do was emphasise the potential embarrassment to all concerned if he wasn't in the studio with us. Bless her, she got the message and with a week to go rang to say that Nigel was in the country and would be with us on the big night.

Two days before the programme the phone rang at home. It was Nigel. 'I'm just ringing to say, Steve, that I'm not going to be there on Sunday night.'

'What?'

'Well you know that I have to feel confident that I've won it. Well, I had lunch with Mohammed Al Fayed today and he doesn't think I have won it because I don't seem to have been in any of the BBC trailers.'

The strength of my language took him (and me) by surprise; he was immediately persuaded and sheepishly took his place on the front row of the celebrity sporting audience for the Sunday-night Sports Personality of the Year. Surely nothing could go wrong now?

However, Sports Personality of the Year is a prestigious night and also a long one. With the build-up and the content, the audience are required to be in their seats for around two and a half hours. It's not such a problem for Desmond Lynam and myself presenting the show, but admittedly for the audience it can be a test of endurance.

With about two minutes to go to the announcement of the Sports Personality of the Year, an anxious Nigel Mansell beckoned me over. 'I'm sorry, Steve. I'm absolutely bursting; I've got to go for a pee.'

Once again the strength of my reaction took us both by surprise, especially with the proximity of a live mike and an audience of about 16 million. Basically I felt we'd been through an awful lot to get this far and I didn't care if he wet himself in front of the entire nation, he was going to stay in his seat and only get up when he was finally required to collect that bloody trophy.

The combination of high drama and low farce that always seemed to accompany Nigel gave many people both inside and outside motor racing the opportunity to sneer. I would have preferred that he could have silenced the cynics with a glorious, triumphant exit from the sport. But that wasn't to be, and I had a reluctant, close-up view of the events that seemed to hasten the end of it all.

In 1994 Nigel had returned to racing from America to drive the last few races of the season for Williams. In the last race in Australia he claimed an unlikely victory that only became a footnote to the season because this was the race in which the collision between Michael Schumacher and Damon Hill controversially gave the title to Schumacher.

With hindsight that should have been the moment for Mansell to go out on a high but Williams declined to take up the option on his contract, and instead Mansell responded to the unexpected overtures from the McLaren boss Ron Dennis.

The two men had been fierce rivals during the previous 15 years, and not always respectful of the other's contribution to the sport. But apparently peace had broken out – Mansell was to drive for McLaren in 1995 and I was called in by McLaren to host a very high-profile press launch at the Science Museum in London.

With an hour to go to the announcement I was called into a back room to join a meeting of the main players, and run through exactly how it was going to be handled. To my dismay it was clear that peace had *not* broken out. Ron and Nigel and a few agents and executives were, seemingly, at the fairly early stage of an acrimonious negotiation, and I ended up hearing the kind of contractual detail that a proper journalist should never have ignored.

But I was there as a hired hand, and shortly afterwards presided over a press launch that was all sweetness and light and mutual bonhomie. It was only when I was helping organise the photo-call afterwards that the big crisis emerged. I was requested to dissuade the photographers from taking pictures of Nigel in the car. 'Use any excuse – say he's got a bad back or something, but he's only doing photographs alongside the car.'

The reality was that Nigel physically couldn't fit in the car, and this very fundamental design problem was to signal the end of the adventure. Admittedly the car was one of the worst that the great team had produced, but within just two races the McLaren/Mansell partnership was over and one of the greatest of grand prix careers ended with a whimper and a whinge.

So I, like everyone else, prefer to remember Mansell at his heroic best, and that usually meant the British Grand Prix, which he won on five occasions. His passing move on Nelson Piquet in 1987 at Silverstone remains one of the classic moments in motorsport, but, for a variety of reasons, it's his victory in front of 200,000 ecstatic fans at Silverstone in 1992 that lives in my memory.

I had put *Grandstand* on the air, and done all the build-up from the grid. The cars were at the back of the circuit on their formation lap when I was approached by Sir Jackie Stewart. He had a strange request. He asked me where I would be watching the race from, and I explained that we would be in our usual studio position alongside Murray Walker and James Hunt at the top of the Shell Tower. 'That's good,' he said. 'If you've got no other commitments I might have a bit of baby-sitting for you.'

The race was just a couple of laps old when the door opened and he rather unregally ushered the young Prince William and Prince Harry into our dubious care for the race.

At first it wasn't too difficult, and we tried to point out the interesting aspects of the race and the encouraging progress of 'Our Nige'. But inevitably their attention began to wander, and in the second half of the race we were letting them play with the camera, sit in the presenter's chair and listen to all that funny talkback coming from the director's truck.

Then with a couple of laps left, with the future World Champion sweeping to victory, we got their attention back again. Their faces were pressed against the window. 'Come on Nigel, you can win it,' they yelled as he crossed the finish line for the penultimate occasion.

This is decent stuff, I thought, and discreetly gestured to the cameraman that he might want to cover the final scenes, with VT making a recording of the two royal princes celebrating the great triumph of the king of Silverstone, a recording which surely would be replayed many times in years to come.

Nigel came into view around Woodcote. 'Yeesss, come on Mansell,' cried one of the princes. At that moment the celebrating crowd could also be seen preparing themselves for a mass track invasion. 'But look at those morons,' screamed the other young prince. He was jabbing his finger at the window. 'Morons, they're all morons.'

I turned to the cameraman, but he was already in the process of lowering his lens to the floor, and they had swiftly hit the stop button in VT. Posterity could wait, but Mansell had already filled the archive with more glorious endeavour than any other British driver.

Chapter 4

SENNA: SNETTERTON TO SAN MARINO

C ircuits like Snetterton in Norfolk represent the heartland of British motorsport. It gave me my first prolonged exposure to motor racing, and taught me that Formula One is merely the distant summit of a mountain of endeavour and excitement.

Snetterton is set on a windy and cold plateau of agricultural land, but in the 1970s it managed to bring together both the superstars and the wannabes; grand prix teams and club racers all found a welcome at Snetterton and could often be seen sharing the track, which was one of the best testing facilities in the country.

It was at Snetterton that I watched Andretti testing for Lotus and Barry Sheene destroying the field in the Race of Aces. We filmed Minis and Sports 2000, Formula Ford and Formula Three; there was even Formula One with the likes of Rupert Keegan and Tony Trimmer. It was where I also learnt an important lesson about pit-lane discipline after Stirling Moss broke our sound engineer's leg as he came in for his first stop in an MG in the early stages of the Willhire 24-hour race.

But despite all the activity, Snetterton in the '70s was struggling to draw the big crowds and the big meetings; its golden years were clearly in the past and it was an unlikely place to witness the early development of one of the greatest and most charismatic drivers the sport has ever seen.

Ayrton Senna da Silva had come to the UK in 1981. Like so many young, aspiring Brazilian racers, he came into the sport from a comparatively wealthy background. He based himself in Norfolk just a short distance from the Snetterton circuit, staying for a while at the home of Ralph Firman, the boss of Van Diemen, the dominant force in Formula Ford.

So it was no great surprise that he won two Formula Ford Championships that season; but it was a surprise that he remained unconvinced by his own ability, and had decided to return home to the family business when the offer came to continue racing the following year. It was something we discussed across a typically greasy Snetterton breakfast. We got on well, probably because he was keen to make whatever contacts he could, but it was easy to dismiss him as just another talented young man still searching for a clear direction in life.

He made the decision to continue racing in Britain in 1982, won the two major Formula Ford Championships on offer and the following year was engaged in an epic duel with Martin Brundle for the British Formula Three Championship, and took the title in the last round at Thruxton. Martin, as he would reflect many times in years to come, along with the whole of motorsport, had been introduced to the brilliance, self-belief and occasional madness of Ayrton Senna.

His astonishing career has been well documented to this point, and the legend and mystique surrounding Senna has gained further impetus from the award-winning documentary feature film, so I will only reflect on my memories of him, including the experience of hosting *Grandstand* from the pit wall at Imola that fateful day in 1994.

I am often asked who is the greatest sportsman I have interviewed, or who is the one who has made the biggest impression. Through my involvement in other sports I am lucky enough to have a decent choice. It sometimes depends on the occasion and circumstances in which you are interviewing the major performers. So Redgrave in Sydney, Nicklaus or Faldo at Augusta, Seb Coe at the Moscow Olympics all provide special memories.

But the sportsmen who mesmerise you every time you

interview them are rare. In fact I would narrow them down to two – Seve Ballesteros and Ayrton Senna.

It is best described as a kind of passion and intensity, a burning belief that seems to communicate itself so much better with a Latin background and temperament, and takes on a special kind of power when delivered with that appealing kind of broken-English accent; try and convey the same kind of fiery emotions with a Birmingham accent and it doesn't work so well.

It enables you to get away with a blinkered self-belief that both Ballesteros and Senna exploited so well; Seve, when he was arguing with a European Tour referee about a rabbit-scrape or a ruling on an obstruction, was an unstoppable force; Senna when he was raging to the FIA that the whole of Formula One was against him, could sway any jury and win any debate.

It was not something that was apparent across that greasy breakfast at Snetterton, but as his status in the sport grew he became a compelling interviewee. Not for him the routine of a standard sound bite in a routine interview. If you pointed a microphone at Ayrton, whatever question you asked, no matter how daft, he would treat as the meaning of life itself.

An example of this was an interview we did, with McLaren's encouragement, at Estoril ahead of the start of the 1991 season. Senna was going into the season as reigning World Champion but McLaren were struggling to maintain their dominance into the new season because of the strength of the Williams FW14B. At the BBC we of course needed to hear from the Champion before the season began, and McLaren made time at the Estoril test session where they were sure Ayrton would put a confident spin on the prospects, especially the development work that had been done on the new Honda V12 engine.

We set our equipment up in the draughty old dilapidated restaurant above the pit complex. The cars stopped running at about 3:00pm and we were expecting Ayrton about half an hour after that. He went into a debrief with his engineers: 3:30pm came and went, so did 4:30pm, and 5:30pm as well. Then, when we reckoned we had barely ten minutes of light left, the door opened and Senna came in with Jo Ramirez of the McLaren management team.

He shook hands with every member of the film crew, as was his style, but we were desperate to get the interview under way so I asked the first question while he was still being miked up. It was one of those soft questions that serve as a sound check as much as a telling probe.

'First time you got to drive the revised car today, Ayrton. What's the verdict, on the V12 in particular?'

He took a deep breath, gazed into the distance, and thought long and hard about this apparent time bomb of a question.

'I was with my team last in October,' he answered, 'it is now nearly March. There was a programme established by the engineers, some targets to be reached on power output and driveability. They work hard, it is many months between October and March. Today I drive the car for the first time, and they have made no progress whatsoever. That is the truth and I have to tell the truth however hard it is to hear.'

There was a splutter from Jo Ramirez at the back of the room as the World Champion went on to describe, not only the failings of the car in very precise detail, but also the shortcomings of the McLaren team and much of the management. He concluded by saying that he had already totally written off any prospect of challenging the front-runners in 1991. A few days later he would win the opening grand prix of the season in Phoenix and would successfully defend his world title.

Ayrton once again had listened to a question and simply given an answer, and clearly would have no patience with the corporate party line that exists in modern Formula One. You got the impression, also, that every answer would contain a subtext aimed at different individuals. In other interviews we did he would relish the occasions when he had a bit of extra time to explore topics such as religion, motivation and the psychological demands of Formula One.

Bits of interviews we did around the early '90s survive on the Internet and give, I think, an insight into the level of confidence and self-belief that the rest of the grid partly admired but were also very wary of. This is a clip from another interview we did with Ayrton that exists on the Internet. This was Silverstone, later in that 1991 season:

'I have always been a man to have very strong principles and I use those principles to guide me as a man and a competitor. I'm doing things for the right reason. Some understand, some don't, most of them I'm sure admire what I am doing... the reason is for one thing, to succeed, to win.

'Religion has always been an important part of my life and has become more important over the last two years. It gives me the peace and equilibrium that I need to perform under strife, under pressure. I have found, through God, a special way of living and a special way of understanding many things in life that I did not have before I found God.'

In 1990 at Jerez, in practice for the Spanish Grand Prix, Martin Donnelly somehow survived a horrifying Friday-morning crash, but those who saw his crumpled body in the middle of the track were convinced that they had seen him die. One of those was Ayrton Senna, who went to the crash site and was so affected by what he saw he considered quitting the sport. But this is what he said to me in a subsequent interview.

'A million things went through my mind, but after a while I realised I was not going to give up my passion even just having seen what I had seen. And I had to put myself together, walk back to the racing car and do it again... and do it again and do it even better than before, because that was the way to kind of cover that impact it had on me. I was not ready to give up, as much as I was scared, I was not ready to give up my aim, my target, my ambition, my passion, my life.'

Hours later Senna claimed a brilliant pole position, the 50th of his career.

Since 1989 I had been the presenter of the annual Autosport

Awards at the Grosvenor House Hotel, an end-of-season celebration of all things motorsport. Some prestigious awards were on offer, but it was also an opportunity to take a (not always light-hearted) snipe at rivals who had been irritating or upsetting you during the course of the season.

Ayrton joined us at the event at the end of 1991. He was World Champion, but he was also a character who had outraged the sport with his headstrong approach and his aggressive and, sometimes, downright dangerous approach to racing; and some of his fiercest critics were here in the 1,200-strong black-tie audience at the Grosvenor.

After I announced him as International Racing Driver of the Year and Stirling Moss had made the presentation, he was interviewed by Murray Walker and answered every question in his slow, thoughtful, compelling style. For the first, and only, time in my experience there was total silence in the vast room where the wine had been flowing for three or four hours. After ten minutes or so Murray thanked him, but Ayrton took the microphone and addressed the audience directly.

He said: 'I am still young, 31, but I have been involved in motor racing since I was four years old, believe me. When I came to England in 1981 to compete in the Formula Ford Championship, it was my first season in racing cars. Until then it was only go-karts, and I have been through different categories – successfully, fortunately – and lots of the things that I learn and subsequently used in Formula One, have come from England. Because here I learn to race as a professional, here I learnt how to obey the flags and how to follow the marshals, the starting procedures, set-up on cars, the relationship with the engineers and mechanics, team owners and team managers and it has made a lot of my personality in terms of motor racing.

'I know that often I don't get the best press in England, but I suppose nobody's perfect. I try hard and I try hard to be better and improve. I would just like to say thank you to all those people in England that have given me the opportunity in '81 to come through all the way and help me in such a short period to get so much success – thank you.'

From my position on the stage I could look directly at the audience's faces. They were the household names of the sport, but you could see spellbound expressions, awe, and a kind of hero worship. He had understood the requirements of the occasion to perfection and left the stage to a prolonged standing ovation. He had committed some dark deeds down the years, but it all was forgiven that night. We had seen the very essence of sporting charisma.

Chapter 5

MAY 1, 1994, IMOLA

The events of that dreadful weekend at the San Marino Grand Prix had a profound effect on everyone involved in the sport, and those who were there were all left with a vivid personal perspective on the death of Ayrton Senna. For me, it was always going to be a busy and varied weekend, combining the live presentation from San Marino with introducing the Rugby League Challenge Cup Final live from Wembley the previous day.

And it always had the feeling of a weird weekend. Early on Saturday morning I got a phone call from the Simtek Formula One team. Was I coming to Imola on Saturday evening, and would I be able to take an important suspension part with me as hand luggage? These were the days before sophisticated logistics solutions and I was happy to oblige, making arrangements for it to be delivered to the BBC Outside Broadcast unit at Wembley Stadium.

I then turned my attention to the preparations and build-up for Wigan against Leeds.

The pre-match sequence would take in *Football Focus* as well as all the Rugby League prospects. There would not be time for any coverage, live or otherwise, of qualifying for the San Marino Grand Prix, although Murray Walker would be filing a report around 1:30.

About half an hour before this we got a newsflash from the Imola circuit. Roland Ratzenberger had been killed in a high-speed crash, the first Formula One fatality since 1982. Murray filed his report and referred back to the horrendous crash that Rubens Barrichello had somehow survived in practice the previous day; but poor Ratzenberger apparently had no chance.

He was a driver that Murray and I had got to know pretty well in the previous couple of years as he contested the British Touring Car Championship. The step up from the BTCC to Formula One is an unlikely one but Ratzenberger had got his opportunity with Simtek. As Murray described the sombre mood at Imola, I noticed the brown cardboard parcel lying on the floor behind the camera, covered in labels saying Simtek Formula One.

The rest of the afternoon carried no more shocks and upsets, Wigan won the Challenge Cup for the seventh straight year, and immediately the programme finished I headed to Heathrow with my extra luggage.

By the time I was met at Milan airport by producer Mark Wilkin and we had driven the 100km to the hotel in Ravenna – which was still some distance from Imola – the hour was pretty late. We talked on the way about the accident to Ratzenberger, which came when his car speared off the road at 200mph after an apparent front-wing failure. However, there was still much anticipation for what was to come the next day.

It seemed to be a defining time for the sport, not just in terms of safety but also from the point of view of the balance of power. Ayrton Senna's move to Williams was expected to re-establish his dominance. He had taken pole position, but had then crashed out in both the season's two opening races in Brazil and Japan. The sport had a new pacesetter – Michael Schumacher in the Benetton, who led the World Championship with two victories. Now, at Imola, Ayrton Senna was on pole yet again, but Schumacher was with him on the front row.

On the Sunday morning we arrived early as the paddock was just stirring. The dreadful events of the previous day seemed to have been absorbed for the time being, but it was still deserted at Simtek, where I was happy to drop off the package and leave.

A lot of people, it seems, have subsequently thought back to the mood that morning and tried to attach an almost mystical significance to what they might or might not have seen. I can't offer any of that. There was a small acknowledgement from Ayrton as we filmed at Williams, but according to others there was an eerie calm about the former World Champion, and apparently that morning there had been a timely reconciliation with Alain Prost after their years of acrimony.

Once the cars had come on to the grid we had to concentrate on getting *Grandstand* cleanly on the air and, in the build-up, do justice to the memory of Ratzenberger and also give thanks for the survival of Rubens Barrichello, whose Friday crash had so nearly meant a double fatality.

Then of course there were the race prospects for myself and Jonathan Palmer to discuss from our position in front of the grid. This was the race where Senna surely had to reassert himself, and resist the growing pressure from the hard-charging Michael Schumacher. Jonathan felt, quite simply, this was a race Senna had to win.

Behind us Senna hadn't got out of his car and was talking to no one apart from his Williams crew. Tucked alongside him in the monocoque of the car was the Austrian flag he was going to unfurl in tribute to Ratzenberger, once the victory had been secured.

The race began in chaotic fashion. Senna led Schumacher away, but back down the field JJ Lehto had stalled on the grid and Pedro Lamy in the Lotus failed to avoid him. Wreckage was everywhere – some of it, including a wheel, had cleared the safety fence, injuring spectators. It wasn't until the start of the second lap that the runners were collected by the safety car, just after they had swept past the scene of the accident at near full speed. The safety car would stay out for another four laps.

Meanwhile, I had reverted to the role of reporter, and it was still a scene of some chaos down in the pit lane. I headed for the Lotus garage, tracked down Pedro Lamy, and was standing by to ask him exactly what had happened at the start, but at that moment the cars were released by the safety car and blasted away down the straight behind us.

We watched on the garage monitor as Senna kept his lead, harried all the way by Schumacher. The interview could wait, this was a pivotal point of the season and a huge test of the Brazilian's resolve. When they came past again the Williams of Senna was still under huge pressure from the Benetton, but third-placed Gerhard Berger was being dropped. The Lotus garage shuddered and vibrated as the San Marino Grand Prix swept by just a few feet away.

It was about 15 seconds later at the flat-out curve known as Tamburello that disaster struck. At the apex of the corner Senna's car just kept going straight, at undiminished speed. It slammed into the concrete wall, the right side of the car crumpled into the cockpit and the wrecked chassis slewed back on to the track.

In the garage there was the horror and disbelief that you would expect, especially within a team that helped launch Senna's Formula One career. This soon gave way to a grim concentration: the day had been disrupted, there was work to do once again.

I moved up the pit lane to Williams, where there was still a numb horror. I did not go there to intrude, but if there was any kind of positive news or encouragement then this was the place to get it. The helicopter coverage above the crash site was showing no sensitivity, and was probing deep into the cockpit as the rescue team went to work. In the garage they saw arm movement, maybe his head moved; there was hope and they were clinging to it.

The cars were parked while the rescue went on, many drivers returned to the paddock, and I positioned myself on the pit wall and contributed what I could. There was quick thinking from producer Mark Wilkin and director Ken Burton, who used my pit-wall camera to offer alternative shots to those of the Italian director whose coverage was becoming more and more obtrusive. Murray and Jonathan tried to remain upbeat. So much progress had been made in terms of driver protection and cockpit safety. Just look at the astonishing impact that Rubens Barrichello had survived on Friday with merely a sprained wrist; but then again, barely 24 hours earlier there had been Roland Ratzenberger.

The delay went on, and for a while the other components of *Grandstand* took over, so as well as getting what pit-lane reaction and updates I could, I was also, in these tense and sombre circumstances, linking into frames of snooker from the World Championship that was under way in Sheffield.

Time went on, and there was a growing sense of foreboding. There was no news from the crash site, or from the medical team who helped the unconscious Senna into the helicopter that took him away to the Maggiore hospital in Bologna.

There would be a race, of that there was no doubt. In a previous season I had asked Bernie Ecclestone what exactly happens in the event of a fatality at the circuit, so I could anticipate it correctly, report it accurately and adopt the appropriate tone. He wasn't being callous when he told me that, whatever the circumstances, no driver ever dies at the circuit. They are airlifted away, the race goes on, the crowd disperse, an announcement is made. It makes the logistics of a tragic situation easier to manage.

That was very much in my mind as we got ready for the restarted race. The helicopter had departed, the race programme was back under way. Would the next thing be an announcement? Surely not Senna!

We didn't need an announcement. As Michael Schumacher headed to the most subdued of victories out on the track, I went to find what official information I could. There were no press bulletins, nothing reliable to pass on, but among officials and contacts and friends, especially at Williams, there was already a desolate sense of tragedy, blank faces and tear-filled eyes. Those expressions and that silence was as definitive as any official announcement. But nothing could be acknowledged or confirmed until the race had been completed and, ideally, the crowds had departed.

Schumacher took the win, Damon Hill to his great credit and that of the team brought the second Williams home in sixth. There were no celebrations. On the pit wall I linked into more frames of snooker and promised whatever updates we could provide, but hopefully the tone would prepare the audience for the solemn announcement that was a short time away. Then at 6:40pm local time it finally became official. Ayrton Senna was dead.

There was no time to dwell on the enormity of it all. Within minutes Murray Walker had joined me on the pit wall and we were going live into the BBC evening news. Murray and Jonathan had to make similar contributions to a whole range of broadcast outlets and then came the decision to scrap the pre-recorded edition of *Grand Prix* and go live with a special edition of the programme that did its best to tell the story of such a tragic weekend and paid tribute to one of the greatest drivers the sport had ever seen.

At the end of that programme we had been on air in some form or another for almost nine hours, and seen a news story unfold that now left us numb. There were five of us heading out of the circuit in the hire car – Ken Burton and Mark Wilkin in the front, myself, Jonathan and Murray in the back. Darkness had long since descended (in every sense). It was a long drive back to Ravenna and no one said a word for at least 45 minutes. Murray eventually broke the silence by asking if anyone remembered whether it was lap 10 or 11 that Gerhard Berger came in for tyres.

There was laughter. Murray was coping with it all just like everyone else in Formula One and he had a deadline to meet with his grand prix diary; but we all knew how deeply affected he had been by what he had seen that day and how brilliantly he had handled it. Indeed, there is no right or wrong way to handle something like that. When we got to Ravenna the local restaurant was still open. After several bottles of Pinot Grigio and some dodgy pizza we ended 1 May 1994 on the racing simulator in the neighbouring games arcade. There was adrenalin and anger flowing and Murray was unbeatable.

The enduring image I will take from that awful day, however, came as the sun was setting, the circuit had emptied and we were on the pit wall in the final few minutes of our live edition of *Grand Prix*. A figure emerged from the Williams garage wheeling a bicycle between the trucks and packing cases. It was Patrick Head, the Williams technical director, who, as the right-hand man to Frank Williams, was achieving near legendary status in the sport. Instead of heading to the paddock entrance and the car parks, Patrick pushed his bike up the pit lane and then headed out on to the circuit and cycled slowly towards Tamburello.

The season progressed, the sport reflected and regrouped, no one doing this better than the Williams team. Damon Hill's brilliance, especially in Japan, took the Championship to the final round in Adelaide, only for Schumacher's 'mistake' to give Schumacher the title! A tragic season had ended with more traditional controversy.

But the loss of Senna is what the 1994 season will ultimately be remembered for, and at the BBC we wanted to replace the traditional season's review programme with a documentary tribute programme to Senna. As ever we were told that budgets were tight, facilities were limited, and surely there was enough material in the archives just to hack something together?

Mark Wilkin and myself wanted something better than that. We scraped together what resources we could, cut a few corners and, most importantly, enlisted the aid of a brilliant young sports documentary maker named Stuart Cabb.

We tried to build the tribute on Senna's entire racing career, not just his time in Formula One, and there were contributions from Alain Prost, John Watson and many others that eloquently captured the essence of a mercurial talent. Nigel Mansell relived the fantastic battles they had in Barcelona and Monaco, and Martin Brundle talked about his wild and unpredictable side that first showed itself in their epic British Formula Three rivalry. We also went back to Snetterton, filming in the grubby cafe where Senna and I had sat some 12 years earlier, and got contributions from people like Dennis Rushen, Dick Bennetts and Ralph Firman, the architects of his early progress in the sport.

But like the big-screen documentary that was made 17 years later, our programme opened with the horrifying events of the San Marino Grand Prix and the outpouring of grief that followed, especially at Senna's funeral in São Paulo. To build this part of the programme we felt we had to go back to Imola.

We had scheduled the trip with a film crew in the middle of November, which gave us barely three weeks before transmission, and like any race circuit in the close season it was a cold, bleak, rather desolate place. The temperature was only a little above freezing, fog shrouded the pit lane and as we made the ten-minute walk from the paddock to Tamburello the trees were disappearing into the mist and everything was damp and dripping; a very eerie atmosphere.

There was no mistaking the fateful corner. Flowers and tributes were hanging from the catch fencing, graffiti messages covered the concrete wall, framing the ugly black smear and the scar of missing masonry that signified the deadly point of impact. It was a chilling scene, made even more haunting by the movement we slowly became aware of in the trees. At first we saw just one or two people, but as we got closer many more became apparent, some in groups, others standing alone, some holding the catch fencing, others deep in the trees both inside and outside the circuit.

All were in silence. I saw some clutching rosaries and praying. Senna had died here on 1 May; it was now over seven months later, and a member of the circuit staff said 'pilgrims' like these had been at the site every day since the accident, and their numbers were still growing.

It was like being in church and we found ourselves talking in hushed tones. But there was a piece of filming to do which was to serve as the introduction; and then Mark told me, rather mysteriously, that I might want to retreat into the background because Stuart Cabb had something else he wanted to 'put in the can'.

I recorded my pieces and had strolled back up the circuit when I suddenly heard a stifled scream and some raised Italian voices. Stuart had a small hand-held video camera to his eye and was running at the graffiti-covered wall, stopping just short of the point of impact. To the outrage of the onlookers he repeated this three or four times.

We apologised for this apparent insensitivity, but Stuart had got a shot that with post-production helped provide an astonishing and moving opening sequence to the programme. I suppose the end result is everything, but sometimes artistic film-making can be a terribly undignified process.

The production procedure for documentaries can also be the most satisfying experience in television. Live outside broadcasts are fine (when everything goes well) but you can only make a limited contribution to the product as a whole. With a programme like the Senna documentary there was the opportunity to get involved in every aspect, from its content and shape to its scripting and editing. We had some earnest discussions, quite a few arguments, and I probably got on their nerves on several occasions. But the finished product satisfied us all, and certainly encapsulated my experience of Senna from Snetterton to San Marino, and it was a proud presenter and production team that a few months later picked up the Royal Television Society Award for Sports Documentary of the Year.

But the ultimate accolade came a few years later when renowned pit-lane reporter Ted Kravitz rather sheepishly admitted that when he was at University, and looking to make his way in broadcasting, he recorded the programme then played around with the components, and even re-dubbed it with his voice, because he felt it was an object lesson in how such a programme should be put together, and the perfect tribute to someone who was his hero as well.

Chapter 6

INVENTING THE
FUTURE

My involvement at Anglia TV from the mid-'70s through the early '80s had given me great experience of the breadth and depth of motorsport. There had not only been Snetterton and Silverstone, but rallycross, motocross, trials and the Anglia Speedway outside broadcasts, which were both tremendous fun and fantastic sport.

I have always felt that Speedway was the perfect kind of televised motorsport – easy to package, plenty of starts and finishes, a strong fan base and a multitude of stories and intrigue around the garages. In East Anglia we had strong teams like Ipswich and also King's Lynn, who boasted the World Champion, Michael Lee. A supremely gifted but volatile character, Lee's regular conflicts with authority eventually proved his undoing and he would quit the sport. He reached rock bottom with a spell in Brixton prison for drug offences, but has now completely rebuilt his life and self-respect and is back in Speedway, promoting Mildenhall's Fen Tigers.

I relate all this because Michael showed us every angle of a great sport. I never knew a Wembley atmosphere quite as thrilling as when Michael was contesting the 1978 World Final in front of 80,000 fans and we were filming from the infield. But the contrast was Mildenhall. We would turn up there in West Suffolk with an outside broadcast unit and strangely would get told to park in a particular corner of the car park and to leave the cars unlocked. Along with 300–400 fans we would enjoy the action and then when we returned to the car park every member of the crew would have a couple of sacks of potatoes in their boot. I wish Michael well at Mildenhall – he was fabulous to watch as a rider, and Mildenhall is what Speedway is all about as a club.

But my career was moving on and in 1980 I was plucked from the prairies and potato fields of Suffolk to host the ITV coverage of the Olympic Games in Moscow. It was the kind of big-network break that everybody dreams of and I was determined to make sure it was the foundation for a decent long-term future, and on my return I became part of the presentation rota for *World of Sport*, ITV's late-lamented Saturday-afternoon sporting showcase.

Along with pretending to be Dickie Davies every now and again, while on the programme I had also worked with an independent production company on coverage of the British and World Rally Championship. It was an experience that gave me a further impression of what worked on television and what struggled, and what forms of motorsport had hidden potential.

So when I joined *BBC Grandstand* five years later I was not only joining the most famous programme in sports broadcasting, but also a team that was on the top of its form and, in comparison to ITV, had seemingly unlimited resources and airtime available.

But you did not have to look too far below the surface to discover that airtime was not being well used, especially where motorsport was concerned. My first edition of *Grandstand* was in July 1985, and the very first item I introduced was coverage of round seven of the Metro Challenge, a support Championship to the previous weekend's British Grand Prix at Silverstone. There was no reference at all to what had happened in rounds one to five in the Championship, and no great concern with what was going to happen in round six onwards. This was just a motor race randomly selected and delivered to the viewing public in very arbitrary fashion.

The problem for *BBC Grandstand* was that they were prevented from doing anything else. The rights contracts for motorsport had been done with circuits rather than Championships, which meant the programme was obliged to visit Oulton Park and Thruxton once a year and maybe Brands Hatch and Silverstone twice a year, and whatever was being staged on the day selected would be broadcast; therefore there was no continuity in the coverage and no ability to follow a story through the whole season.

In 1987 there was an opportunity to break out of this arrangement when the contracts for the circuits ran out. An informal meeting was called in the *Grandstand* office with John Phillips, a pioneering, freethinking *Grandstand* editor; Tiff Needell, who was becoming an occasional contributor and really had his finger on the pulse of British motorsport; Murray Walker and myself. I was being perceived as the new enthusiast who might shoulder much of the hard work involved in taking the coverage in a new direction.

The feeling was that the circuit contracts should not be renewed, despite the outrage this might provoke among some of the circuit owners, and the BBC's domestic coverage should be built around two major Championships, the choice of which did not require much debate.

The first was the British Formula Three Championship, which at this time was unchallenged as the principal step into Formula One, and the great battle between Senna and Brundle a few years earlier emphasised that it could produce supreme competition. The other choice was the British Touring Car Championship, a long-established cornerstone of domestic motorsport. First contested in 1958 it boasted the likes of Jim Clark among its former Champions, and although it had fallen on comparatively thin times it had the ability to pull in the fans, and it also had strong potential to bring in sponsors and rekindle manufacturer interest.

The next problem was how we would cover it. Each Championship would comprise about ten rounds, and the budget would not come close to putting a live outside broadcast unit at all ten, or even 20 if the Championships did not run together at the same locations. The decision was taken that the coverage would not be live, instead it would be post-produced; in other words several cameras recording remotely would generate the coverage, it would all be edited together over the following couple of days and the commentary put on as the last component.

However, the BBC, for all its facilities, could not handle such an operation, so the responsibility for mounting the coverage and delivering the final broadcast version would go to an independent producer. Not only that, but the independent producer or its agent would also have the responsibility of generating the budget, because the BBC would only pay a nominal £1,000 per race, feeling that its side of the bargain was covered by providing the *Grandstand* airtime and a four million audience. In other words, motorsport at this kind of level was seen to be a cash-rich sport that needed the oxygen of television coverage to survive, so it could damned well generate that coverage itself, and pay for it.

From a television licence-payer's point of view it made sense, and from the point of view of the cost of the modern Formula One rights deal it *still* makes sense. In 1986, from the point of view of British motorsport, it was a brave new world. From every other point of view it was a nightmare.

The one thing you cannot do, or be seen to do, with the BBC is sponsor programmes or effectively 'buy' airtime. If there is independent funding there must be no relation between the money raised, how it was raised and what appears on the screen. And when Tiff and Murray looked across at me, delighted that around 20 hours of prominent airtime had been secured for British motorsport, the responsibility of picking a route through this minefield of production, funding and (to use a modern word) compliance had clearly fallen to me.

We had about four months to put it all together. There was no time to have a beauty parade of television production companies; instead Barrie Hinchliffe's BHP were selected on the understanding that they would be under great short-term scrutiny. It was Barrie I had been working with on the World Rally Championship coverage for *World of Sport*, when his company had been rather grandly titled United Motion Pictures. They were based in Fitzroy Square in London and he was a brilliant motorsport film-maker. His work on the World Rally Championship and the European Touring Car Championship still graces the archives, but he worked on film and needed to switch rapidly to the newfangled video; and as for funding – he didn't care whether it was a World Championship or not, what appeared on the screen was only ever an accurate reflection of who had paid the money; that was how his business had survived.

Barrie was in touch with the best motorsport cameramen in the business and block-booked them for the season to come. We urgently had to get the message out that the two Championships were now receiving comprehensive coverage so that teams and sponsors could decide on plans and hopefully make an extra commitment.

The funding would be raised by a substantial levy on the entry fee administered by the RAC Motor Sports Association on behalf of the Touring Car Championship, and by the British Automobile Racing Club and the Formula Three Association on behalf of F3. Their assistance came as a great relief because it seemed to provide the 'laundering' element in the funding, and created distance between the competitors and the TV producers that prevented there being a connection between who paid the money and who featured in the ultimate coverage.

However, we were still struggling for entries in both Championships, resulting in a shortfall in the funding. There was no way to make the coverage cheaper; after all, it costs as much to cover a grid of 10 cars as a grid of 20. Inevitably the offers of 'assistance' came in from some of the more affluent entrants. 'We're happy to pay a bit more in return for more coverage' – precisely the scenario that would outrage the BBC and probably take us off the air.

A solution came with the introduction of on-board cameras. The technology was still primitive and, although they are now an integral part of Formula One coverage, back in 1987 they were not an option, especially when it came to single-seater racing. However, we had all seen what had been achieved in the groundbreaking coverage of the classic Bathurst race in Australia, demonstrating how well on-board cameras could operate in a saloon-car environment.

So our more wealthy entrants could pay to have an on-board camera mounted on their cars; it was no guarantee that they would get extra coverage, but if the camera worked it would certainly heighten the probability, especially if they were prominent at the front of the field. Then came the request to put sponsors' logos on the cockpit area in front of the camera. Back we went to the BBC. I will not burden you with all the legal arguments about foreground advertising, but miraculously we got a concession. The sponsor's name or logo could be mounted in front of the camera but had to conform to very specific dimensions, and we were given a cardboard template to carry around to make sure that everyone complied.

I suppose all this BBC guidelines stuff was familiar ground to the average producer, but I was a mere presenter and it meant that I arrived at the opening round at Silverstone exhausted and confused, having barely given a thought to the coverage or the prospects of the season ahead; I was just grateful that we seemed to have cars on the track and cameras around the circuit. For the majority of the season the Touring Car Championship and the British Formula Three Championship were to run alongside each other, which was a help in terms of shared cost. But even though it offered a high-quality line-up for the live spectators, only about 4,000 turned up for that first meeting at Silverstone.

Unfortunately the BBC contracts manager was one of those who did attend, along with his cardboard template, and was horrified that those who had bought on-board cameras had mounted the name of their individual sponsor in front of the lens, instead of the name of the series sponsor, Dunlop in the case of the Touring Car Championship and Lucas for Formula Three. For a tense hour it seemed that our brave new coverage might be over before a camera had rolled. Eventually after concessions had been made regarding the framing of the shot we were allowed to go ahead, but the rules had to be obeyed for the rest of the season. An important revenue stream had been blocked, but this was nothing compared to the problems that were still to come.

As the season progressed, some of the circuits – Brands Hatch in particular – were getting upset at the loss of the revenue that they were receiving directly from the BBC under the old agreement. We argued that because the new form of coverage was raising the profile of the Championships they were hosting, they would be making it up from the extra attendances, awareness, and perimeter advertising, and surely this would make it better off in the long term? But Brands, under its ambitious new owner Nicola Foulston, did not see the potential.

She attempted to use many sanctions, like charging BHP an inflated television access fee, or attempting to cover the racing with her own television crew – which, of course, would not come cheap and would probably not comply with the required production standards and guidelines. The BBC stood firm against that proposal, and the RAC Motor Sports Association and Formula Three threatened to boycott her circuits (which also included Snetterton and Oulton Park) if she put up any unreasonable barrier to the TV coverage going ahead.

The dispute got very acrimonious, and then it got personal, with questions being raised about my dual involvement with BHP (of which I was now a partner) and as presenter of the commissioning programme *Grandstand*. Approaches were made to *The Sunday Times*, which resulted in a full-page feature questioning my role, suggesting a corrupt commissioning system and effectively accusing me of taking backhanders to enable sports to get airtime on *Grandstand*.

The telephone call I got from Jonathan Martin, the BBC Head of Sport, at about 1:00am on the day of *The Sunday Times* publication was, as you can imagine, frosty and formal. Jonathan was a strong, feisty personality who knew television inside out and was easily the best Head of Sport I ever worked under. On this occasion he was making no judgements, but I had to be in his office at 10:00 on Monday morning with documentary proof of my complete innocence.

I turned up with invoices for car purchases, servicing and tyres plus all the correspondence that had been generated so far in putting the coverage together. He was convinced and he was supportive, helped by the fact that he was excited by the quality of the coverage so far and the very positive reaction it was getting.

But the BBC had to be seen to take action. I agreed, in the long term, to distance myself from BHP, and it was agreed that rival bids would have to be considered to provide the coverage. A form of tender went out and the stipulated requirement was that the successful bidder had to cover the events in precisely the manner in which it was currently being transmitted. Murray Walker immediately committed himself exclusively to the BHP operation, so all the others had no chance.

It all felt a bit grubby, but there had been times during the wrangling when this great television opportunity for British motorsport was going to be lost. There was no way a rival bidder was going to offer better coverage or reliably meet the deadlines that *Grandstand* imposed week after week, and already there were clear signs that the coverage was having a very positive effect.

As the season went on and television helped to develop storylines and personalities, so the live attendance grew, sometimes reaching 15,000 or 20,000. The great advantage of doing post-produced coverage is that you could second-guess every event in the race. Every crash or overtaking move had been recorded remotely and could be shoehorned into the final edit. The dullest race (and with the Touring Cars there were not too many of those) could be made a maelstrom of non-stop action and incident. It might not have been completely faithful to the pace and tone of the original, but it was working wonders in growing a new audience for the sport.

Because it was all off-tape we could also be a lot more confident about tackling controversy and talking to angry drivers choking on red mist. Mike Smith, the trendy, blond-haired radio DJ, was a good driver and was teammate to the millionaire car dealer Frank Sytner. It was not an ideal partnership, and Sytner's expletive-laden rant against his teammate while striding the length of the Snetterton pit-lane would have been a disaster live, but after a few hours work with the bleep machine it became a classic piece of television.

The Championship was developing heroes and villains at a rate that would have delighted any modern reality game show. Sytner actually emerged as Champion in that first season of coverage in 1988. The television foothold had been established and now the manufacturers were circling. The future looked assured for the Touring Cars, but Formula Three proved to be more of a battle.

Despite its worthy reputation as the final stepping-stone into Formula One, it has always proved hard to sell to the big sponsors, and large motor manufacturers would struggle to use single-seater racing to sell their wares. But its pedigree could not be challenged – the Championship where Senna had triumphed over Brundle in 1983 had been won by Johnny Herbert the previous year.

Now, at the end of March 1988, Formula Three shared the Silverstone billing with the Touring Cars. JJ Lehto, who would go on to make an impression in Formula One if not a great impact, won the race and went on to win the Championship. Half an hour after the racing, in a TV crew-room laden with packing cases, equipment and the odd plate of sandwiches, a youthful Damon Hill sat cross-legged on the floor with Eddie Irvine looking over his shoulder. On a shaky monitor they were reviewing the output of Damon's on-board camera, the first time either of them had had the chance to look back on a race from this perspective.

'Fantastic, this is the future,' said Damon. For a moment all the contractual complications and legal threats were forgotten. I felt we were on the right track.

All this was barely 20 years ago, but on-board technology was in a very primitive state. It seems unthinkable now in the age of faultless, rock-steady, crystal-clear pictures from battling Formula One cars, but back then we were struggling to get mounts that could absorb vibration, and were forced to toughen up recorders so the tape did not tear from the heads (microwave linking being far too advanced and expensive).

But when it worked, the pictures – and the significance of the pictures – was fantastic. There was not only Damon Hill in his formative years but also a first look at another future World Champion, Mika Häkkinen. His style was evident from every angle but he was also capable of getting it wrong in spectacular fashion. The sequence of him crawling out from underneath his inverted chassis at the Snetterton Bomb Hole would be replayed at regular intervals throughout his career. Others to play a starring role through the next five years of coverage would include David Brabham, Paul Stewart, Gil de Ferran and Rubens Barrichello, as well as the ill-fated Roland Ratzenberger. But despite the cast-list the budgets became harder to sustain. Dave Price worked tirelessly on behalf of the Formula Three Association but it became especially difficult when more political problems forced it to split from the Touring Car race-day line-up.

By contrast the British Touring Car Championship was becoming a reborn phenomenon from both the sporting and marketing points of view. A small committee representing the various interested parties managed the first couple of seasons, the line-up including the experienced Andy Rouse, who could put the viewpoint of both the driver and the teams; Dave Cook of Vauxhall on behalf of the manufacturers; team boss Vic Lee; and Dave Richards of the emergent Prodrive team, whose talents as an innovator were second to none. For a while the RAC Motor Sports Association and this group, known as the Touring Car Association, handled the running of the Championship and also the raising of the television production budget, and they passed it on to BHP with no strings attached. This protected me from having to handle any accusations of participants 'buying time' in the coverage.

Although the product was good and the Championship was growing in popularity there was a very temporary feeling about this arrangement. That would all change when Australian Alan Gow arrived on the scene in 1991. A former Melbourne car dealer and former manager of Australian touring car legend Peter Brock, Alan also worked closely with Andy Rouse, especially when the four-time British Champion moved from Ford to Toyota in 1992.

But Alan also proved to be the ideal man to guide the BTCC toward a more solid, structured future. He found himself running the Touring Car Association, which then became TOCA Ltd when he negotiated the purchase of the Championship rights from the RAC Motor Sports Association. He was then the architect of the move to the 2-litre Super Touring formula, which has now been globally accepted, and has given a strength and consistency to Touring Car racing worldwide. He was also (eventually) a supporter of live coverage of the Championship on British television, but that was still a couple of years in the future.

With Alan Gow's invaluable input everyone involved from back in 1988 could take a great deal of satisfaction from how well the package had worked. It was achieving everything we hoped for, especially from the manufacturers' point of view. Vauxhall and Ford were doing battle, BMW often set the pace,

Alfa Romeo added spice and took a lot of honours, but it was when Volvo came on board that we realised how much of a marketing man's dream it had become.

Volvo had no great motorsport history – indeed, their image seemed to be the very antithesis of what motor racing represented. But they had seen that any kind of success in the Championship could introduce them to a whole new market. They did a lot of research and planning, and in one meeting at BHP I wondered what model they were thinking of running, and jokingly asked 'Why not the estate?'

They agreed there was no reason why they shouldn't run it; if they were going to make a statement, why not make the ultimate statement? The estate, beautifully prepared, made its debut at Snetterton, and on the drivers' parade – to the crowd's delight – there were two large golden retrievers gazing out of the tailgate.

A few rounds later they were right on the pace at Brands Hatch and were rewarded with Murray Walker delivering the kind of commentary line that was a Volvo marketing man's dream. 'Just look at the Volvo Estate going round outside of the BMW M3 at Clearways. Unbelievable performance!'

Murray Walker's commentary was an integral part of the success of the coverage, but its preparation and delivery would be in great contrast to the 'pants on fire' performance he would save up for live grand prix. After a Sunday Touring Car race, heading for a Saturday transmission, the initial edit would be available for Murray on a Wednesday afternoon. Murray would come into the central London studios of BHP around midday and would sit in front of a monitor for about six hours. He would then repair to a pretty decent hotel and return the next morning to put in another four or five hours of preparation.

Every shot would be studied, every move would be analysed, every fact would be checked. He didn't exactly script the commentary, but with the help of notes that filled about a dozen A4 sheets of paper it was the next best thing. Then about four o'clock on the Thursday afternoon the buzz would go round the edit suite and the production office, Murray was ready.

The microphone was raised – because Murray always stood – and we settled back in the dubbing suite for the performance. It was always a remarkable tour de force. His finger would jab at the screen, his voice would stray a few octaves too high; even with two days' preparation he gave the impression that every incident and development in the race came as a complete shock. It came across as the perfect live commentary, accurate in every detail, convincing in every emotion. At the end of the commentary he would always solemnly join us on the other side of the glass and insist on a complete playback of the recording. We dutifully sat with him, safe in the knowledge that Murray had nailed it once again.

But deep down I had the feeling that the whole thing was on borrowed time. We could never put a co-commentator with Murray because, in terms of the edit, the action and incident was relentless. There was no time for analysis or reflection. This post-produced recording method was terrific television, but it was also a misrepresentation of the narrative and pace of the actual race. Twenty years ago I held a view (a view which is taken for granted now) that unless a sport, and a sports broadcast, is transmitted live, it is decidedly second division.

Murray held the opposite view – and expressed it forcibly in his autobiography – that if you went live with the British Touring Car Championship, the genie would be out of the bottle, and the viewing public would have to confront the fact that the Touring Cars could at times, like any other sport, be boring. Up to this point, thanks to the BHP editors, there had never been a boring Touring Car race.

There was merit on both sides of the argument but thankfully progress intervened and, in the long term, reliable microwave on-board cameras were developed, digital television made extra airtime available, and the video-editing has become astonishingly swift and slick. The end result has become the seven hours of live transmission that ITV4 provide of every TOCA race day. Reality television, it turns out, has not been a problem to the Touring Cars.

Along the way its strength as a marketing device has wavered. With some honourable exceptions manufacturers have not been in it for the long term; instead they achieve their ambitions and move on. During the '90s the manufacturer-count swung from eight or nine down to two or three.

But it is hard not to look back on those days as a kind of golden age. There was Cleland and Soper, Winkelhock, Harvey and Hoy and, as we reflected a little earlier, on a couple of occasions there was Mansell as well.

And if there was one race that defined the British Touring Car Championship as being short on purity but strong on soap opera, it was the climax of the 1992 season, the race at Silverstone that made Tim Harvey Champion. His success only came after a race-long duel with John Cleland and Steve Soper, who resolved it by taking out Cleland in seemingly uncompromising fashion at Luffield. There weren't actually punches thrown, but some aggressive gestures were made and Soper was accused of being an animal. We were all shocked and outraged, of course, but deep down we were reassured. All the battles had been worth it. The British Touring Car Championship clearly mattered.

In the late '80s and early '90s motorsport on the BBC had never been stronger. Formula One was backed up by the premier domestic Championships, and *Grandstand* had also been persuaded to make a strong commitment to British and World rallying. McRae and Burns were about to get everyone excited on the gravel, Mansell and Hill were poised to take us into a thrilling era of grand prix glory. It was all on the BBC. Inevitably there was complacency, and for everyone who felt this dominance was here to stay there was a shock in store.

Chapter 7

THE BBC DISCOVER
FORMULA ONE

In fairness, sports broadcasting at this time was, as far as the BBC were concerned, pretty much an open goal. Football rights were still strongly contested between ITV and BBC, there was the occasional spat over athletics, ITV still had a slice of horse racing and the Rugby World Cup, but after the demise of *World of Sport* there was no serious opposition to the BBC and its *Grandstand* flagship when it came to sports like motor racing.

It was a good thing and a bad thing. It is always good, in any television sports operation, to at least be under the impression that you're in it for the long term. Relationships, contacts and experience can be built up, as well as that all-important long-term contract with the viewers. They want to be able to identify with 'the voice of cricket' and 'the home of golf', and that usually meant the BBC.

However, having that sense of security also encouraged complacency; too much was taken for granted, and I'm sure I was part of the self-satisfied mood that was around.

Formula One was an integral part of the Sunday *Grandstand* afternoon, but forget the pit-lane news and the grid-walk – it would be a kind of a 'macho' thing to hand to Murray from the London studio at the last possible second before the start of the race, and if everything worked to plan this would be about ten seconds before the green light. This would be regarded as a triumph of timing rather than an editorial betrayal.

Equally, once the race had begun the running order would dictate that around two o'clock we would move away from the Belgian or Portuguese Grand Prix and head probably to the Sunday League cricket or Hickstead, with the promise that 'you can see the climax of that race sometime after 5:30pm'. Astonishingly, given the high standards and expectations these days, the audience accepted that, even though the amount of motor racing they saw at 5:30pm might be dictated by whether Somerset had been bowled out or not.

But there were those within the department who were fans and defenders of Formula One, and I would count Head of Sport Jonathan Martin among them, and slowly the tide began to turn. With the help of the *Sportsnight* programme we would do features, and on maybe three occasions a year we managed to get *Grandstand* trackside at places like Monza and Imola; and there was always the grand prix highlights programme to make sure that the full story was eventually told.

The case for making a stronger commitment to the sport was not helped by the coverage itself, which was still dependent on local producers providing the world with coverage that was biased, sometimes outrageously, towards the local audience. Needless to say when the BBC hosted the coverage of the British Grand Prix, the brilliance of our director Keith McKenzie provided the model for Formula One coverage that is still being followed to this day.

Through it all, good and bad, we had Murray Walker, the great enigma of commentators, and the great survivor. All his shortcomings in terms of insight and delivering research in the right order were redeemed by his overwhelming enthusiasm. Other commentators, to my mind, did the same thing without ever finding the same magic ingredient. Rugby League commentator Eddie Waring was certainly one of those, but the view in that sport is that Rugby League 'survived' Eddie Waring, whereas Murray Walker was one of the 'architects' of the modern passion for Formula One.

Also, Eddie Waring never had to work alongside James Hunt. Internally within the BBC, Murray never disguised his objections to working alongside this ill-disciplined, out-of-control co-commentator, who may have been a World Champion but seemingly broke all the rules of professional broadcasting and civilised behaviour.

I once put *Grandstand* on the air from the British Grand Prix at Silverstone. I had stood at the trackside as the cars fired up and blasted away on the formation lap, one of those bonus front-row moments that you sometimes get in broadcasting.

I headed for the Shell Tower and was making my way up the exterior steps, anxious to be in position for the start itself, when I was conscious of a voice behind me.

'There's a man who'll know.' It was James. 'Hi Steve, by any chance is there any cricket on after we've done racing here? I'll hang around if there's some cricket to watch, otherwise I'll be legging it before the finish.'

He was coming up the Shell Tower steps in his own good time carrying a pint of lager in each hand. I held the door open to try to hasten his arrival in the commentary box. The cars were heading toward Woodcote. He put the two pints down on Murray's notes, smearing the near-perfect calligraphy, picked up the microphone and offered a succinct 30-second assessment of race prospects, contradicting most of what Murray had been saying, before handing back for the start. It was no wonder Murray got so pissed off.

Then there was the time he failed to appear at all. I was in the *Grandstand* studio completing the final build-up to the Belgian Grand Prix at Spa, when the instruction came to just hand to Murray because James was not yet in the commentary box. The race came and went. There was no sign of James, no message, and no clue to his whereabouts, although he had been at the circuit the previous day. Murray needed some help and it was at this race that Martin Brundle was plucked from the pit-lane to make an impressive first contribution in the commentary box.

As time went on Murray would make regular complaints about the lack of studio etiquette from James, but deep down he knew that these two extremes of approach were producing the perfect live commentary. The two commentators would often hold completely opposite opinions about the progress of a race, but rather than alienating the audience the viewers became embraced in the debate – they stopped being a passive audience and started to become involved in the argument, and almost by default involved in the sport. With Senna, Prost, Piquet and Mansell there was plenty to get excited about, and in the BBC coverage every extreme of opinion seemed to be on offer. Murray and James, whatever their irreconcilable differences (and there were many), were perfect for the time and lifted the profile of Formula One, not least internally at the BBC.

The tragic irony was that at the time of his shockingly early death at age 45, James had become a dramatically reformed character. A new woman had entered his life, and with this there came a new sense of responsibility, also encouraged no doubt by the realisation that his finances were in a desperate state. He stopped drinking, got himself fit and became a total professional in the commentary box. A few weeks before he died from a heart attack we had met for lunch at a restaurant in Bayswater, with other members of the broadcast team. James had cycled from his home in Wimbledon, drank only water and was full of excitement for the new season and brimful of ideas and energy for expanding the coverage. The fact that the BBC seemed to share his enthusiasm and ideas became part of James's legacy over the next few years.

Slowly the coverage developed, the occasions when we would link live from a grand prix increased, and we became slightly more ambitious in the coverage. There was a willingness to produce Formula One documentaries, and the tribute programme we did for Senna was followed by further profiles of Damon Hill and Michael Schumacher.

Chapter 8

THE BBC LOSE FORMULA ONE

In the first half of the '90s the BBC was quite simply the best sports broadcasting organisation to work for. The summer of 1992 typified it for me. I worked on the presentation of Wimbledon with Sue Barker, who had just joined the team. From there it was straight to Silverstone to watch Mansell's victory, along with our junior royal guests. From the Silverstone car park I headed north to Muirfield to host coverage of Nick Faldo winning one of the most dramatic of Open Championships. Then it was straight back to London for a Monday-morning flight to Barcelona and a glorious Olympic Games in which Linford Christie and Sally Gunnell were the gold-medal stars for Britain and we watched each success from our presentation position above the finish line.

ITV were not serious rivals, the satellite revolution was not yet up to speed and we were able to work in the secure, warm glow that if it was major sport (and it wasn't football) then we would be bringing it to the nation on the BBC; and no sport felt more impregnable in this respect than Formula One.

Then we got to Tuesday 12 December 1995. We were in the final stages of an end-of-season documentary on the World Champion Michael Schumacher. We were barely a week away from transmission and the programme was simply titled *Michael Schumacher*. We had every possible contribution on film except an interview with... Michael Schumacher. The situation was getting desperate.

All our attempts to secure any time in Schumacher's schedule had so far failed. In the end the Benetton PR staff, sensing our panic, managed to get us half an hour on the afternoon of 12 December in the team hotel in Portugal during a break in testing at Estoril. We had booked ourselves on the first available TAP flight out of Heathrow, and now we were sitting in the departure lounge staring at the screens. There was a minimum four-hour delay and the gloomy assistant on the check-in desk felt it could be more; and no, there were not any other flights.

The gloom now became total. Without Schumacher we had no programme, and yet somehow a programme had to be delivered. Back in London the *Grandstand* Christmas lunch was in full swing, while we were marooned in a crowded, bad-tempered departure lounge thinking that life couldn't possible get any worse. Then producer Ken Burton's mobile phone rang.

It was a researcher who had been left alone in the *Grandstand* office with instructions only to disturb any of the senior programme personnel if it was of extreme importance.

'Hi Ken,' he said. 'I didn't think I'd get hold of you. You're in Portugal aren't you?'

'No, I'm not. What's the problem?'

'Well I may have got completely the wrong end of the stick but something has just come up on the screens here saying that ITV have won the exclusive television rights to Formula One from 1997, and the BBC are kicked into touch.'

'I'm sure you have got the wrong end of the stick,' said Ken calmly. 'Read it to me.'

And that was how we heard. A five-year deal, a figure of around £60 million was mentioned, but the story was keen to emphasise that BBC Television's 18 years of broadcasting Formula One were coming to an abrupt and completely unexpected end.

Still disbelieving, we found a television in the corner of Terminal Two, and there it was, the lead item on the lunchtime news. There was little mention of production values, or the part the BBC had played in making Formula One the high-profile sport it was. But there was an awful lot about whether or not this was the end of Murray Walker, and whether the voice of motorsport was preparing to switch channels as well.

As that grim day wore on the initial shock turned to anger and complete mystification as to why an organisation like ITV, with no continuous commitment to motorsport, would suddenly bid three or four times what the BBC could afford for a sport that was ill-suited to their schedules, and also had no natural format that could accommodate commercial breaks. There was also anger at Bernie Ecclestone for the kind of cold commercial decision that seemed to have no regard for past service to the sport and also seemed to have involved no element of negotiation.

But most of all we were angry at ourselves and the hierarchy of the BBC for not anticipating the challenge, and so becoming a complacent victim of the comfort zone built up over the past few years.

But the fallout from this astonishing bit of news could wait – we had a programme to try and complete. Thanks to the Portuguese airline we arrived in the team hotel far too late for any interview time with Schumacher. The Benetton staff confronted us with the ITV news, anxious to know the detail and our reaction and what on earth was going to happen to Murray Walker? We did our best to provide what information we could, and I think it was out of sympathy that they managed to get us ten minutes, and no more than ten minutes, with Michael over breakfast at 7:00am.

It had been a very long day, but because of the early start the next morning we felt it was a good idea to get all the equipment set up so we would be ready to go with the interview bright and early at dawn. It was then that the cameraman asked nervously who had packed the batteries. Once again panic set in. This vital part of our gear was still at Heathrow, somewhere in the bowels of Terminal Two, and there was no chance of getting it to us overnight.

All credit, then, to the crew for spending the next three hours plundering the battery from the hire car, begging another one from a hotel van and getting it all to work with two sets of jump leads.

Michael Schumacher arrived promptly at 7:00am, raised an eyebrow at the two dirty car batteries and the flickering lights, and with Teutonic wit expressed his sympathy that apparently we were all going to be out of a job. We reassured him that at least Murray would be fine and pressed on with the interview before our ten minutes ran out, along with our electricity.

Back at the BBC the blow was slowly absorbed. At least we had one more season before Formula One switched sides. But clearly life was never going to be the same. I felt sorry for Jonathan Martin, the head of sport, whose commitment to the sport had been total but, like many others, had to appreciate that Bernie Ecclestone would always have more flexible priorities.

Once all the anger had subsided it was clear that in theory this was a great opportunity for the future broadcasting of the sport. The BBC coverage had evolved slowly, the new innovations having to exist alongside the bad habits. But ITV, through the efforts of a yet to be appointed independent producer, would approach Formula One with a blank sheet of paper – no history and no preconceptions; the imagination could run riot and the best ideas would end up on the screen.

Around February 1996 I was approached by a talented producer/broadcaster at Anglia named Kevin Piper. Kevin had joined Anglia at around the time I was moving on to network television, and Norfolk and the East of England had clearly given him the same sort of enthusiasm for motorsport as it had for me, some 20 years earlier.

He told me that Anglia, in conjunction with Meridian Television in Southampton, were exploring the possibility of putting in a bid for the ITV Formula One production contract. Would I be interested in joining them, at least to help in putting together some initial ideas? My immediate reaction was 'Of course not' – I was under contract to the BBC and could not imagine this would enable me to work for the opposition in any form.

But then again my convoluted reasoning convinced me that I would be working on behalf of ITV Formula One. BBC had lost the contract, and from 1997 there would hardly be a frame of grand prix motor racing on the BBC; therefore I could not be in conflict with the BBC's output.

I put this strange logic to Jonathan Martin; he smiled and told me to get on with it, but he and I would have no more discussion on the subject. Generously I think he felt I had the exciting prospect of being involved in the formation of a new style of Formula One coverage, just as he had some 15 years ago, and could see no reason, contractually or otherwise, to stand in my way as long as it did not compromise my role with the BBC.

And it was precisely that. A group of us met on several occasions, sometimes in Norwich, sometimes in London. We analysed how the sport had been covered up until this point and came up with ideas of how it might progress. Some of them were outrageous and were thrown out immediately, others are very much part of the coverage now.

We brought Martin Brundle into the group to add the driver perspective, and we regarded him as the man who could communicate the sport to a new and growing audience. We argued about the style of presentation, whether it would be studio based or pit-lane based, but there was agreement that from now on Formula One would travel the world, and every race would be presented from location, with live coverage of qualifying a definite part of the package.

The mission was partly to present the sport to a new audience, but also to introduce the sport to ITV itself, because it became clear as our research went on that the contract had been signed without much consideration to the component parts of Formula One and a grand prix schedule. There seemed to have been no concern about commercial breaks interrupting the coverage and no thoughts on the need to schedule qualifying; in fact there was no reference to the rights to broadcast qualifying in the ITV contract, and this was to have serious consequences a few months into their first season. Also there was no great awareness that a couple of the races, Canada and Brazil, cut into the lucrative peak-time audience on a Sunday evening.

Our meetings and discussions tended to focus on the potential for features and spin-off programmes, and beefing up the pre-race build-up and post-race analysis. Apart from the British Grand Prix there was little opportunity to influence race coverage itself.

We evolved from an occasional pub-lunch to more formal meetings. Mark Wilkin came on board and slowly the word got around the industry that this ad hoc little group might be making some progress. Some muscle was needed and it came in the form of Chrysalis Sport and their boss Neil Duncanson, who had been working on similar lines. The two bids joined forces and turned into a powerful line-up. Meridian and Anglia alongside Chrysalis became MACh 1, a high-octane name for what was now a very serious and well-researched bid.

Also we seemed to be first out of the blocks and had most of the details and philosophy in place by the time of the tender invitation on 5 June 1996. But among ourselves there was no great confidence, because there were some big rivals who were yet to show their hand, including Mark McCormack's mighty TransWorld International, Sunset and Vine, and the clear favourites ISN, the internal bid from ITV. In all we reckoned there were about nine or ten companies and consortiums bidding to provide ITV's Formula One coverage.

Guidance from ITV was in short supply but they had made it clear that they did not want the new coverage to just pick up where the BBC had left off. So did this mean that they wanted Murray Walker or not? No one was going to take a chance, ourselves included, and we had persuaded Murray to commit himself to our bid. This was important to us – after all, it was Murray's commitment that had kept BHP in the Touring Car Championship a few years earlier.

In July at Silverstone I walked around the Formula One paddock with Murray. The British Grand Prix that year was the first and only meeting place of the rival bids, and was full of gossip and intrigue. I became aware as we walked that familiar-looking TV executives were coming up to Murray, putting an arm round his shoulder and greeting him like a long-lost friend. Murray grinned rather sheepishly: 'That was Jim, he thinks I'm exclusive to his bid', or 'That was Joe, apparently I signed something and I might be exclusive to his bid as well.' There was only ever going to be one winner, and Murray quite rightly wasn't going to take any chances. He was probably exclusive to every bid in the line-up. Good luck to him.

Time went on and ITV were leaving it late. We were heading into September and the key production staff involved in the winning bid would want to get to some races, ideally in Europe, before doing it for real in Adelaide the following March. We were also getting nervous, and some supporters decided to head off to the more substantial ISN bid. I could understand their thinking, but I wasn't under the same kind of pressures; my future was not on the line in quite the same way, or at least I did not think so.

I was playing golf at Moor Park in Hertfordshire when the news came through. It was Neil Duncanson. 'Congratulations, you're part of the winning bid and, congratulations, you're the new presenter of ITV Formula One.' The first part of all that was a great thrill – I knew the work, the detail and the very sociable dialogue and discussion that had gone into putting the bid together. The second part filled me with a lot of contractual trepidation.

I had been nominated in the bid as the presenter and we had talked loosely about the practicalities of making it stick. I had, perhaps naively, been assured by Chrysalis that 'getting you out of the BBC contract won't be a problem, we have guys who talk to the BBC at a pretty high level, we can do them a couple of favours and so on...'. All the members of the winning bid met for a drink in London that night, their working futures in Formula One excitingly guaranteed. I felt less convinced.

This outcome had never been part of the discussion with Jonathan Martin six months earlier. Jonathan had now been replaced by Brian Barwick, one of my former producers on *Sportsnight* and *Grandstand*, who a few years down the line would be a high-profile Chief Executive of the Football Association.

We were good friends and there was no need for small talk. He knew I wanted to leave and knew that I felt let down by the BBC's inability to hold on to a property of the status of Formula One. But it seemed that the cavalry promised by the top management at Chrysalis wasn't going to arrive, and I still had two years left on my contract. There was no need to be legalistic about that side of things – Brian didn't want presenters who had been bullied into staying. There followed long discussions about the pros and cons of staying or leaving and a couple of lunches in which Brian put a good case for the good times that lay ahead at the BBC for all of us, despite the absence of Formula One.

In the end I was not worn down, I was actually convinced I should stay – the BBC was still the place to be. I conveyed my decision to MACh 1. But it wasn't too long after this that Brian Barwick himself left the BBC to become Head of Sport at ITV. Television is a daft industry but this was an about-turn of such spectacular proportions we both laugh about it 14 years later.

It was December, three months to go to the new season, and ITV were without a Formula One presenter and, in a sense of panic, some truly silly names were being mentioned, and also some eminently sensible ones, including John Leslie and Philip Schofield, who remains a keen and knowledgeable Formula One fan. My role as part of the winning bid was over, and I had precious little influence on what happened from this point on, but I took it upon myself to contact ITV's long-serving presenter Jim Rosenthal to tell him that I was out of the running, and if he fancied Formula One to go for it. ITV would eventually decide that he would bring just the right kind of experience that the new venture needed.

At ITV the planning was getting frantic and the anticipation intense. However, at the BBC, in the last few months of 1996, we still had the loose ends of the season to tie up, and the great consolation was that it was a season potentially bringing us another British World Champion in Damon Hill.

So from the BBC point of view it was not a season that could be allowed to just drift to a close, although within the upper reaches of the BBC there were those who were already sneering that Formula One was overpriced, overcommercial and probably shouldn't be counted as a 'real' sport anyway; a sour reaction to the loss of one of the undoubted crown jewels in any broadcaster's portfolio.

For some reason Michael Jackson, the Controller of BBC 2, decided to join us at the Portuguese Grand Prix at Estoril, and I'm sure it wasn't simply because this was the last chance to go to a sunny Formula One race before the contract disappeared. Even so, it was difficult to decipher what message he was trying to impart. There seemed to be no great enthusiasm for the sport and no great knowledge of exactly what the sport had contributed to his network down the years.

On the night before the race he hosted a solemn, dull gathering in an Estoril restaurant for the BBC team who were all together that evening for the very last time; and if the message he was trying to convey was that Formula One would actually be far better off on ITV, then he succeeded.

Portugal had been the race where Damon was set to clinch the title, and I suppose ideally the Controller of BBC 2 would have liked to have seen the contest resolved so that he could say 'That's it, season's over, Formula One is finished for us, maybe we don't have to spend so much money now, covering the last round in Japan.' But Damon had one of his more indifferent days; his teammate and great rival for the title, Jacques Villeneuve, took the victory and the Championship race went on to Suzuka. We at least left Estoril with the knowledge that the last grand prix on the BBC would be surrounded by huge headlines and great national interest.

In Japan, Damon rose to the occasion in style, taking the lead from the start, and was never headed. I was manning the studio in London with Nigel Mansell as the guest. He was good company and fully appreciative of the achievement of Damon, although he was understandably less aware of the emotions being felt that day by all members of the BBC Formula One team. When Damon crossed the line as World Champion and Murray said 'I have to stop talking because I have a lump in my throat...' he struck a chord with the nation; but Murray was the only front-line member of the team who would be starting the next season with ITV.

Back in the studio Damon's world title was the only thing that mattered, but it was only when *The Chain* played us out for the last time and we left Studio Three and walked out into the early Sunday-morning sunlight that we began to appreciate exactly what had been lost.

There were still opportunities to add to the discomfort of the BBC management. A significant moment came at the end-of-year Sports Personality programme, a title that Damon had won two years earlier despite not winning the World Championship. He had received a kind of sympathy vote, having been a victim of Schumacher's bullying tactics at Melbourne, and I still remember the look of outrage on a senior BBC Sports producer's face (broadcast to millions) when Damon's name was read out ahead of Colin Jackson and Sally Gunnell.

In 1996 he won it as World Champion, although he still conceded that he felt uncomfortable at getting the vote ahead of Steve Redgrave and Frankie Dettori. But it was as nothing compared to the discomfort of the channel controllers and contracts managers seated behind the presentation, who were getting told, quite firmly, by the viewing audience that they had, in fact, lost a championship of huge broadcasting status.

Our final production in our last contract year was to put together a documentary on Damon's achievements, similar to the programme we had done on Michael Schumacher the year before. Given Damon's family background and motorsport heritage it was a fascinating story to tell, with a great deal of archive footage and 'family album' material available.

The purpose of the programme was also to acknowledge those who had provided help to Damon along the way, and one of those was the ex-Beatle and great Formula One fan George Harrison. At this time George was a pretty reclusive character who performed only occasionally, and very rarely gave interviews. But with a few guarantees about the ground we would cover, and a little persuasion from Damon, he agreed to face our cameras one evening at his very distinctive home, Fryer Park in Henley.

It started off in an uncomfortable atmosphere with George seemingly confused and concerned about what he could actually contribute to the programme. But to our amusement, every 15 minutes or so he would leave the room and come back just a little bit more relaxed and co-operative. The interview was done, and he had been entertaining and knowledgeable about everything connected with Formula One and the history and heritage of the sport. Then instead of us packing up and leaving he insisted that we all had a few beers and talked motor racing. As the evening progressed we managed to expand the agenda to pop music as well, and the Beatles in particular.

It was a fascinating and privileged audience, all taking place in a rather ramshackle den that had no superstar pretensions. I remember there was a juke box in the corner of the room and I expected it to contain the very best of the last 20 years in rock music. The fact that the two most memorable titles were *The Ying Tong Song* by the Goons and Benny Hill's recording of *Ernie the Fastest Milkman in the West*, seemed perfectly in tune with the eccentric Gothic pile of Fryer Park where George had made his home.

A memorable evening was drawing to a close when George, now completely relaxed and convivial, leant forward and said 'Do you know I've written a song about Formula One?'

I said that I was familiar with his song called *Faster*, which I always thought was one of the most evocative songs ever written about motorsport, but George was apparently talking about a new song, specifically about Formula One and the personalities in the sport. Not only that, but nobody had ever heard it and would we mind if he played it for us?

We followed him up the stairs to his high-tech recording studio at the top of the house, now feeling very important and poised for a moment and an experience that would surely go down in rock music legend. He retired behind the glass and settled down with his guitar. I adopted a kind of George Martin pose at the control panel. Then he played.

I would defy even the great George Martin himself to have salvaged anything from one of the worst songs I had ever heard. It was clunky and discordant and there was even one chorus where he had transposed 'Bernie' for 'Ernie' in an apparent homage to Benny Hill. It was dreadful.

He clearly sensed from our discomfort that this was not a winner, and I also sensed that we had heard the first and last public performance of his Formula One song. I resisted the temptation to suggest that while he was there could he do *Here Comes the Sun* for us, but he then turned his attention back to his guitar and performed a perfect impromptu acoustic rendition of *The Chain*.

'That's the sound of Formula One,' he said, smiling.

'Well, it *was*,' I replied.

Chapter 9

ITV CHANGE THE LANDSCAPE

The following March ITV went on air with the Australian Grand Prix from Adelaide, and made an impressive debut. There was a schedule that persuaded the audience to stay up through the night, including the classic movie *Grand Prix* and other great gems from the motor racing archive. Then Jim Rosenthal took it on, live and well prepared, from the Adelaide paddock, with a pre-race show that was the best part of an hour long. Sitting there through the night with a bottle of wine, I could only mournfully reflect on going on the air for the 1986 World Championship decider from Adelaide from that converted weather studio in Television Centre, inheriting an audience that had been transfixed by the slowly turning pages from Ceefax.

But in those early shows for ITV many of the elements we had discussed through the previous year in Norfolk pubs and London meetings were there and working. Some of the more ambitious proposals – of having a permanent studio presence in the paddock and a live operation around the pit-lane garages – had clearly come up against the immovable obstacle of Bernie Ecclestone, but at least their operation had time to grow and time to evolve.

Back at the BBC we had to pick up the pieces. There were no problems for me, as the attractions of golf and rugby and everything else that *Grandstand* provided were still intact. But I was aware that Mark Wilkin, one of the best of the department's producers, was being marginalised in a very petty fashion because of his involvement with the ITV bid, and indeed it would be another ten years before he would be invited back into the mainstream.

Others cast adrift by the loss of Formula One tried to plan the recovery and emphasise to the viewing public and the decision-makers within the BBC that we still had a role to play in motorsport, even without the grand prix. There was certainly a strong argument for the continuing entertainment value of Touring Cars and the relevance of Formula Three plus British and World Championship rallying.

The talisman in all this was to try to preserve and expand *The Chain* as the signature tune not only of Formula One, but of all things motorsport. Mark and I, with Ken Burton, proposed a magazine programme called *Chequered Flag*, which would have the ability to react to what was happening in Formula One as well as looking at action and behind-the-scenes stories of every other form of motorsport around the world.

The proposal was greeted indulgently by the planners and we were granted an occasional daytime slot and precious little budget, but it was an opportunity. There were some good features: we went to America to profile Mark Blundell, making a real impression in IndyCar, and we were in Monaco to do the same with Touring Car Champion Frank Biela. But the programme was without support and existed on borrowed time. The internal opposition, not just to Formula One but to motorsport in general, was growing. Our cause was not helped by ITV – despite high production values – being stuck with a pretty humdrum first season in which Jacques Villeneuve eventually emerged as Champion.

The feeling at the top of the BBC was 'aren't we clever to have off-loaded this boring, expensive, self-obsessed sport', and it was a feeling that eventually infected the rest of the BBC's motorsport portfolio. Within a few years the BBC, the pioneers and architects of modern motor racing coverage, had withdrawn from all forms of four-wheeled competition: Touring Cars, Formula Three and rallying, including the notable production partnership with *Top Gear* that gave us annual RAC rally coverage, had all gone.

These were decisions taken by the new breed of Sports Controllers that came from light entertainment and current affairs and appeared to have no understanding of the ebb and flow and heritage of sport. They would spend the next 11 years sneering at the ITV coverage and what they saw as the bogus and inflated world of grand prix motor racing, and then in March 2008, after a phone call from Bernie Ecclestone and apparently no meaningful negotiation, they would declare that Formula One was 'coming home to the BBC'. But that's another story.

Jim and the ITV operation represented by Neil Duncanson and the progressive MACh 1 production team did an outstanding job without ever being rewarded with epic Championships. Michael Schumacher was taking a stranglehold on Formula One and the British challenge was thin. At a production level mutual respect was guaranteed between the two broadcasting organisations, largely because ITV had engaged the services of BBC Outside Broadcasts and Facilities to provide the majority of the technical backup, especially at the British Grand Prix.

And there was also Murray Walker, who had been saved for the nation and was now forming a very effective commentary partnership with Martin Brundle. We all wished him well, even after a Formula One dinner hosted by the Television and Radio Industries Club, when, with BBC and ITV on adjacent tables, Murray said in a speech: 'I have been in broadcasting for nearly 50 years but I have never received such outstanding professional support as in this 1997 season...!' There was coughing and spluttering on both tables but we all appreciated what he was trying to say.

For me, once the frustration of losing Formula One had been absorbed, I grew to appreciate more and more that I was still in the right place in terms of my broadcasting career. There were no more grands prix, but it was a golden age for golf coverage, rugby was strong and so too was *Grandstand*; and in a couple of years' time Desmond Lynam would be switching channels to host the football coverage for ITV, and I would have the opportunity to lead the BBC presentation team at the Sydney Olympics.

There was also the chance to explore the broadcast possibilities of what the die-hard Formula One fans might regard as the fringes of motorsport, but rallying, club racing and sports-car racing was a rich source of material, especially for the independent producers at BHP, with whom I was still strongly associated.

I had been lucky with my progress through the television ranks. Nothing had been pressurised, there had been time to look around and learn. I got the feeling that I had a thorough graduation, and if I didn't mess up I would be around a while. This was encouraged by the atmosphere around the BBC in the '80s and '90s.

I had gone from local journalism to radio in 1974, to local television in 1977, network television with ITV from 1980, and joined BBC Television in 1985. As now, making the move from ITV to BBC in those days was not easy. ITV were commercial upstarts – the BBC was the home of properly trained broadcasters. But as happened so often in my career, I seemed to be in the right place at the right time.

It was more in hope than expectation that I had suggested to my agent back in 1985 that a move to the BBC would put me in a different league and open up so many different opportunities; so what were the chances? He was not hopeful, but said he would try to arrange an informal dinner with Jonathan Martin so he could meet and get to know me and at least explore the possibilities for a couple of years down the line.

The dinner was at a very smart restaurant in Park Lane. Jonathan came with his assistant head of sport, John Rowlinson, and before the menus had even arrived he leant forward and said: 'Right, cards on the table, we want you to come over with immediate effect. We want you to take over the presentation of the *Sportsnight* programme from Harry Carpenter and eventually replace him as our main golf presenter. And we also want you to share presentation duties on *Grandstand* with Desmond Lynam, hosting a minimum of 35 editions a year.' He added, 'I don't know what the contract situation is, but with these kind of roles we aim to have a working relationship of in excess of 20 years.'

He gave the impression that the BBC (at least in the '80s) never took a gamble with an appointment like this and never 'took a punt' on a presenter; if they were going to take an ITV face and put it in the front line of BBC Sport they were going to be 100% sure of success. Self-belief had never been my strongest quality but this show of confidence was a boost. Equally, the '20-year working relationship' commitment was something that would resonate through the difficult times after the loss of Formula One. In any 20-year relationship there were going to be problems. But if they were going to be loyal and long-term towards me, I would reciprocate.

So 11 years after first speaking into a microphone I hosted my first edition of *Grandstand* in July 1985. Behind me lay Anglia and *World of Sport* and *Midweek Sports Special*. Ahead of me, as far as Jonathan Martin was concerned, lay a great deal of golf, and that was not such a terrible prospect. But on that first *Grandstand* it was symbolic and satisfying that the first action I had linked into was that random round of the MG Metro Challenge. There would be more glorious events in the future, but this would do. It wasn't just motorsport. It was club motorsport.

This is where I had come from and this is what I knew – the wind whipping across Snetterton, long hours at the Bomb Hole or the Russell Chicane, anoraks covered in badges, the smell of onions in the paddock, and trying to be John Frankenheimer in the edit suite.

It was a motorsport education that I was privileged to have, but it was also an *essential* education. To have experienced only Formula One, without getting to know the sport in all its strata, would have been like saying you understood classical music after three hours at the Last Night of the Proms. You had to appreciate what had gone before – the structure of motorsport, its variety, its heroes and its eccentricities.

I was never a great one for the nuts and bolts of racing-car preparation. I could admire the technology without remotely understanding it; and later on, when that technology came via a computer screen, it all felt even more remote. To me it was engineering, and only when you added the human factor of the driver did it become motorsport. Shiny cars always seemed to be the quickest, drivers with shiny personalities turned it all into a compelling sport.

When the immaculate science and diligent preparation met cavalier characters on a rather different agenda the result was hilarious to all but the boffins.

At Anglia we had done a pilot for a new motoring consumer programme that tested cars against each other via a very strictly defined set of scientific parameters. But to make this rather dull format remotely interesting for a television audience the test drivers were the most extrovert and unpredictable characters around at the time in British motorsport. The line-up included Barry Sheene, rally driver Tony Pond, Hot Rod star Barry Lee, Touring Car racer Steve Soper and a few other Stig-like personalities.

Test number one on the long-banked oval of Vauxhall's proving ground at Millbrook in Bedfordshire was a fuel economy test for the Superminis, cars like the Nissan Micra and the Fiat Uno. Each car would contain a litre of fuel, measured so precisely that it had to be certificated by the weights and measures authorities and fussed over by half a dozen white-coated lab assistants.

The drivers' task was to circulate in single file around the banked oval at a rock-solid steady 30mph until the fuel ran out; the last car running would be demonstrably the most fuel-efficient. The mistaken thinking was that only drivers of the quality of Sheene, Pond, Soper etc would have the concentration and self-discipline required to fulfil such a precise task. Wrong.

For the first three or four laps everything was going fine, but around lap five the sport started taking over from the science. I think it was a bored Barry Sheene who realised that there were no cameras or spectators or men with clipboards at the back of the circuit. The next time they went past they were in a slightly different order. 'But this is not possible,' said the boffin alongside me who had designed the foolproof experiment.

The next time past the order had changed again and Tony Pond seemed to have opened a bit of a lead, even though they were all still supposedly maintaining a precise, disciplined 30mph. Next time round Steve Soper had a wing mirror hanging off and they only managed one more lap before word came from the back of the circuit that Barry Sheene had crashed the Nissan Micra. The scientists and engineers were aghast, the men from the weights and measures were confused and outraged, but I was quietly delighted. Cars are great, but it will always be the characters behind the wheel who shape motorsport in the end.

What makes you laugh changes from sport to sport, but perhaps motorsport humour is the most distinctive. I suppose it comes out of the private world of shared peril where your success and quite often your life depends on the competence of those around you. There is locker room humour and terrace humour, but in motorsport it's more a kind of gallows humour.

And you can see where it comes from. In 1982 I was filming Barry Sheene for Anglia at a test session at Silverstone, and during lunch he had the crew in gales of laughter as he recounted what he saw as the 'funny' side of his accident-prone career. That afternoon, while we were heading back to Norfolk, he crashed into debris on the circuit at over 120mph. Among multiple injuries he broke both legs and was lucky to survive one of the most horrifying crashes the sport had ever seen. A month later he was once again cracking jokes about it in his hospital bed.

Tony Pond was another who struggled to take anything too seriously. In 1985 we did a documentary feature of the man who, at that time, was Britain's top rally driver, and was just about to give a high-profile World Championship debut to the MG Metro 6R4. Our filming coincided with Tony taking the final examination for his helicopter pilot's licence, the perfect material for a *Sportsnight* feature.

The first sequence we were due to film was the oral examination on procedure, conducted by a mustachioed ex-RAF tutor who reluctantly agreed to the presence of the camera as long as it did not affect the very formal nature of the test.

The cameras ran. 'Question number one, Mr Pond,' he intoned. 'What steps would you take in the event of a fire on take-off?'

'Bloody great big ones,' answered Tony. 'Next question.'

The answer did not make *Sportsnight* and certainly was not rewarded with a pilot's licence, but it has survived in many well-received rallying compilation tapes.

As, indeed, has my favourite rallying sequence. It's not, as you might imagine, a bit of breathtaking in-car footage, or a high-speed 'off' in a Welsh forest, but a sequence shot by Barrie Hinchliffe involving ex-World Champion Ari Vatanen, broken-down in a Lake District lay-by during the RAC rally. Vatanen is seen full of debonair charm, taking a disproportionate interest in a middle-aged lady's plans for the rest of her caravanning holiday, while in the background Ari's co-driver Terry Harryman is seen doing a cash deal with the lady's husband for the purchase of the much-needed rear differential off their family Cortina.

The same Vatanen/Harryman combination also produced a far more professional sequence that ranks as one of the most stunning in-car moments, complete with that grim rallying humour. It was a high-speed tarmac stage on the Isle of Man. Harryman was calling it flat with the proviso there was the need to lift for the cattle grid that lay ahead, barely the width of the car. Ari didn't lift. The back of the car became loose as the cattle grid approached at about 120 miles an hour. To his credit Harryman did not falter on the pace notes but inserted the words 'Dear God' as the car miraculously made it between the two concrete posts without a scratch.

And I suppose there was divine intervention, of a kind, when the partnership suffered a quite appalling accident in their Group B Peugeot on the World Championship Rally of Argentina in 1984. Vatanen was hauled from the wreckage barely alive, but after he had survived the medical crisis he had the psychological trauma to endure. I met with him on a couple of occasions in the months that followed, and he was a haunted, troubled man, irrationally convinced that he had contracted AIDS from poor hospital treatment; for once there was no way to hide behind humour and no way to crack jokes about another of those 'mad motorsport moments'. Vatanen spent a year confronting his demons and then climbed back into a Peugeot rally car and won perhaps the most gruelling event of all, the 1987 Paris Dakar. It was a performance that tells you all you need to know about motorsport and the men behind the wheel, and made a compelling feature for *Sportsnight*.

From my experience, those qualities of daring and precision exist in top-class rallying more than any other area of motorsport. The combination of instinctive car control, extreme bravery and almost total self-reliance in surroundings that make no concessions to safety, makes men like Vatanen, Mikkola, Röhrl and Loeb the best drivers in the world. Men with Formula One experience like Martin Brundle, Derek Warwick and Derek Bell have taken on the challenge of the old-style Lombard RAC rally and left it, usually well before the end, full of wide-eyed admiration.

In the '80s I had a promotional tie-up with Shell Oils that required a monthly column in *Autosport* magazine which, by its nature, was a layman's inside view of the sport. This included the old journalistic standby of a co-driver experience alongside a competitor known for his humour, reliability and patience. Welshman Harry Hockley fitted the bill and I had an instructive day in the passenger seat of his Vauxhall Nova, doing my best to get him lost in forests and one-way systems.

Surprisingly as a result of this I got a call from the team that was running the Finnish World Championship star Pentti Airikkala in the Audi National, which was a direct preparation for the RAC rally. Would I like to co-drive for Pentti?

Subsequently I got a call from Pentti himself, who I had interviewed on a couple of occasions and knew to be one of the nicest and most knowledgeable men in the sport. He was keen to emphasise that this was a light-hearted invitation for an event that was of absolutely no consequence to him, and the important thing to him was that it should be a relaxed informal day, full of laughs, not caring at all about the performance or the result.

Suitably reassured I headed off to Aberystwyth on the Friday afternoon and met up with Pentti at the rally hotel, and he was as good as his word; we had a convivial evening full of beer and wine and good stories and talked very little about the challenge of the next day. Our potential opponents – like Tony Pond, who was giving an early outing to the 6R4, Jimmy McRae and the great French star Michelle Mouton – left the bar long before we did, but reluctantly around midnight we called a halt and agreed to meet at breakfast at 6:00am, ahead of a day that Pentti promised, once again, would be 'a lot of fun... full of laughs'.

At 6:00am I came down to breakfast with a slightly thick head, and there was Pentti sitting facing the wall at a corner table. With a pot of black coffee in front of him he was slowly and methodically binding the palm of each hand with wide, black gaffer tape. His mood had changed dramatically from the night before. 'We can win this,' he said grimly. 'I would love it, to beat Pond and Mouton even though they have more powerful cars. We can pressure them. The most important thing is we don't make one single mistake. We can win it.'

As we headed out to the Telecom Astra and the support team in the car park, my head was thumping quite a bit more and I was trying to work out exactly where the 'laughs' were going to be over the next ten hours. A black cloud of foreboding was about to descend on the occupant of the co-driver's seat because

I had a horrible feeling that a red mist of rally driver madness was about to surround the man behind the wheel.

On the way to the opening stage we nearly collided with a tractor when I misread the first tulip diagram in the pace-notes. It was the first and last time I offered anything to our challenge that day. Pentti drove the Welsh forest on instinct and memory, and he did it with a terrifying physicality. I watched, mostly through the side window, in a mixture of awe and nausea, only glancing down at the pace-notes on the rare occasions that all four wheels were pointing forward.

His ambitions were justified; we got close to Pond and Mouton before eventually finishing third, comfortably winning our class. I modestly acknowledged the applause at the finish, having contributed absolutely nothing. But what I had seen was an astonishing demonstration of pace and confidence in the most unforgiving of surroundings. Pentti in later years, with a proper co-driver, would win the RAC rally, but I was left with no doubts about his ability in the Welsh forests, and I had seen it all from the most privileged front-row seat that any sport could offer.

The important ingredient for me that day was that he was actually competing, and not just out to impress a journalist on a joyride. The challenge for television, then and now, is also to add that ingredient and portray rallying in a far more competitive tone, and not just as a series of disjointed 'up and past' shots linked together by prolonged 'in-car' sequences. How is a rally won and lost? Why is one driver better than another? What is the difference in technique that can make one driver faster than the others? Then there is the biggest question of all: could all this be done live? Can live coverage of rallying ever make practical, economic or editorial sense?

There was a time when rallying even worked well on radio. My earliest motorsport memories, along with getting Stuart Lewis-Evans' autograph at a boys'-club soap box derby and the angry noises from nearby Crystal Palace circuit, revolved around late nights under the bedclothes with the Monte Carlo rally.

Raymond Baxter was the guide, and names like Hopkirk, Aaltonen and Carlsson peppered the story, which made precious little sense to me, but along with Radio Luxembourg, adjacent to it on the dial of the transistor radio, it was just about the most exotic thing imaginable.

Thirty-odd years later was about the closest rallying got to making it as a television sport. The snarling Group B monsters in the hands of Walter Röhrl, Hannu Mikkola, Henri Toivonen and Ari Vatanen were providing a greater spectacle than Formula One, especially when combined with the mad antics of the huge crowds that turned out for tarmac rallies in Europe. In this country the RAC rally remained the four-day test of endurance and survival that it always should be. It was enhanced by the efforts of Barrie Gill, Tony Mason, William Woollard and the rest of the *Top Gear* rally team who could generate a kind of sporting excitement even when the only visuals involved moving names around on a late-night prefabricated leader board.

Suitably encouraged by this I remember finishing an edition of *Sportsnight* one Wednesday evening in 1986, looking forward to an early morning flight to Lisbon to join the BHP team covering the Rally of Portugal. Then a newsflash came through that a rally car had gone into the crowd on one of the high-speed Sintra stages. There were fatalities, the rally had been abandoned, and it inevitably meant the end of all the spectacle and lunacy of the Group B era in rallying.

Slowly the sport became diluted, and television interest was gradually diverted elsewhere. It was hard to justify the huge costs of covering events like the Safari Rally, although the British Championship, which visited the traditional locations in Ireland and the Isle of Man as well as the Welsh and Scottish forests, still produced strong locations and good stories. On one occasion our report on the Welsh rally even achieved an audience in excess of eight million when we managed to smuggle it into the back end of *Grand National Grandstand*.

But we always felt we were fighting a rearguard action.

Grandstand, as a programme, was supportive of rallying, and wanted to stay committed. But the BBC management were showing the kind of political confusion that was to be even more prevalent 15 years later; their interpretation of the tobacco sponsorship legislation was particularly baffling and destructive.

In January 1991 BHP had returned from the South of France with a thrilling version of the Monte Carlo rally, an event in which Carlos Sainz had taken victory from the unfortunate François Delecour on the very last stage. I scripted and dubbed the 20-minute report and it was duly delivered to the BBC. But at the time of its scheduled slot on the Saturday edition of *Grandstand* all the viewers got was an apology from Desmond Lynam that the report was no longer available.

The BBC had objected to the Marlboro livery on the Toyota of Sainz, the only tobacco sponsorship in the field, which, in the judgement of the BBC, was in breach of the agreement with the Tobacco Advisory Council. A BBC spokesman was quoted as saying the car was 'heavily emblazoned' with tobacco sponsorship when quite clearly the Marlboro logo was secondary to that of Repsol and Toyota.

Astonishingly the BBC then filled the newly available airtime with extra coverage of the Benson and Hedges snooker competition in which the tobacco sponsorship was huge and exclusive. The BBC defended their position by saying they were happy to screen tobacco-sponsored Formula One, snooker and Rugby League because there had been a 'historic' contractual involvement. Rallying was a 'new' event.

Trying to defend this nonsense on behalf of the BBC led to our crews being bombarded with rocks on a couple of stages of the Scottish rally, and a ludicrous situation on the British Championship Circuit of Ireland, when agreement was reached for the Prodrive Subarus to compete without Rothmans livery up to the Irish border, but with the evil name on the side of the cars as the event headed into the Republic. No one could quite understand why, but everyone knew it to be an exercise in muddled thinking and huge hypocrisy from the Corporation. It was sometimes chastening from my lofty aspect as *Grandstand* presenter to be reminded of how certain aspects of the BBC appeared to the outside world.

But, these obstacles aside, it was clear that just like our experience with the British Touring Car Championship, the television coverage of rallying was going nowhere unless it could break out of being merely a movable recorded 'filler' and could establish a live television potential of its own.

And that was when, in 1989, the idea of the Mobil 1 Rally Challenge was born. It came from a conversation with Head of Sport Jonathan Martin, who had been a pioneer and enthusiast for *Ski Sunday* – the coverage of the downhill and giant slalom in particular had the same kind of logistical challenges as rallying. A lot of the action would be in a pretty inaccessible location, and there would only be one competitor on the run at any time. How do you turn that into compelling television with continuity and a competitive narrative?

The answer was to make sure that at least the second half of the course had comprehensive coverage, and the competitive edge was provided by the accurate timing clock ticking away in the corner of the screen, indicating whether the competitor was up or down on the target. Of course, a downhill would be decided on just one course of maybe a couple of miles. A rally required 20 or 30 stages totalling hundreds of miles, but the *Ski Sunday* approach was the only possible way to progress the television profile of the sport.

Jonathan promised that if we could come up with a fully financed proposal he would give it support. The only format would be to create a completely new made-for-television rally. It would be run on six stages, each of about two miles in length. There would be a variety of locations and surfaces. Welsh forests, the military range of Epynt, Scottish and Yorkshire forests and the tarmac of the Isle of Man. Every yard of the stage would be covered by at least one exterior camera. The series would focus on the man behind the wheel as opposed to the machinery. At the end of it all there would be a winning driver but no winning car.

Six manufacturers would take turns to provide the car for each individual round. The appeal for them was that there would be a half-hour of television with no other car apart from their own in front of the camera. The drivers would be as high-profile as we could make them – Mark Lovell, Russell Brookes and Dai Llewellyn from the British Championship, and Scandinavian class in the shape of Airikkala and Stig Blomqvist. Also in the line-up was Louise Aitken Walker, Britain's best woman driver and always a strong performer against the best of the men.

The whole thing had to be put together from scratch. There needed to be co-operation from the individual manufacturers, or at least their designated teams, and in this respect we received great support from Vauxhall, Ford, Toyota and BMW. There was also a new team finding its feet in rallying. David Richards' Prodrive team brought along a rather routine-looking, unbranded car called a Subaru Legacy RS. If the Mobil 1 Rally Challenge can claim nothing else, it was the first public appearance of what was to become one of the most iconic World Rallying brands of the next 15 years.

Stages had to be selected and we were keen to run in forest locations that had helped produce great action down the years in the RAC rally. There was no great debate about the tarmac venue, the Isle of Man had rallying pedigree and also had a great appetite for any television coverage that could be generated on the island.

As regards the airtime, *Grandstand* could give it the usual 15-minute bite-size chunks in between the horse racing, but the event needed to achieve more than this. A longer self-contained slot would provide the opportunity to do features on how pace-notes were prepared, how the partnership was formed between driver and co-driver, the contrast in driving technique and style, as well as an excuse to rerun some great archive footage. A 45-minute slot would be ideal. Also there would be far more potential for a title sponsor to receive decent exposure if it was broadcast as a self-contained programme.

So I was dispatched into the hinterland of BBC Television to try to achieve six stand-alone programmes. We were not being fussy; we would settle for a late-afternoon slot on BBC2 if necessary. Alan Yentob was the BBC2 Controller in those days and I prepared myself for a lofty discussion on the philosophy of the programme, its structure and its production values. But I never got that far. I was swiftly passed down the line to the new chap who seemed to be in charge of daytime BBC2 scheduling.

Nevertheless, I went into the meeting well prepared and feeling passionate about the programme; none of that was required. Michael Jackson hardly looked up from the spreadsheets covering his table. 'You want five 45-minute programmes... I could do them stripped across one week in... let's see, week 40', and he put five red stickers on his spreadsheet in the same way you would book five seats together in the dress circle. He didn't seem too concerned about the level of sponsor recognition in the programmes, but had to be reassured that they would be delivered to his network without any charge. And that was it. Michael Jackson seemed as involved and interested in the start of the Mobil 1 Rally Challenge as he would be in the demise of BBC Formula One seven years later as Controller of BBC2.

These programmes, however, were vital in securing our title sponsor, because the venture had no potential as a spectator event and only existed as a television product. Mobil 1 would be restricted to branding and the opportunity to bring a few guests to a hospitality marquee at the last round on the Isle of Man.

At the back end of the summer of 1989 we started the filming, and it turned into a pretty dull task. We would have one car, which would do one run before it was brought back to service, to be restored to pristine condition for the next driver. There would be at least an hour between each run, and it was a struggle to hold on to any sense of continuity of a rallying competition. But then again we were making television, not sport.

All this would be smartened up in the edit suite, of course, when the exterior cameras were added together with the on-board material, and then the timing clock would be inserted into the corner of the screen, and suddenly it was *Ski Sunday* on wheels.

We learnt very little that we did not know already. Rally drivers were the most patient, good-humoured group of sportsmen you could work with, keen to learn and keen to try to explain the dark secrets of their craft to the wider audience. The stages were decided by fractions of a second, but we also learnt that Stig Blomqvist, with his World Champion pedigree, was quicker on every stage and in every car; and despite all the clocks and the camera we failed to really work out how.

As a result we came to the final stage on the Isle of Man, where the key clients of Mobil 1 were to be wined and dined, with Stig having the demanding task of trying to defend a 12-second lead over a two-mile tarmac stage. The day wore on, the six drivers did their runs, the car was brought back to service, the guests headed back to the hospitality tent for the one compensation that this tedious day on the moorland of the Isle of Man could provide.

And then it was the turn of Blomqvist, and from the start in the BMW he did not seem to be his normal fluent aggressive self. The post-produced timing clock would tell the story of seconds lost throughout the run and the audio track brought us a growing sense of panic inside the car.

In the end the 12-second lead was almost completely used up, but he still managed to claim the title of Mobil 1 Rally Challenge winner. But what had gone wrong? It was then we began to realise that Stig had overstretched himself in entertaining the clients of Mobil 1 for the previous five hours and had lost what can only be described as the sense of focus you need to prove that you are among the best in the world.

We dispensed with the interview, gave him the trophy and the director called a wrap.

So what had we learnt, and what had we proved? People are still kind enough on various websites to say that we broke new ground. We had certainly opened up a new dimension in rally coverage, but in a lumbering post-produced manner that cannot be replicated in the real world. Ten years after this at the Autosport Awards I stood alongside David Richards, who had just taken over the television rights to the World Rally Championship, when he declared that in two years' time the television profile of rallying would be as big as Formula One. It did not happen then, and now –15 years further on, even with all the technological advances in broadcasting – meaningful live television still seems to be beyond the reach of rallying.

Bernie Ecclestone – who for a long time, rather alarmingly, had control of the ultimate destiny of World Rallying – once said to me: 'I like watching the sport on television but I don't like it so much when it goes off into the woods.' It's naively put but it's absolutely right. Top-class rallying somehow has to live without a top-class television profile, and needs to stop diluting itself in order to accommodate television But it can do so in the knowledge that it has the bravest, most brilliant drivers, and if the example of Stig Blomqvist is anything to go by can provide the most congenial company as well.

We did manage a second series of the Mobil 1 Rally Challenge the following year, which Malcolm Wilson won, but there was no chance of selling any more to *Grandstand*, BBC2 or anyone else. The last big chance for rallying on British television came when Colin McRae and Richard Burns traded blows in the battle for the world title in the '90s. The sport had the personalities, but not the television product. BBC Sport combined forces with the *Top Gear* rally team and were able to tell a powerful story, but it was not enough to spark any enthusiasm from the executives, who clearly felt that motorsport had finished with the loss of Formula One.

Chapter 10

INDEPENDENT DAYS

Over at BHP, the British Touring Car Championship continued to provide a much-needed financial lifeline, but there was a constant requirement to try to find 'the Next Big Thing'. Production budgets were put together for events ranging from the Schneider Air Race to the Camel Trophy. Ultra 30 dinghy racing packed with on-board cameras and on-board commentary added a new dimension to sailing coverage before the money ran out. Broadcasters, including the BBC, were happy to provide free airtime but none of the events really lit the blue touchpaper in terms of public interest.

Some events failed even to get airtime and funding. We were visited by motorsport enthusiast Lord March, who wondered if we could find any television interest or appropriate funding for coverage of his planned 'motorsport garden party'. We failed, and so missed out on the first year of the Goodwood Festival of Speed.

What we were trying to do on behalf of promoters and events was hold back the tide of motorsport that seemed to be inevitably heading into the clutches of the emergent satellite outlets. They seemed to offer everything – airtime, repeats, on-air promotion and a relaxed attitude to sponsors; everything, in fact, except an audience. Only the terrestrial outlets could do that; but ITV were overflowing with Formula One and the BBC were sulking and becoming more and more opposed to anything on wheels.

Group C Sportscar racing had prompted occasional interest from the BBC. Jaguar had won at Le Mans and drivers like

Martin Brundle, Derek Bell and Derek Warwick were star performers. The BBC were keen to take summaries of World Sportscar races, in particular those in the UK, but only on a post-produced summary basis and definitely without any payment involved.

The Brands Hatch round of the Championship in 1995, with the spectacle of the Silver Arrows Mercedes, was one that we were particularly keen to see on terrestrial television, but finding the budget was a big challenge. With less than a week to go we had barely half the required funding and we had tapped up everyone involved, from the circuit and the governing bodies to manufacturers and sponsors. But with or without the money we were committed to delivering the coverage.

Then an apparent saviour emerged in the form of a Japanese network who were prepared to pay decent money for what we were able to produce. So against all odds it seemed we were actually going to make a profit. But on the Friday came a chilling phone call from Mr Nakamura at the network, saying that he would be at the Fitzroy Square offices of BHP at nine o'clock on Monday morning to collect a full recording of the six-hour race. He was clearly under the impression that we were at the circuit with a state-of-the-art, fully-linked live outside broadcast unit.

The reality was that the race, like all the others, was being covered by 16 cameras all recording remotely around the Brands Hatch Grand Prix circuit. These cameras would generate about 120 video cassettes; even working flat-out it would be hard to expect the tapes to be collected, delivered, logged, collated and assembled into even a rough edit of the race before midday on Wednesday. But our valued Japanese client wanted a full version, complete with graphics, barely 12 hours after we had all left the circuit. Impossible.

But maybe there was half a chance. Steve Saint, the chief editor at BHP, loved a challenge, and this was the ultimate test of his organisational skills. The only possibility was to hire 16 video players, each representing a camera, and mix a master version between the tapes as if it were a live event. We decided to go for it as our only chance of saving the budget and our reputations.

As the race was into its opening laps at Brands Hatch we were shipping tapes back to put together the pre-race build-up in the edit suite. However, access problems around the circuit meant that we could not pick up tapes from the race cameras until the chequered flag had fallen.

So it was around 10:00pm that a van with all the tapes arrived back in central London and the mind-boggling operation got into full swing. The first batch of race tapes were put into the machines, time codes linked and the mix began at around midnight. At first the best runs we managed were around a minute long before technical problems struck; it was desperately frustrating. But slowly the sequences lengthened and the spirits among the 20 or so people slamming tapes into machines in the edit suite began to rise.

At 7:30am the winning cars crossed the finish line. Then followed the requirement for graphics and a guide commentary. A job that usually took a full day was crammed into an hour.

At 9:00am Mr Nakamura rang the doorbell of BHP. I opened it in a rather off-handed manner and said, 'Ah, you've come for your tape of the Brands Hatch race. I believe one of our editors was able to run you off a copy last night. Yes, here it is…'

He then took delivery of what seemed a very routine item, said thanks, and was on his way to Heathrow Airport.

I returned to the edit suite, where the temperature must have been well over 100° and machines were whirring and lights were flashing with the intensity of the engine room of a nuclear submarine. Bodies were everywhere, slumped across consoles and prostrate on the floor. Tapes, clipboards and half-eaten pizza covered every surface. Eventually Steve Saint spoke: 'OK, that's the Japs,' he said. 'Now let's start thinking about the BBC version.'

Sometimes the most memorable days in television are not in front of a camera, but at the back of an edit suite.

There were many good and satisfying days at BHP, especially in regard to the work being done with the British Touring Car Championship. One of the consolations of doing this kind of post-produced coverage is that the full richness of the material did not reveal itself for about 24 hours.

You would come away from a race meeting excited by the quality of the action and anxious to see if it looked just as dramatic from a particular camera angle or on-board recording. Similarly, you could come away uninspired and despondent, but then in the edit suite be transfixed by the intensity of the battle for fifth, sixth and seventh that just had not been apparent to the live spectator.

Equally the drivers were becoming aware of the benefits of this delayed production process. It became a bit of a Monday afternoon tradition that drivers involved in the previous day's race would 'coincidentally' find themselves strolling through Gough Square and decide to drop in to take a look at some of the recorded action.

A regular in this respect was the 1991 Champion Will Hoy, who still worked in the City as a surveyor and regularly felt the need to call by. This usually coincided with a controversial race or a contentious incident the day before. He would propose, for example, that we should look at an aggressive overtaking move from his point of view, then the perspective of the opposition, then maybe a replay from the exterior camera would be worthwhile. As a last resort he would even suggest being available to do an interview to justify and explain whatever illegality he had performed. On each occasion we would listen to his prepared argument with great interest and humour and do completely the opposite in the edit.

Some Monday-afternoon visitors were less good-humoured, and one in particular was downright sinister. In 1992 we got an unannounced visit from HM Customs and Excise demanding to immediately review the weekend's rushes from the meeting at Brands Hatch. We dutifully piled up all the tapes and installed two of their officers in a small edit suite and were given instructions not to disturb them.

However, after a couple of hours we felt obliged to at least offer them a cup of coffee and so dispatched an office junior on the errand with specific instructions to spot what, in particular, they were examining. Out he came a few minutes later having established that both took white with one sugar and that they seemed to be watching not race action, but pit-lane and garage material.

Sensing that they may have been investigating some tax or VAT scam we felt that the decent thing to do would be to ring round the various team principals to alert them to the investigation. They were all grateful and they all declared their innocence, including Vic Lee who had been setting the pace in the Championship for the last two years and had taken Will Hoy to the Championship title.

The rise of Vic Lee and his run of success had been so dramatic that we had sent a feature crew down to his race headquarters to show the sophisticated facilities and the state-of-the-art car transporters and discuss the new 'nothing but the best' philosophy of the extrovert team boss.

A month later the visit of the HM Customs and Excise and the new-found prosperity of the team all started to make sense, as Vic Lee was arrested and charged with importing £6 million-worth of Class A drugs in the team's much-admired transporters; the suspicions of the drugs officials had been apparently alerted by the disproportionate number of times the team felt it necessary to go testing at Zandvoort in Holland.

It was clear, right from the start, that the team personnel were not involved. This alternative source of funding had been misguidedly organised by Vic himself. Driver Tim Harvey was as shocked as anyone at the arrest of the team boss. The easiest thing would have been to close the operation down, but Tim and others set about marshalling and consolidating the demoralised team and it is to their credit that they kept going and were able to deliver the title for Harvey in that dramatic showdown at Silverstone.

Lee was released early from his 12-year prison sentence and, astonishingly, was able to re-establish himself in motorsport. But then in 2005 he was arrested again, at the Holiday Inn in High Wycombe, and was convicted of further, significant, drug-trafficking offences. And this time he took others with him, including Jerry Mahoney, who had become a close associate. The television team had a particular affection for Mahoney, as he was the man who had won the first BBC televised race (in an Arquati-sponsored Ford Cosworth) back in 1988. He, like Lee, was sentenced to 12 years.

Some tried to portray the crimes as a symptom of the poor hard-up privateers trying to compete with the major manufacturers who were starting to dominate the BTCC; after all, the sport had always been prey to a colourful, criminal fringe. In reality it was the most evil and selfish of crimes committed for reasons of plain greed. The domestic sport survived, but this was a long way from being its finest hour.

Through the '90s the manufacturer support for the BTCC had been solid and at times spectacular. Big-name drivers like Derek Warwick, Frank Biela, Alain Menu and Jo Winkelhock had been thrilling the crowds. Behind the scenes the Touring Car Association, or TOCA, under the strong leadership of Alan Gow, was professional and progressive and the whole thing, at last, had the feel of a Championship that was going to prosper for a long time.

By 1997, however, the all-important commitment of BBC Television felt less secure. ITV had Formula One, BBC Television was no longer the natural home of the best of motorsport, and the BTCC was fighting a rearguard action to keep the BBC interested.

We did have a growing live commitment, though, and although it could not guarantee the intense kind of racing we were able to portray with the recorded version, the personalities rose to the occasion. Anthony Reid squaring up to Alain Menu during a live interview in parc ferme was just the kind of action we needed if we were going to offer an alternative to the anodyne, Schumacher-dominated world of Formula One.

However, my own performance during an outside broadcast at Brands Hatch did little to add to the credibility of Touring Car racing. It was the lunch-break, with about 20 minutes to go to the start of Saturday qualifying. The producer wanted to make the point about the close relationship and similarity between the racecars and the showroom version. It was a comparison that was obvious to the spectator, and non-existent to the TV presenter, unexpectedly installed behind the wheel.

I was to take a couple of laps with Rickard Rydell in a hastily fitted passenger seat in the Volvo. We lapped the short course at Brands Hatch in reasonably invigorating fashion with me providing a few well-chosen words on the experience without fully understanding what the talented Swede was doing.

At the end of it all we pulled into the pit-lane. Qualifying was about ten minutes away and Rydell leapt out of the driver's seat and gestured me across. 'Now you drive, now you drive,' he yelled, clearly misunderstanding what this little production was all about.

But before I could protest the belts were being adjusted and commentator Charlie Cox had climbed into the passenger seat to provide further observations. I was not able to make any prolonged objections because even if we headed out now we would barely get in three laps before qualifying began.

What I *could* do was to provide a perfect illustration that this was a very different beast to the Volvo in your local showroom. With about 8,000 watching in the circuit I kangaroo-hopped along the pit-lane and spent the first lap in a ludicrously low gear, trying to work out where everything was in a left-hand-drive cockpit that seemed straight out of *Days of Thunder*. I also spent the lap with my head down trying to unravel the mysteries of a sequential gearshift.

On the second lap I found time to look out of the windscreen and attempt to map out the best route around the Brands Hatch

Indy circuit. Towards the end of it Charlie Cox looked across at me as if I was some kind of idiot and suggested that I had only one more lap to put on any kind of decent show. I decided to forget trying to work out which gear I was in, I would just try to find one that I liked, gun the car as hard as I could, and hang on for a lap.

The plan seemed to work. I got the encouraging sound of tyre squeal around paddock and a lot more at Druids, where there also appeared to be a bit of crowd reaction. I must confess to running a bit wide at Surtees but the very highly animated commentary from Charlie suggested I was getting it right. I felt confident going into Clearways so gave it a bit of extra right foot, but the long right-hander just never seemed to end. I kept my right foot down because I was a racing driver, but now realised that Charlie was yelling desperate instructions instead of commentary.

It was all to no avail and we ploughed into the Clearways trap at about 80mph, the big Volvo digging itself deep as the gravel clattered against the bottom of the car. There was one minute to go until the start of official qualifying and I was not popular.

It took 15 minutes to retrieve the car and it took an all-night session from the Volvo crew to get the last stones out of the chassis and the bent bits replaced; some of those bent bits still adorn my study wall.

It all seemed to be a shambolic metaphor for the way things were heading. Within two years, amid a spirit of self-congratulation, BBC Television – once the trailblazers of televising motor racing – had pulled out of all coverage of four-wheeled sport. The once proud pioneer of grand prix coverage confined Formula One to just a 13-second segment of *Sports Review of the Year*. The administration of the British Touring Car Championship changed hands and the BHP coverage became a victim of the new management, as the BBC used it as an excuse to pull out of that as well. As a result I was heading for a period in my career that, completely by accident, would contain very little of the sport that had given me so much enjoyment.

Chapter 11

OUT OF THE
FAST LANE

So 1997 would turn into a bit of a crossroads in my television career, certainly as far as motorsport was concerned. Formula One was the new headline event for ITV and, in its absence, any BBC enthusiasm for the sport seemed pretty superficial. However, the commitment to the British Touring Car Championship continued and, indeed, made some serious progress in the live screening of the Championship.

But matters elsewhere were about to conspire against the future of the event on the BBC. At Brands Hatch, Nicola Foulston – who had provided so many obstacles to the coverage when she took over as an enthusiastic but misguided 22-year-old chief executive – had now fallen out with her mother Mary, who had installed her in the position. All this followed in the wake of Nicola's attempts to buy Silverstone and the apparent commitment of Bernie Ecclestone to bring the British Grand Prix back to Brands Hatch.

Into this mess stepped Octagon, the sporting arm of the giant American Interpublic Group. Sensing profit, they bought Brands Hatch circuits and, as a small spin-off of the deal, installed their own production company to generate the Touring Car coverage. They also tried to renegotiate the broadcast contracts, exploiting what they saw as the greater commercial potential of the event. The BBC saw it as the perfect opportunity to step aside, and it was 2002 before the BTCC once again found a respectable permanent home at ITV as the commercial network tried to boost its growing motorsport portfolio. Even this was only achieved after Jonathan Palmer's MotorSport Vision organisation had bought the circuits from Octagon, and Alan Gow had returned as the Touring Car Championship supremo.

Around this time Neil Duncanson at Chrysalis acquired the production contract for the television coverage of the World Rally Championship and took it off to what he hoped would be a brave new world at Channel 4. Once again there was little resistance from the BBC, and one of the great attractions of the new outlet for the coverage of both events would be that ITV and Channel 4 could provide self-contained, scheduled slots that could be promoted and trailed, unlike having to take their chance in the movable feast that was the *BBC Grandstand* line-up.

Within the BBC there were, in fact, growing rumours that the days of *Grandstand* were numbered, and the Corporation was seemingly divided between those who thought it was a glorious flagship and those who felt it had declined into a tired old warhorse. What could not be denied was that Formula One, a cornerstone of the programme, had gone, rapidly followed by everything else with an engine and four wheels. Murray Walker was now an ITV man, and apart from bikes the BBC was a motorsport-free zone, and very few people seemed to care.

And to be honest I was one of those who had given up the fight. I had been involved in the presentation and production of the sport for the previous 20 years and felt I had seen it all. The low points with the deaths of Peterson, Ratzenberger and Senna contrasted with the exhilaration of seeing Mansell and Hill take the title. I felt a contribution had been made to take Touring Car racing to another level; it was frustrating not to be able to do the same for rallying, but the experiences and the personalities in that sport would live with me forever. Time to move on.

Of course, I felt a whole range of mixed emotions watching ITV go on the air with the start of the 1997 season. Coulthard was a great first winner, the production was right, and Jim Rosenthal was clearly going to be around for a while as a very competent and fast-learning frontman. But a month later, when Jacques Villeneuve completed back-to-back victories in Brazil and Argentina, it was clear this season was taking a more routine shape. On the day that Villeneuve crossed the line for that win in Buenos Aires I was in Augusta, watching a young Tiger Woods breaking every golfing landmark to win the Masters in record-breaking fashion. My recovery was complete; I'm sorry, motorsport, but for me this felt more like the future.

While I was looking on the bright side others seemed eager to take the opposite view. This, for example, is from the Giles Smith column in the *Daily Telegraph* of 28 April 1997:

'Over on *Grandstand* (BBC 1), where Formula One used to be, touring cars now were. I suspect I am not alone in finding the sight of Jacques Villeneuve in a Williams more exciting than the sight of some bloke in an Audi. I can, after all, get the latter in my street fairly regularly.

'But these days, *Grandstand* must take what it can and make do. Later in the show, an overrun at the snooker forced Steve Rider – once hotly tipped for the ITV Formula One job – to issue the following poignant apology: "We've lost the time that we originally allocated to our world championship curling coverage." What a total professional Rider is. He brought to this sentence a tone of nicely judged sobriety which carefully included the possibility that someone, somewhere, was actually going to be disappointed about this.

'This is a strange phase for *Grandstand*. The time may not be far away when someone on the show has to apologize that, owing to an earlier delay at the 65-and-over badminton from Framlingham when the shuttlecock got lodged in the church hall rafters, there will be no time to show the scheduled chocolate egg hunt from the beer garden of the Dog and Forget-Me-Not at Epsom. And when that moment comes, the programme is going to need Rider more than ever.

'How peculiar though, the fates of television sports jockeys. Rosenthal is out there in the sunshine cultivating his new role as TV's Mr. Smooth; Rider is back in London, cancelling the curling.'

There were times, I must confess, when *Grandstand* in the late '90s was taking on the hilarious irrelevance of ITV's *World of Sport* in the late '70s. It was still a great broadcasting brand, worthy of protection, but Giles Smith in his own inimitable way was able to emphasise the damage done by the loss of Formula One.

In the short term the live broadcasting of selected rounds of the BTCC instigated in 1997 were proving a success, and with Charlie Cox and John Watson forming a fine commentary partnership the fears that the entertainment value would be diminished proved unfounded. On this occasion the flexible nature of *Grandstand*'s running order proved an asset in accommodating the unpredictability of live motorsport. Although there was no coverage of the support races, it was also proving the perfect template for what would come ten years later with ITV.

Of course, in motorsport terms it hardly made up for what I was missing in Formula One, especially as I had spent the previous 12 months helping to put the components together for ITV's great adventure in the sport. But although there was no longer any involvement in the broadcasting of Formula One, there was still plenty to do at a corporate level, in particular the new car launches that, as with Nigel Mansell in 1994, could provide such an insight into the inner workings of the teams.

I helped unveil new cars from Benetton, Jordan and Stewart, each production revealing a little of the character of the team, or more possibly the man at the helm; suave sophistication on the shores of a Swiss lake for Flavio Briatore; wacky cars on wires surrounded by Cirque du Soleil acrobats for Eddie Jordan; solid heritage at Lord's cricket ground for Jackie Stewart.

But all this paled into insignificance alongside the efforts of McLaren on the evening of Thursday 13 February 1997. The 'Night of Stars and Cars' at the Alexandra Palace in north London was a gala evening to celebrate the tobacco sponsorship move from Marlboro to West, and the McLaren cars changing from their red and white livery into the silver machines we are familiar with today.

I had worked with McLaren on a number of launches. As well as the ill-fated Nigel Mansell announcement two years earlier, I had also presided over the launch of the McLaren F1 road car at the Monte Carlo Sporting Club – a tense night, Prince Albert and his entourage, sitting in the front row, and a large number of the audience about to see for the first time the car for which they had each paid upwards of half a million pounds. But that night in February in north London raised the bar for such functions to a record and, maybe, nonsensical height.

The theme for the evening was a rock concert, and the core of the audience was about 2,000 members of the public, with the whole thing being transmitted live on MTV. Performing live were the Spice Girls, who were at the height of their powers (they would each receive a brand new Mercedes for their 15-minute lip-synching efforts), along with Jamiroquai and Jools Holland. On the stage I would handle all of the F1 element of the evening while a young DJ from MTV named Davina McCall would handle the showbiz.

There were, as I recall, three tiers of VIP guests, ranging from Silver to Gold and Platinum, the last level containing a substantial amount of royalty, government ministers, Sean Connery, Mick Jagger and a couple of Beatles. There were themed restaurants and reception areas throughout the complex, where according to your invitation status you could freely partake of the great cuisine of the world, prepared by Michelin-starred chefs.

At about five o'clock we all appeared from our individual Winnebagos at the back of the car park for a final rehearsal and soundcheck. The Spice Girls were very concerned about the number of journalists and potential paparazzi in the cavernous hall and I was dispatched to the microphone to ask them to leave. I was about ten seconds into my polite request when Sporty Spice grabbed the mike and put the message across a lot more forcibly – an expletive-laden tirade of which the only word I am able to reprint is 'parasites'.

The clock ticked on to the time that the doors were opening, Jamiroquai did a hurried soundcheck, there was a brief moment to rehearse the reveal of the car and how the drivers Mika Häkkinen and David Coulthard would make their entrance, and then the attention switched to the arena itself and a specially constructed 300m runway around which the roller-skaters from *Starlight Express* would continuously circulate with the sponsors' logos and the flags of all nations.

It was while they were gathering speed and Davina McCall was cranking up the volume on stage that I was approached by Ron Dennis of McLaren and the Mercedes motorsport boss Norbert Haug, both looking rather solemn. I was about to congratulate them on the scale of what they were putting on when Ron expressed his reservations about the evening. 'Norbert and I are worried,' he said. 'We reckon we might come in for a lot of criticism for going a bit over the top with this. We wondered if, when you went on stage to welcome everybody and do the launch... you could try and keep it as low-key as possible?'

I was speechless and mentally filed it under the heading of 'great impossible requests'. The evening went fine, Marlboro went West, MTV went live, and even the BBC repeatedly showed great chunks of the show, abandoning the tobacco sponsorship principles that had cost us the Monte Carlo rally coverage six years earlier.

But the days of tobacco sponsorship were numbered and so too were lavish launches like this one. In fact it would be ten years before I hosted McLaren's huge welcome for Vodafone and Lewis Hamilton in Valencia; and in the meantime nothing else came close. The sport and the industry seemed happy to go back to pulling off a dust-sheet and offering a press release and a glass of warm wine. Formula One would sensibly 'keep it as low-key as possible'.

Chapter 12

ENTER THE NEXT GENERATION

O n a summer afternoon in 1999 I was walking the dogs along the banks of the Thames when my mobile phone rang. It was my agent. An hour or so earlier Desmond Lynam had held a press conference and announced that he was switching from BBC to ITV with immediate effect. For everyone at the BBC it was a bolt from the blue, and clearly Brian Barwick had been as persuasive in getting Des to leave as he had been in getting me to stay three years earlier.

I am not embarrassed to acknowledge that my first reaction was a selfish one, wondering where it all left me in the BBC scheme of things. This was reinforced by a call from Dave Gordon, the Head of Sport, telling me to stand by to take over as presenter for the World Athletics Championships that were a couple of weeks away; I had, after all, spent much of the summer presenting the sport for *Grandstand* at glamorous locations like Glasgow and Gateshead; now Gothenburg was set to host the biggest event for the sport outside the Olympics.

My inflated opinion of myself lasted just a couple of days before the ruling came down from the higher reaches of the BBC that they preferred the glamour that Sue Barker would bring to the job. This was before the days that presenters would cry foul or prejudice at such a decision and rush off to law. However, I mentally made a note that loyalty does not always have its rewards. Needless to say, my good friend Sue would subsequently prove herself the perfect choice for the role.

We all knew that BBC Sport was coming under pressure.

It was not only the loss of Formula One, cricket and other major events like the Rugby World Cup, but the growing presence and potential dominance of Sky that was changing the sports rights' market and viewing habits as well. But even with the defection of Des, it still felt the right place to be.

There was a strong sports portfolio, the Sydney Olympics were about to produce a huge boost and some epic sporting moments, and although there were some strange things happening at management level, the mood on the shop floor was good. Each presenter had their own strengths and responsibilities and there was no sense of rank or a pecking order. However, when it came to the big productions like Olympic Games and Sports Personality of the Year, it was flattering to be regarded as Desmond Lynam's successor as 'senior pro'.

There was regular reassurance that I had made the right decision in turning down the ITV F1 offer. In 2000 I would have hated to have missed the experience of the Sydney Olympics and in particular standing on the pontoon at Penrith Lake presenting the build-up to Steve Redgrave's attempt to win a fifth gold medal, and being there to get the first reaction to one of British sport's greatest achievements.

In terms of the coverage, this was always going to be the BBC's big moment of the Games. With the backing of a BBC producer I had argued that we should present it on location with a small linked crew. But the technology at this time was not totally reliable and such an approach was regarded as far too risky for an event that was generating a midnight audience of around seven million back home.

In the end they agreed to our request, with the proviso that Hazel Irvine would be standing by with a fully crewed back-up studio in Sydney. In the end our operation went fine and the pictures that were generated by our lakeside team added a great deal to the drama of the occasion, and were later honoured with the award of a BAFTA. For me it was all reminiscent of cold mornings alongside a rally stage or running up a pit-lane and reinforced my view that there was no longer any justification for cosy, studio-bound sports presentation.

This had long been the style of presenting the occasional live Touring Car events that found their way on to the schedule and, of course, ten years on it would be unthinkable that there would be any alternative. It had its perils, however, and one race at Silverstone in 2000 nearly sent us scuttling back to the safety of Television Centre.

We had decided to complete our build-up to this particular race from the middle of the front of the grid. As the cars left the pit-lane we went through a gap in the pit wall with all our gear, which included two cameras, a sound engineer, a lighting man, floor manager, a trainee floor manager and a rather cumbersome TV monitor. It was raining pretty hard, and we had a minute to set up all the equipment, but no problem – this, after all, was part of the challenge of live, location presentation. We were just about sorted when a marshal came strolling over in leisurely fashion and said, 'Good afternoon, gents. I assume you've all got the right passes, and that you all know it's now been declared a wet race so the cars will be coming through here on a flying lap before taking their places on the grid?'

At this point the cars were 15 seconds away at the Luffield complex. There was no time to designate responsibilities. I grabbed the monitor, the soundman seized a tripod, no one left empty-handed except the trainee floor manager, who was already 50 yards away. When the cars thundered across the line, with Jo Winkelhock heading the charge with a great rooster tail of spray, we had equipment and personnel on both sides of the track. A minute and a half later we were back in action welcoming the *Grandstand* audience from the front of the grid, hopefully in the usual composed fashion.

Nowadays at the BBC there would be about 16 pages of forms to fill in after an incident like that. The battalions of health and safety guardians patrolling the corridors of Television Centre were ever a potential barrier to taking *Grandstand* on the road.

One internal report even advised us against linking from live rugby or football matches because their research showed that the crowd noise could cause permanent ear damage to the production crew. Needless to say we refused to allow them anywhere near Brands Hatch or Silverstone.

I had been a *Grandstand* presenter for about 15 years and, for reasons of seniority alone, I had a pretty influential voice on the programme. I was campaigning strongly to take *Grandstand* on location whenever the content justified the move. At the Cricket World Cup, for example, it was nonsense to present a match at Lord's from inside a studio two miles down the road in Shepherd's Bush. It was lazy, overcautious and denying the audience an extra dimension to the event.

What I did not expect was that the BBC would take up my suggestion with such enthusiasm, and within a couple of years it seemed that every edition of the programme would be presented from a Rugby League touchline, a golf tournament, a snooker championship or a race meeting; all very challenging and satisfying from a presenter's point of view, but this all or nothing approach would end up damaging the fabric of the programme and the justification for the famous *Grandstand* studio. It would also provide more ammunition for those who argued that the programme should actually be dismantled and that, when available, stand-alone events should fill the weekend afternoons.

When the Touring Car Championship and World Rallying disappeared off the *Grandstand* schedule my connections with the sport became more remote. I was identified with golf and rugby and the Olympic Games, and for a period of four years my only regular connection with motorsport was my role in hosting and helping to produce the annual Autosport Awards at the Grosvenor House Hotel.

The *Autosport* evening had, down the years, boasted an amazing roll call of star guests, with Ayrton Senna, Richard Petty and Mario Andretti being among the highlights. James Garner was a popular visitor to the stage by virtue of his role in the feature film, and to be honest my own motorsport credentials were becoming equally tenuous. Martin Brundle certainly sensed this, using the occasion to flaunt his growing number of (highly deserved) broadcasting awards for his work with ITV, and every year producing a different variation of his 'your sport's got small balls' joke, of which he was obviously especially proud.

Over the previous 15 years the Autosport Awards seemed to have absorbed all the smaller prize-giving occasions into one huge evening. It could be both long-winded and worthy; on one occasion we were struggling to the end of things at about 11:30pm and the patient audience only had thoughts for the bar, when at that moment Michael Aspel came through the curtain at the back of the stage clutching a red book and announced, 'Tonight, John Surtees, *This is Your Life*, and we're going to be doing the show right here in half an hour's time.'

In recent years, however, the evening has built up toward a more natural climax with the announcement of the McLaren *Autosport* Young Driver of the Year. The award was instigated in 1989, the year I took over hosting the evening, and was the brainchild of the team at Haymarket Publishing, who then enlisted the valuable support of Ron Dennis at McLaren. It was their hard work and generosity, along with great contributions from Mercedes and the BRDC, which made the award the number one target for young drivers making their way in the sport. The prize was made up of both cash and opportunity. The cash rose to £100,000 in 2010, but the opportunity came in the form of membership of the British Racing Drivers' Club and, most importantly, the chance to test-drive a McLaren Formula One car under the discerning eye of senior team management.

The prestige of the award was helped in no small degree by having David Coulthard as the inaugural winner. He was the handsome embodiment of a young talent, backed by the support of a great family, but – like so many others – needing the extra muscle that the award offered in order to start achieving his potential. His first experience of a Formula One car would be his prize drive at Silverstone in the McLaren. He would go on to drive for Williams, McLaren and Red Bull and become one of Britain's most prolific grand prix performers, as well as an excellent broadcaster; but he was always ready to acknowledge the career launch-pad that the award had provided.

It has been a privilege to host the awards throughout their 22-year life, and although I might have overstayed my welcome in the broadcasting of many sports it is satisfying to have the December night at the Grosvenor as an enduring commitment. Every subsequent winner of the Young Driver award has gone on to a professional career in the sport, and some have achieved great things.

Dario Franchitti, for example, the winner in 1992, is a huge star in America where he has won the Indy 500 and the IRL Championship on three occasions. Ralph Firman and Anthony Davidson have both gone on to drive in Formula One, but strangely Lewis Hamilton does not figure in the Young Driver roll of honour; he would use the Autosport Awards evening to take a more direct route to the top.

To date only one Young Driver award winner has gone on to become Formula One World Champion. Just like Dario Franchitti, Jenson Button was the British Formula Ford Champion when he was nominated for the Young Driver award in 1998. But it was not Jenson's first trip across the Grosvenor House stage. He had been there in 1991 to take the applause as an all-conquering junior kart champion. But in 1998 it was the big one, announced at the end of the evening amid strident music, flashing lights, fireworks and dry-ice; this was an opportunity that Jenson was going to grasp with both hands.

The year 1999 had seen Jenson make solid progress in the British Formula Three Championship, taking three wins and third place in the title race; but most importantly his talent and his approach to the sport had made an impression on those who could usher him into Formula One. In November 1999 he had his prize drive in the McLaren, performing sensibly on a wet track with fading tyres, and his maturity certainly impressed the team.

Another opportunity came courtesy of Alain Prost to test a Prost F1 car at Barcelona, and this time Jenson showed both style and pace, eclipsing the times set the previous day by the experienced Jean Alesi with a comparable set-up and fuel load. That prompted the phone call from Frank Williams for Jenson to come down and show what he could do in the Williams FW21B with the new BMW engine. Once again the performance was impressive, but, as far as Frank Williams was concerned, inconclusive; all of which led to the Barcelona shoot-out of 23 January 2000.

Jenson brought talent and undoubted potential, but Bruno Junqueira – his rival for the seat vacated by Alex Zanardi – brought a lot of productive testing experience, plus significant sponsorship as well. It was a close call and a deadline was looming. On 24 January, at the Circuit de Catalunya, the team were due to announce their driver line-up, in particular who was going to be teammate to Ralf Schumacher, and I had been hired to host the press announcement.

So the previous day it was Junqueira vs Button for a Formula One drive, the biggest race of their respective careers. The press were largely excluded, but because of my Williams commitment I was a privileged onlooker. I soon discovered this was an onerous burden. Bruno and Jenson just got on with the driving and there was precious little to separate them on the track. But their supporters and agents, none of whom wanted to pressurise Frank Williams or Patrick Head, soon identified me as a potential source of indiscreet information.

I was positioned on the large flat roof above the Circuit pit complex; a nervous John Button would pace slowly past once every ten minutes; we would exchange observations on the progress of the day, the tension of the occasion... then there would be a dismissive 'Any indications yet...?' I would apologise and shake my head and then the pacing would start again. I felt bad, because considering the time and sacrifice John and his family had put into reaching this moment, the wait must have been unbearable.

And the same goes for Bruno Junqueira, who as the afternoon progressed also saw me as the only non-Williams spectator who might be privy to inside information as to who was going to get this huge opportunity. The potential for me to make mischief was enormous, but nobody was getting any sort of indication as to what the decision would be. On the occasions that I went down to the Williams trucks, Patrick Head would be transfixed by the computer screens and swathed in armfuls of printouts. Frank Williams was nowhere to be seen, and I was starting to get the impression that although Jenson was a couple of tenths faster, Patrick Head was favouring the Brazilian. But then again, Jim Wright the Williams head of marketing had prepared press packs for both Junqueira and Button and was starting to think that we would only be announcing Ralf Schumacher as a confirmed driver the next day.

As darkness fell I found myself on the fringe of a discussion between Frank and Patrick on what the shoot-out had produced. There was a lot more poring over printouts and telemetry and the only agreement was that it was impossible to separate the two of them. At this point Frank looked at me, smiled and winked and said, 'That's sorted; we'll give it to the British lad, then.'

It wasn't quite strong enough for me to rush to the phone with a world exclusive, and it wasn't until the next morning, barely an hour before the packed press announcement, that Jim Wright got the phone call that enabled him to go to the shredder with the Bruno Junqueira press releases; but I did feel that I had been present at a defining motorsport moment. Junqueira would never get his chance in Formula One, but ten years later Jenson Button would be World Champion.

Five years earlier at Grosvenor House the 1995 Autosport Awards had the feeling of being a pretty routine occasion. Michael

Schumacher won International Racing Driver of the Year but maintained his record of being one of the few modern Formula One World Champions not to attend the event. Damon Hill was the British Competition Driver of the Year but had missed out on a world title he should have won, and anyway the loss of Ayrton Senna was still leaving a numb feeling across Formula One.

I probably contributed little extra to the occasion but at least the evening had begun with a moment that, at the time, merely seemed sweet and charming, but on reflection, like Jenson Button in Barcelona, it was another moment of great significance in the sport. Ten-year-old Lewis Hamilton was attending his first big motorsport gathering. As British Cadet Karting Champion he had borrowed a green velvet jacket and black patent shoes from the previous year's Champion and in his own words 'felt really good'. And that opinion was shared, in a different kind of way, by the more maternal members of the audience as, oozing innocence, he made his way across the stage with his large and hard-won trophy.

In his pocket, however, was a home-made autograph book that also included spaces for addresses and phone numbers. Into this book during the course of the evening went the signatures of some of the great stars of the sport – John Surtees, Jackie Stewart, Stirling Moss and Colin McRae. From my position on the stage I am blissfully unaware of the kind of things that are going on in the dark recesses of the Great Room, but Lewis described it perfectly in his autobiography:

'... eventually that night, my dad said, "There's Ron Dennis, go and get his autograph." I walked up to Ron. I remember standing in front of him. I remember being so nervous but confident at the same time; nervous of speaking, but I also had my own self-belief, too. I knew what I wanted but I was not confident that I could speak the words properly. I was uncomfortable to the point that I really did not want to say too much. So I went up to him and said, "Hello, I'm Lewis Hamilton. One day I'd like to be a racing driver and I'd like to race for McLaren..."

'Ron sat down and spoke to me for what seemed like ages, ten minutes or so, although I'm sure it was really just a minute or two. I remember looking in his eyes – and I never lost contact with him. He said, "You have got to work hard at school. You have got to keep that spirit and keep going." So I got him to sign my autograph book and I said, "Can you also put down your number and address please?" and he said "Okay." He wrote down his address and said, "I tell you what – phone me in nine years and I will sort you out a deal." I said "Okay" and he wrote down his phone number. He just wrote, "Call me in nine years."'

A television interview recorded at that time and much replayed has Lewis casually, chin on hand, gazing into the distance and nonchalantly saying: 'I've got Ron Dennis's phone number, I'm going to give him a call in a few years and he's going to offer me a drive...' In fact it was just over two years later that Ron himself would call Anthony Hamilton, offering to support Lewis's career technically, financially and in whatever way necessary as part of the McLaren Mercedes Young Driver support programme. It was an offer, gratefully accepted, that would make Lewis ineligible, of course, for the McLaren *Autosport* Young Driver award; but Lewis, by his charm and his karting championships, had taken the short cut to all the big opportunities.

And that was my view from the wings, as Lewis Hamilton and Jenson Button put themselves in a position to become the latest heroes of British Formula One as the sport moved into the new century.

Chapter 13

Taking the Hint – Making the Move

The impact of Jenson Button and Lewis Hamilton was still a little way off as motorsport entered the new century. ITV were in desperate need of their heroics, as Michael Schumacher's dominance of Formula One had become total. In Germany the grand prix audiences were sky-high. In the UK the audiences were respectable, but were down to the hardcore who would never desert the sport.

ITV's coverage was justifiably still winning awards, especially for technical innovation and the contribution of Martin Brundle, but the dynamism of the early years had gone. The glossy air-conditioned studio was abandoned, which was no bad thing, but the presentation now seemed marooned in a paddock no-man's-land and it was clear that Jim Rosenthal's big moment of job satisfaction came from describing the England success in the 2003 Rugby World Cup; Formula One was not even threatening to provide such celebration for the home audience.

Within the BBC motorsport was rarely even discussed; apparently Formula One had been proved to be a bloated, cripplingly expensive non-sport, and the BBC hierarchy needed no encouragement to congratulate themselves for their foresight in 'ditching' the whole thing back in 1996.

BBC Sport was now under a new style of leadership, with executives like Pat Younge, Peter Salmon and Andrew Thompson – all good television pros but from other areas of the industry, such as drama, documentaries and current affairs. They offered the potential for fresh thinking, but to someone who had grown up in the straightforward days of Bryan Cowgill, John Bromley and Jonathan Martin the signals being sent out were, to say the least, baffling.

One good idea that Peter Salmon tried to get going, or so it seemed, was to recognise the knowledge and experience that the BBC commentators, as a group, could offer in helping the Corporation plot a course through the jungle of sports rights, and prioritise where BBC Sport should be, and what it should be doing.

So for the first time in my experience, in 2004 all the BBC Sport commentators and presenters gathered in a Television Centre conference theatre. It was humbling to look around the room. There were Olympic Champions and World Champions and legendary commentary figures like Peter Alliss and Bill McLaren. Surely, with this kind of experience and insight in the room we could make some real progress in shaping the future of televised sport and the immediate priorities of BBC Sport, especially in terms of style and content?

Instead, the day began with a 45-minute address by some kind of consultant, on 'BBC journalistic guidelines in the post-Hutton era'. I was sitting alongside the Rugby League commentator Ray French, a great pro, diligent and attentive and without a shred of the cynicism I had clearly become infected with. But even Ray, I felt, was struggling to work out how he was going to incorporate these complicated instructions into Saturday's commentary on Widnes against Warrington.

At least there was a brainstorming working lunch to look forward to – except that someone had forgotten to organise the lunch and we were all sent scurrying off to the BBC canteen. At this point we started to lose some of the legendary broadcasting personalities, because word had got out that the afternoon agenda included being divided into working parties to design the ideal floor layout for the prospective BBC Sports Department at Media City in Salford; big questions such as where should the cappuccino machine go... and should there be a games area?

Eventually, towards the end of the day, we got to talk about the content and shape of the year ahead, and were solemnly told that the big challenge for the department was making a success of Sport Relief; that is what we would be judged by. At this point Steve Cram put his hand up and suggested that surely the Athens Olympics was the big event of the year. I'm not sure our bright new bosses were convinced.

As it turned out the Athens Olympics were comfortably the highlight of the year for me. The drama of Matthew Pinsent winning his fourth gold medal helped my rowing crew win another BAFTA for best sports coverage, and when Sue Barker and I hosted a homecoming for our Athens heroes in front of 75,000 in Trafalgar Square, there should have been an atmosphere of euphoria; but for me there was a sense of 'perhaps that's as good as it's going to get'.

The other impression I had was that the 20-year lifespan at the top of the profession that Jonathan Martin had promised, and Harry Carpenter, Des Lynam, David Coleman and many others had enjoyed, was fast running out. All the feelings of irritation I had at the direction that BBC Sport was going were surely symptoms of an old-style sports presenter failing to keep pace with the new technology and new media that the BBC was about to embrace so effectively.

I plead guilty to all of that but could not understand why the traditional BBC qualities of confidence, team spirit, humour and a strong leadership providing a clear sense of direction needed to be lost along the way.

So much has been written about the BBC at this time – the cloying bureaucracy, the producers suffocating in paperwork and email traffic. I saw all of that, and like everyone else suffered the isolating lack of internal communication. Out went all the initiative and the sense of adventure, in came the image consultant who told me to abandon the tie and wear my shirt out of my trousers, along with that health and safety adviser who told me crowd noise at rugby matches could do me permanent damage.

▲ *First day as a sports presenter. Anglia TV, Norwich, October 1977. Rather more Alan Partridge than Desmond Lynam.* (ITV/Rex Features)

▼ *Already crowned as Constructors' Champions in 1978, Team Lotus personnel gather for a celebratory photograph before all the mixed emotions of Monza.* (Sutton Motorsport Images)

▲ *Monza 1978. My first time in front of the camera in a Formula One pit-lane and I'm trying to explain ground-effect to an ITV audience. Team Lotus senior mechanic Glen Waters listens and learns.* (Author's collection)

▼ *The aftermath of the multi-car accident at Monza that would eventually claim the life of Ronnie Peterson and confirm Mario Andretti as a tragic World Champion.* (Sutton Motorsport Images)

▲ *Formula One at Snetterton, 1979. Rupert Keegan giving his reaction after winning the Aurora F1 Championship race. The coverage is still on film and Phil Jacobs is the first cameraman I ever worked with and certainly one of the best.* (ITV/Rex Features)

▼ *Formula Ford, Snetterton, 1981, and the victory wave of a young Ayrton Senna that would be seen many times over the years to come.* (Mike Dixon)

▲ Film-maker Barrie Hinchliffe with Pentti Airikkala at the 1980 Lombard RAC Rally. Working with Barrie at BHP through the late 1980s taught me a lot about the best way to get motorsport on the screen. (Author's collection)

▼ I learned a lot as a one-off co-driver for Airikkala as well. We're on the Audi Sport Rally in Wales, the co-driver is looking cool, Pentti in the background is looking rather more stressed. (Guy Davies)

▼ A top-three finish in Wales and I watched the whole thing through the passenger's side window. (Author's collection)

▲ *A dominant car and a dominant driver, Nigel Mansell crowned 1992 World Champion in Hungary – the title was never in doubt.* (LAT Photographic)

▶ *It was less certain that Nigel would be on hand to pick up the 1992 BBC Sports Personality of the Year award... but that's another story.* (Mirrorpix)

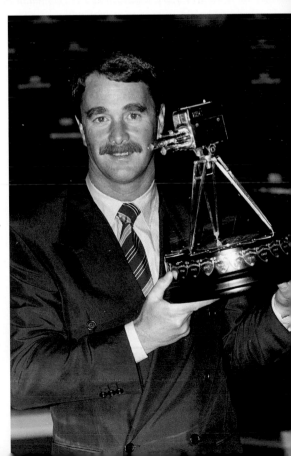

▲ *The kind of action that helped build the audience for the British Touring Car Championship... and Will Hoy and Julian Bailey were team-mates!* (LAT Photographic)

▼ *November 1993, a huge crowd at Donington to see Nigel Mansell in the TOCA shoot-out and he suffers one of the biggest crashes of his career, right in front of the BHP cameras.* (LAT Photographic)

▲ *The fateful last few minutes at Imola, Senna sits pensive in the Williams…*
(Sutton Motorsport Images)

▼ *…and leads the Benetton of Schumacher towards his final lap.*
(Sutton Motorsport Images)

▲ *The* Grandstand *studio: the hub of BBC Sport could feel aloof and out of touch with the atmosphere of big live events.* (Mark Lloyd/Daily Mail/Rex Features).

▼ *On the 40th anniversary of* Grandstand *I am joined by the other long-term presenters of the programme, Frank Bough, Des Lynam and David Coleman. We were delighted also to welcome Peter Dimmock, the presenter of the very first edition.* (Author's collection)

▲*Putting* Grandstand *on the air from an empty grid at the 1996 British Grand Prix at Silverstone. Floor manager Chris White marshals a crew of minimum size, and I'm clearly saving money on ties as well. See Portugal below...* (LAT Photographic)

▼ *Forcing a smile on the grid at Estoril, the last Grand Prix in Europe before ITV took over. The visit of Michael Jackson, the Controller of BBC1 and BBC2, had done little to lift the mood.* (Author's collection)

Pre-season launches in 2003. I struggle with BAR team-mates Jenson Button and Jacques Villeneuve, who were not on speaking terms in Barcelona... but a few days later in Lucerne a youthful Fernando Alonso was clearly a composed champion of the future. (Sutton Motorsport Images and LAT Photographic)

▲ *Ringmaster Bernie Ecclestone creating mischief in the Spa paddock in 2007. I follow dutifully; Mark Blundell is still making his mind up.* (Sutton Motorsport Images)

▼ *The best job in the world? Sometimes this view is as good as it gets.* (LAT Photographic)

Jenson Button and Lewis Hamilton at the 2007 Autosport Awards. Within two years they would both be World Champion, and then team-mates as well.
(LAT Photographic)

▲ *Lewis's final pit stop in the 2008 Brazilian Grand Prix, with the high drama of becoming World Champion just laps away.* (LAT Photographic)

▼ *A few days later the new World Champion is welcomed back to Woking. The victory-red shirts of the McLaren staff are reflected in the futuristic glass walls of the McLaren Technology Centre.* (LAT Photographic)

▲ *Our own celebration in April 2008 – the second of three straight BAFTA awards for the ITV F1 team. From left are Neil Duncanson, Gerard Lane (Editor), Kevin Chapman (Producer), Steve Aldous (Pit-Lane Producer), James Allen, Mark Blundell and Martin Brundle.* (Getty Images)

▼ *At the Goodwood Festival of Speed for ITV and these are the perks of the job. A run up the hill with Sir Stirling Moss in the Porsche RS60 that he almost took to victory in the 1961 Targa Florio, and a similar thrill alongside Sir Jackie Stewart in the Mercedes that won the 1951 Carrera Panamericana driven by Juan Manuel Fangio.* (Nick Rose and author's collection)

▲ *Goodwood 2011 and Dario Franchitti and Dan Wheldon are amused to hear stories of how Nigel Mansell paved the way for their double Indy 500 success. Tragically this was just a few weeks before Wheldon lost his life in a crash at Las Vegas Motor Speedway.* (Author's collection)

▼ *Sebastian Vettel arrives on stage in party mood at the end of a long, hard night at the 2011 Autosport Awards.* (LAT Photographic)

▲ *Maybe the best racer, certainly the best storyteller. Sitting down with the likes of Sir Stirling Moss for the SKY F1 Legends series has been a pleasure and a privilege.* (Alex Rodger/Sky Sports)

◄ *Make your choice. The learned approach of SKY F1 or the light-hearted appeal of the BBC. Whatever the style, it was hard to tell them apart at the 2012 British Grand Prix. Simon Lazenby and the SKY team on the left, Jake Humphrey and the BBC boys just a few feet away in the Silverstone pit-lane.* (Jack Rider)

144

BBC Sport used to be a proud flotilla, forging on, line astern, behind the flagship *Grandstand*; but now, in 2005 it was becoming little pockets of resentment clinging to the wreckage of ever-diminishing sports rights. But from my point of view, with probably five years left in front of the camera, there was still great quality in the BBC Sports portfolio, and on the horizon there was also now the inspiring prospect of the 2012 London Olympics.

What was not on the BBC horizon was any more motorsport, and definitely no prospect of Formula One. In 2005 my contract was due for renewal, which had always been a fairly routine process, and despite constant reminders from my agent I had given it precious little thought. I was content to remain as part of the BBC's golf and rugby team, and would do whatever I could to prolong the life of *Grandstand* despite constant rumours of the programme's imminent demise.

In the summer of 2005 I was in Scotland covering the Scottish Open before moving across to St Andrews for the Open Championship itself. The requests to sort out my contract became more insistent; I offered to discuss it all when I got back to London, but apparently it was even more urgent than that. So, over the phone, I agreed a contract that would be roughly the same as what had gone before, maybe a little bit down in terms of money and, for admin reasons yet to be fully explained, only two years; but everyone, so I was told, was being treated the same. So I thought, 'I'm a BBC man, I'm clearly not going anywhere else... do the deal.'

On the Monday of the Open Championship, at the start of perhaps my busiest week of the year, I agreed the renewal of the contract with the proviso that we would meet when things were a bit quieter to discuss more of the detail of the next few years. Two days later the BBC announced a new five-year deal with the Royal and Ancient Golf Club to continue exclusive coverage of the Open, and Director General Michael Grade came to my presentation position to be interviewed about the great boost it provided for BBC Sport. I had been the BBC golf presenter for 15 years and allowed myself to pompously wonder whether the haste to complete my contract had anything to do with the signing of the Open Championship deal. Surely not.

It was only in discussing the detail of the contract a couple of weeks later it emerged that the contract had been reduced by about 20%, a drop in money that was being justified by a lessening of my responsibilities; rugby league presentation was going elsewhere, there was a strong feeling that Gary Lineker was going to get involved in the golf, and the BBC were reluctant to give more than a two-year contract, seemingly because of uncertainty about the future of *Grandstand*.

Every aspect of the discussion seemed to confirm that the BBC was keen to move in a direction that would not suit or include me. I had no problem with that and it is the absolute right of the BBC to shape things as they wish, but despite constant promptings no one would concede that this was in fact the case. Instead, with the 'reassurance' that I was a 'vital and essential part of their long-term plans', I resigned myself to a contract of less money, fewer responsibilities and a shorter duration. But despite its shortcomings it at least kept me as the theoretical number one in the department as the BBC started its build-up to the London Olympics in 2012.

And then another of 'those' phone calls. I was in the wilds of Devon, and it was my agent. There had been an approach from Neil Duncanson, the boss of North One Television, producers of the ITV Formula One coverage, and my partner in the successful production bid for Formula One in 1996. Would I be interested in taking over the presentation of Formula One from 2006? Of course I would be interested, but the answer was no for two reasons. Firstly, I had just signed a new BBC contract, and secondly this was the third such approach and my answer had always been no. Regrettably, but encouraged by the attitude of the BBC, presenting Formula One was a thing of the past.

But as the day progressed I thought more and more about

the suggestion; after all, the recent discussions had indicated a BBC career in reverse. I had nothing to prove in terms of loyalty, having rejected previous ITV advances; perhaps this deal worked for both myself and the BBC? Both of us could go off in the new directions we wanted. Also, jumping ship like this seemed to leave no permanent scars. BBC executives would go back and forth to ITV and Channel 4 as a matter of routine, and even after the brutal, abrupt way Des Lynam switched sides, 18 months later he was a front-row guest at Sports Personality of the Year, mischievously trying to trip me up at the start of the programme. The time seemed right and it was clearly a last chance. That night I rang my agent; let's talk about it.

The approach had been made by Neil Duncanson, but the first meeting was with Mark Sharman, the Head of Sport at ITV. As head of sport at Meridian, Mark had been involved with us in the successful Chrysalis bid for the F1 production rights back in 1996 and was aware of my rather distant pedigree in the sport. We covered a lot of ground in our discussion. I wanted an assurance that even if Jim Rosenthal was not voluntarily stepping aside he was being treated fairly in the whole process. He wondered whether I would be available to handle any of ITV's football coverage alongside Formula One and I said I was not a football man and, after 20 years on *Grandstand*, I was looking forward to spending the last five years of my career concentrating on the demands of just one sport.

The contract would be for the full five years and the money would be the best part of three times what the BBC were offering. Perhaps I should have done a Des Lynam and held an ITV press conference the following morning, but I wanted to think it through properly before doing anything rash, and fortunately a trip to Japan to cover the World Rowing Championships would provide that opportunity. It was an intensive few days but it was everything I loved about working for the BBC – a genuine fast-moving, complicated outside broadcast that left you drained but satisfied at the end of the day. At night I lay in the wooden hot tub out on the patio that doubled as a bathroom in our rather strange hotel, and tried to work out the best course of action.

I thought back to ten years earlier when I lay in a hotel bedroom in Estoril, devastated by the manner in which Formula One had been grabbed by ITV. I remembered nine years earlier, the satisfaction of being part of the winning production bid, and the long conversations with Brian Barwick that persuaded me to stay at the BBC. On balance, I reflected, a month earlier I had assumed I would see out my career at the BBC. If my new contract could take on a sensible five-year duration, and go back to roughly where I was a month earlier in terms of money and responsibility, then thank you ITV, but I would be happy to stay a BBC man.

But it seems it was not all as straightforward as that from the BBC point of view. On my return from Japan I went into a meeting with the contract manager and the newly appointed Head of Sport, Roger Mosey, the former editor of *Today* and Head of Television News who was a couple of weeks into his new job. I explained I had had an offer from ITV to present Formula One and, given my reading of the situation at the BBC, I was tempted to take it.

I don't know whether their reaction was outrage or mock outrage, but they said it was impossible, of course, because I was under a two-year contract that had been signed a matter of weeks earlier. They had a point there. Then I suggested that, as had been previously discussed, the new contract was merely an illustration of how they no longer saw me as the future of sports presentation on the BBC; and if we could both be honest about that, then the ITV move would be the perfect opportunity for us all to head off in the directions that we clearly wanted to go.

Absolutely not, they countered, I was the number one for the foreseeable future; the long-term future of *Grandstand* was also assured according to them, and when I expressed further reservations about the content of the new contract I was told it was only two years because they were not able to plan too far ahead, and it was reduced by 20% to reflect the amount they were cutting back on my presenting role.

I am not a negotiator and this was not meant to be a negotiation. I was looking for an adult conversation about our respective ambitions. But instead I was just sinking in a BBC quicksand of contradictory statements and contractual glue. In fairness they came back with an improved financial offer, but despite the generosity of the ITV deal this was not about money as far as I was concerned.

I decided to go away and put a proposal on paper. I did not want to be accused of contract breaking, and deep down I did not want to leave the BBC. So I proposed a long-term deal that would leave me working on the major events that I had become associated with. There would be no demand for number one status, but I wanted to be in a position to use my experience of 12 Olympics to help the department prepare and deliver great coverage of London 2012. In terms of pay I suggested pegging my contract to the July 2005 level and freezing it for the next seven years; and considering I was on about 25% of the highest-earning presenter in the department this struck me as a pretty good deal for the BBC.

I thought that if that proposal was rejected then BBC Sport was definitely heading in a direction that was never going to involve me and I could leave with no guilt about the contractual position, and could feel that I had behaved honestly and unselfishly in trying to reach a compromise. On the Friday morning I delivered my proposal in writing and it was immediately rejected. I was given the weekend to decide what I was going to do.

I was in the middle of presenting the World Match Play Championship at Wentworth so had little time to dwell on the situation. There were a few people on the team who appreciated that my future had become a little uncertain, to say the least, including my loyal colleague and *Grandstand* floor manager

Chris White. I told all of them that we were having a meeting to sort it out but gave no idea that it was probably all over. I had a lot of good friends on the golf team in particular and did not want the weekend to become downbeat or sentimental; however, I knew that after 20 years it was almost certainly my last weekend presenting the programme.

The golf finished early on Sunday afternoon and I was left filling with football scores and rugby news from a bush behind the 16th green, trying to decipher information from a distant, dodgy monitor. I was going to make some flippant remark to get us off-air, but then, with about 90 seconds to go, I was handed a sheet of paper bearing the sad news that Michael Park, the co-driver to Markko Märtin, had died from his injuries after a crash on the Wales Rally GB. There was just time to say a sombre goodbye, and as the credits rolled it was that story that occupied my thoughts more than the realisation that my *Grandstand* days were over.

When I got back to the television compound the production cabin was empty; I had one last look round and then drove out of the car park. The following morning I handed in my resignation at Television Centre, and to the time of writing I have never been back and have never been invited back.

A short time later, Roger Mosey, in an interview for *The Guardian*, said that I only went to ITV for the money, a comment for which he later apologised. I, for my part, made a few supposedly humorous observations about the Corporation in after-dinner speeches and as a result would get rather pompous letters from the BBC legal department which would be the only formal communication with the old place; they went straight in the bin. In 2006 it was announced that *Grandstand* would finish in three years' time; but the axe actually fell, with comparatively little notice, in January 2007. Clare Balding presented the last edition from the Indoor Bowls at Potters Leisure Centre in Norfolk, and with that, 49 years of sports broadcasting history was at an end.

With the benefit of hindsight it was clear that the programme had to evolve and probably change fundamentally, and the opportunities to expand audience choice with all the digital options available have been exploited brilliantly by the BBC. But it was surely not necessary to lose such an evocative brand or the framework that allowed small, less fashionable sports to get a bite-size showcase in front of a large terrestrial audience. The British Touring Car Championship would have struggled to establish a decent television profile without the springboard of *Grandstand*. Admittedly there are now a vast number of satellite and digital outlets for all sports, but none of them has the *Grandstand* potential to develop that vital new core audience.

Later in 2007 there was a BBC Television Centre reception to mark the passing of the programme. Those who had worked on the show throughout its history were invited, but I was not, despite having presented more editions of the programme than anyone else and having been one of only four regular presenters. It was the final confirmation that the spirit of the old BBC Sport that I had known and loved no longer existed, and the decision I had made to move on was definitely the right one. Especially as the last years of my television career were going to be the most varied and eventful of all

However, the first few days of the rest of my life began rather quietly. The BBC reached a modest financial settlement for my services and triumphantly imposed the condition that I should not appear on ITV screens for three months. As it was now October and the new Formula One season did not start until March, this was a blow that we were comfortably able to absorb.

For the first time in 30 years I did not feel pressurised or hemmed in by programme schedules and deadlines and I was able to take a deep breath and look around.

One of the first things I wanted to do was meet with Jim Rosenthal, who lived close by in Berkshire. I suppose it was wrong to expect the whole new arrangement to have met with his approval and it was clear that, despite what I had been told, he was keen to have continued with Formula One. I hope he was reassured that I had in no way tried to force the situation, and we were able to shrug our shoulders, shake hands and stay friends. Six years later we would once again be sitting in the same Marlow coffee bar bemoaning the unfairness of the business, and this time I would be the victim; but all that is another story.

Chapter 14

GARDENING LEAVE

It is fair to say that in 2005 the ITV Formula One coverage lacked the zeal of the early days of the contract, although they had been desperately unlucky with the action on offer since 1997. They had seen only four different World Champions crowned, Michael Schumacher having won the title for Ferrari in 2000 and not relinquishing the crown until Fernando Alonso won it for Renault in 2005. They had the excitement of a last-round decider in 1997, but in 2002 Schumacher had won it with six races remaining, and he'd claimed the title with four races still left in 2001 and 2004. It was hardly the stuff to build an audience or get the TV production juices flowing. Instead these were the kind of statistics that were encouraging all the self-congratulation over at the BBC. Not only that, but no British driver had won a single grand prix since David Coulthard took victory in the opening round of the 2003 season in Australia.

Ironically it had been the sport's lowest point that brought out the best in ITV in this period. When Formula One arrived at Indianapolis in 2005 without tyres that could cope with the demands of the famous circuit, the American audience, yet to be convinced of the merits of grand prix racing, were left howling their derision at a meaningless six-car procession. ITV covered the three-hour farce in a style that said everything about the journalistic instincts of Jim Rosenthal and the interviewing tenacity of Martin Brundle.

They deserved all the plaudits they received, but this scarcely compensated for the abuse that ITV had encountered just a month earlier when they were either forced, or chose (depending on your point of view), to take a commercial break with three laps remaining of the San Marino Grand Prix at Imola. As a result the audience missed Michael Schumacher's battle with Fernando Alonso that was providing a thrilling climax to the race, and the broadcaster only just managed to get back for the final lap.

Everyone who appreciated the juggling act that was going on in the production gallery that day had sympathy with the predicament of the ITV broadcast team. Jenson Button had been leading the race, the ITV director had decided to stay with that, then the Schumacher/Alonso battle developed, the commercial breaks had become backed up, and in the end ITV were trapped.

With hindsight my feeling is that ITV as a network had become far too complacent over the probability of a situation like this; I only had to recall the immediate discussions following their move into the sport in 1996 when, clearly, no one had given a thought to the problems of taking a commercial break while a Formula One grand prix was actually in progress. To my knowledge no serious consideration was given to alternative methods of accommodating in-race advertising, such as split-screen technology, after the advertisers had signalled their opposition. As a result ITV had missed Damon Hill's brilliant move on Michael Schumacher in the 1997 Hungarian Grand Prix, and the puncture at Suzuka that had ended Schumacher's title hopes the following year. But Imola was the big one.

Far too much responsibility had been placed on the production team on site, with little authority or flexibility coming from the network in London. There should have been a panic button that would enable the director to make the decision, in extreme circumstances, to stay with a critical situation in a race and, as a result, cancel a commercial break entirely and sort out the financial implications on Monday morning. I know that advertising is how ITV gets its revenue, so the advertisers are important, but not as crucial as the viewers, especially when ITV had taken a broadcast monopoly of the sport.

No advertisers want to be be associated with a cock-up like this. A few years later ITV I was hosting the Everton–Liverpool FA Cup tie when a computer in London randomly went to a Tic Tac mints advert as the only goal of the game was being scored; and in 2010 a rogue Hyundai advert prevented ITV HD viewers seeing England's first goal of the World Cup finals. On neither occasion did the advertiser appreciate the extra exposure, or being seen to be an obstacle to the viewer's enjoyment. After each incident it was largely left to the broadcast teams to absorb all the criticism, with ITV management very slow to mount a defence until all the ridiculous 'ITV Sport can't cover football' headlines had been written.

So it was at the San Marino Grand Prix – Jim Rosenthal, James Allen and Neal Duncanson were 'obviously' to blame for letting down the viewing public. The events at Imola merely fired up all the critics who felt that Formula One should never have gone to ITV in the first place, and should never be interrupted by commercial breaks, let alone with three laps to go in one of the best races for years. It all had a demoralising effect on the ITV team and I was still very aware of it being an open wound when I joined the team for 2006. All I could do was try to freshen things up and provide a little of the authority and experience that ITV Head of Sport Mark Sharman thought he was buying.

Three months after my appointment those qualities were not especially in evidence when I hosted that year's Autosport Awards. Jenson Button's career had spluttered and stalled after his high-profile arrival on the Formula One scene but he was still ITV's main hope of enticing back that part of the TV audience who wanted British success.

So when he came on the stage at the start of the evening and posed for a photograph with the group of young Kart Champions, my comment 'Place your bets now, which member of this line-up will win a grand prix first?' got a laugh, but in the context of my future role can best be described as 'ill-judged'. It was no problem to Jenson, who saw the funny side, but apparently some of his table companions that night were outraged. Complaints were made, and a more formal complaint was made by Jenson's Honda team, along with a threat to withdraw co-operation for the new season. Jenson was more mature than all that, though, and was happy to take a lunch off me to discuss what lay ahead.

It turned out to be a very useful opportunity to catch up with someone whose driving talent was undeniable, but who had had his share of frustrations since that successful Williams audition at Barcelona.

Jenson spent just one year at Williams, having to move on to partner Giancarlo Fisichella at Benetton when Frank Williams decided to honour a long-term obligation to Juan Pablo Montoya. The results had been disappointing, the relationship with team boss Flavio Briatore did not seem supportive, and midway through 2002 Jenson learnt that he would be surrendering his race-seat to the team's test driver, Fernando Alonso.

David Richards, who had progressed from rallying to Touring Cars to become team principal at the hitherto underperforming BAR Formula One team, saw Jenson as a future World Champion and had eagerly signed him up to drive alongside Jacques Villeneuve. But the 1997 World Champion had been in at the instigation of the team, which had been set up by his former manager Craig Pollock. Jenson represented the first David Richards' signing and Villencuve hardly gave him a warm welcome.

I was master of ceremonies at the press launch in the Conference Centre in Barcelona when the new BAR 005 was launched along with the Villeneuve/Button partnership; and just like Mansell with McLaren eight years earlier at the Science Museum, it failed to give you much encouragement for the future. As the new car was on the point of being unveiled,

I announced the drivers on to the stage and only Jenson Button emerged from the wings. Villeneuve was sulking behind the scenes at having being instructed to wear a particular cap for the photo-call, especially, it seems, because Jenson had been asked to convey the instruction.

Villeneuve's petty behaviour and obvious insecurity showed itself more publicly in the first race of the season in Melbourne, when Button found himself backed up behind Villeneuve in the pit-lane, the Canadian claiming that he had radio communication problems. However, by the end of the season an uneasy working relationship had been restored and Button had proved himself quicker and more consistent than his teammate.

During this period Jenson had been characterised as a playboy, more interested in enjoying the fringe social benefits of the sport than developing his outstanding potential. Some of that was true for a while, as it has been for just about every young driver in Formula One, but what could now be seen in Jenson was a strong personality ready to rededicate himself, and reinvent himself when circumstances required.

This he did in 2004 and 2005 with the Honda team, being rewarded with a series of strong qualifying performances and podium finishes which underlined that he was certainly going to be a winner in future, if not a Champion. The year 2005, however, had been overshadowed by a contract dispute, with Jenson enthusiastically anticipating that Williams would take up their option on his contract and David Richards defending the position on behalf of BAR Honda. Eventually the FIA Contracts Recognition Board ruled in favour of BAR Honda and a rather chastened Button had to stay where he was for a disappointing and frustrating 2005 season when the prospect of a first victory seemed as far away as ever; and that victory, now long overdue, was vital to his progress in the sport.

Hence the clumsy comment at the 2005 Autosport Awards when, to his credit, Button retaliated by comparing his contractual adventures with my own situation on 'gardening leave' from the BBC. We discussed it all over lunch and the important concession he agreed to was to be interviewed by ITV every Saturday evening at every grand prix, whether the story was good or bad and whether the team was making progress or struggling. I felt that this regular dialogue with one driver was an important missing element of continuity in the ITV build-up; a large part of the television audience was homing in on the British interest and they had to be served and informed, however tough the message.

During this period around New Year 2006 I tried to visit as many of the British-based Formula One teams as possible and was fascinated by the different outlook they seemed to have to their sport and business compared to my previous involvement ten years earlier. I had left a sport wondering how on earth it was going to compensate for the loss of tobacco and alcohol sponsorship, and now it was underpinned by big money from the banks and finance worlds, and sky-high sponsorship budgets from the high-tech, computer and mobile communications industries.

McLaren were the embodiment of this supposed progress. I had worked with the team as a journalist and broadcaster from their original home in Boundary Road, Woking, to their nearby glass-walled headquarters complete with bonsai trees, presentation cinema and trophy-crammed reception area. But in 2003 they had moved into the Norman Foster-designed McLaren Technology Centre, which had been under construction for four years and along with its artificial lakes and ecological principles had been described as 'the largest, privately funded construction project in Europe'.

Now here I was on the eve of the 2006 season with Ron Dennis in his office that occupied a first-floor corner of the building. He was talking about the difficulties of working with Kimi Räikkönen, and how problematic it was aligning Kimi's chaotic social life with the standards and professionalism of McLaren; although he described it all in rather more colourful language than that. It was early December and Ron was starting to hint at the spectacular deal that he was poised to announce that would bring the current World Champion Fernando Alonso to McLaren for the 2007 season.

I had been given a fascinating tour of the spotless new complex, seemingly a haven of order and calm. I was not at all surprised to hear the McLaren boss describe how it all reflected his philosophy of life and Formula One. The working environment had to be clinically prepared and free of clutter and distractions; the staff, Ron felt, rather worryingly, would probably enjoy these surroundings even more than their home environment; he himself especially relished having his own private washroom facilities; the gospel was organisation and efficiency at all times.

I have always liked Ron Dennis and I have long been one of his greatest admirers. But a couple of years later on a private jet flight to Valencia, he and his then wife Lisa laughed about his obsessive attention to detail and how it showed itself in their home life; it was also evident in every aspect of the design and function of the McLaren Technology Centre. A lot of those traits I had also seen in Colin Chapman 20 years earlier; it had made Lotus powerful but also brittle and inflexible, and I saw McLaren as the same kind of animal.

Walking around the MTC I was desperate for the sight, or at the very least the smell, of an oily rag. Instead I was put in mind of that legendary film of production-line life, *Modern Times*. Charlie Chaplin... Colin Chapman... Ron Dennis. I suppose it was all the perfect preparation for my first grand prix with the ITV team at the spectacular but absolutely soulless Sakhir Circuit in Bahrain.

I had decided to immerse myself in the first three 'flyaway' races without returning home, so the grands prix at Bahrain, Malaysia and Melbourne would keep me away for the best part of five weeks. Mind you, even before Formula One had come back into my working life I had expected to be on the other side of the world at this time, but with the BBC. It was a strange feeling to walk into the departure lounge at Heathrow Terminal Three and see virtually the entire BBC Sport production staff ready to fly out to the Commonwealth Games. Five months earlier I had been in discussion about the shift-patterns I would be working at the Games, and that Sue Barker and myself would be joint main presenters just as we had been at the Athens Olympics four years earlier.

Now, at Heathrow, when the BBC team walked through the door marked Melbourne and I headed for the Bahrain gate, it was the last of many symbolic moments that underlined the parting of the ways. I found it a tough moment as well because I always, rather weakly, tend to dwell on what is in the past rather than what the future holds. But sitting on that plane to Bahrain it also seemed that everything had fallen into place. Ahead lay a five-year contract working on the television sport that excited me as much as any other. After that, at well past 60 years old, I would be more than happy to step aside from a regular on-screen role, maybe retire completely, and enjoy everything else life had to offer.

Chapter 15

GETTING BACK UP TO SPEED

It was because of the Commonwealth Games in Melbourne that the start of the Formula One season had been moved to the Middle East. The Sakhir Circuit had come on to the Formula One schedule in 2004. Designed by Herman Tilke, who, it seems, was single-handedly creating the new generation of Formula One circuits, it was built in the space of 18 months on a former camel farm, 20 miles south-west of the Bahrain capital, Manama. In 2007 it was still well before the spotlight had fallen on the civil rights issues in Bahrain that served to make it feel like an even more inappropriate place for Formula One.

Having left the sport in the evocative, raucous surroundings of Monza and Estoril nine years earlier, this first glimpse of Bernie Ecclestone's brave new world was a shock to the system. The architecture was stunning but the desert location seemed at best random, and the vast empty acreage of the paddock with the teams shut away in air-conditioned offices said everything about corporate image and very little about the sport.

It was not the fault of the location, but compared to the heartland of the sport there was no history, tradition or great racing stories attached to the circuit, and the fact that the previous two grands prix had been won from pole position, by Schumacher and Alonso respectively, gave rise to the suspicion that this was a highly technical circuit with little opportunity for risk-taking or racing.

That hardly made it unique on the Formula One schedule, but it did make it especially unsuited to host the first grand prix of the season, the one race that comes with questions to be answered, surprises to be sprung and race-starved appetites to be satisfied; the one race that every fan would have been anticipating for at least three months. Every fan, that is, except those in Bahrain. The modest, largely silent crowd that braved the sky-high ticket prices to fill barely a third of the circuit on race afternoon had a deflating effect on the whole occasion.

But my job in these first three races was not to admire the scenery but to learn and get used to the ITV way of doing things. It was fascinating to see from the inside exactly how they had moved the coverage on. A live outside broadcast always will be a perilous, vulnerable operation, especially if you abandon the security of an on-site studio and link the whole thing in whatever the environment is throwing at you, as close to the action as you can get. And when that action is the adrenalin-fuelled, sometimes ear-splitting chaos of a grand prix build-up, the problems and difficulties increase still further.

In terms of presentation, the impression I got was that ITV wanted to get closer to all that excitement than ever before. They had begun their coverage of Formula One nine years earlier surrounded by chrome and smoked glass in a self-contained studio that looked glossy and impressive but, by its nature, was remote and aloof. When they abandoned that, Jim and his guests had a rather itinerant look about them, setting up their cameras and monitors in some pretty nondescript corners of the paddock. Even the BBC these days find themselves in those kind of locations; but an hour before the start of a grand prix the only place to be is amid the tension of the pit-lane, just as with half an hour to go the only place to be is on the grid.

So would I be happy to work amid all the logistical difficulties, communication problems and apparent perils of the pit-lane? After all those years marooned in the *Grandstand* studio I could hardly imagine anything more challenging or satisfying.

It was not something that would have been even considered back at Estoril or Monza in 1996; the technology did not exist to generate reliably a signal from that sort of location, or to provide the talk-back communication to guide the presenter through the running order and get the programme on and off the air. The digital age had changed all that, and in terms of communication the big breakthrough for me were the deep-set earpieces that cut out all ambient noise and enabled you to concentrate on the programme. They worked so well that two Ferraris could fire up in the garage ten feet away, and you would barely notice. The downside was that you would also not hear anything if a Ferrari was hammering down the pit-lane straight at you. It was a wonderfully atmospheric environment, but one in which you had to be extra vigilant.

In that respect it was great to be reunited in Bahrain with a former colleague from my days at Anglia TV, Steve Aldous. He was a very junior film assistant when we worked together in 1978 on the Lotus film at Monza, among many other more mundane projects. Now he was my pit-lane producer and had become just about the best in the business. Over the next three years it was Steve who broke the rules and rewrote the rules of how to present live television from a busy pit-lane. He made the all-important contacts, and got the trust of just about every garage. He understood movement and access and, crucially, safety. At every race he guarded our backs, mine and all of the crew, and I was delighted that his services were considered indispensable by the BBC when the contract shifted back three years later; certainly Jake Humphrey would agree, judging by the footage of Steve shoving him out of the way of a speeding Renault.

Steve would be my right-hand man, but the rest of the ITV operation were equally well qualified. Ted Kravitz, who had come through local radio at LBC and Capital, had been with the ITV operation from the start and had turned into one of the most accomplished pit-lane reporters in the sport. Louise Goodman, with her background in Formula One public relations, had a comfortable rapport with everyone in the paddock, and my regular pit-lane pundit was Mark Blundell, a delight to work with though his entertaining failure to master the English language had made him a cult figure on some of the more spiteful Formula One websites.

Most impressive, though, was the hard work and professionalism of James Allen, which made him a perfect, almost telepathic foil for Martin Brundle in the commentary box. But it was that feeling of a well-oiled machine, in which each person knew their responsibilities and how they fitted in with everyone else's roles, that was also a weakness for ITV. The years had lulled them into a safe routine that would get them through a very demanding schedule with few risks or alarms. Running orders varied little from one race to the next, features followed a similar pattern, the mind-numbing cheapskate viewer competitions imposed on the programme by sales departments on the South Bank were an immovable fixture, and all this was crammed into the straitjacket of a rigid schedule of commercial breaks. In these circumstances the easy, safe option was always attractive and I would take it as readily as anybody else.

What they desperately needed was a British challenger among the Championship pacesetters who would excite the UK audience and pump some adrenalin into the UK broadcaster. Bahrain would not provide too much hope in that regard. Jenson Button qualified on the second row, but a clutch problem at the start left him out of position, and his fourth-place finish was respectable in the circumstances.

Fernando Alonso started the defence of his title with a comfortable win, and Renault emphasised their dominance a week later in Malaysia. But this time it was Giancarlo Fisichella leading home his teammate Alonso. Button had qualified on the front row and was on the podium in third, but the fact that he was disappointed with that gave us all encouragement that his breakthrough win was not too far away. Maybe it would come in Melbourne two weeks later.

One rather tedious observation that people made about my occupation was that 'it is quite simply the best job in the world... all those great events, all those exciting places'. It made me feel a bit spoilt and selfish that I was not a more grateful custodian of 'the best job in the world'. But as often as not I have watched all those great events on a small monitor with a producer screaming in my earpiece; and as for the travel, the schedule is so tight that you are blissfully unaware if you are in Augusta, Athens or Kuala Lumpur.

March and April 2006 was the first opportunity I had to build some slack into the schedule. I watched live coverage of the Masters golf in the departure lounge at Kuala Lumpur airport, the first time since 1983 that I had not spent Masters weekend in the lush surroundings of the Augusta National. But ahead lay a few free days in Sydney, a weekend spent walking in the Blue Mountains and even a diversion to stroll around the mist-shrouded Penrith Lake, where the rowing heroics that took place six years earlier had just been voted Britain's favourite all-time sporting moment. Then it was on to Melbourne and the definite prospect of another performance to celebrate.

The empty grandstands and bleak corporate paddock of Bahrain had been replicated at the Sepang circuit in Malaysia, so it was reassuring to arrive in Melbourne, a proper sporting city that, even though it had just gorged itself on the Commonwealth Games, was ready for Formula One. The Albert Park circuit is laid out on public roads, and the grand prix has not been immune to local environmental opposition and robust political debate concerning its future. But they understand motor racing and know how to stage a grand prix in the 'old-fashioned' way.

This means dawn to dusk entertainment on each of the three days of the meeting; lots of surrounding attractions that include historic cars, fairgrounds and rock concerts, and a full track programme which involves celebrity races and the fantastic Aussie V8 saloon cars. Formula One is merely top of the bill in an action-packed day. And all this is played out in front of a busy, noisy, knowledgeable crowd who create a fantastic atmosphere. The people who sign the cheques and make the deals seem to feel that these are not important ingredients, but without such vibrancy venues like Bahrain, Abu Dhabi, Malaysia and China will never feel like the real thing.

Apart from Silverstone itself it seemed like the ideal venue for Jenson Button to finally make the transition to grand prix winner. When Jenson stormed to pole position, only the third in his career, ITV probably – myself included – did not hold back in their anticipation of the great event. His teammate Rubens Barrichello, in an identical car, could only manage 17th on the grid, and we saw that as a further endorsement of Jenson's talent. I walked alongside him through the race-day crowds at the paddock entrance. There was huge and vocal British support. Jenson urged caution in his thoughtful interview, we were more upbeat, but neither of us could anticipate that this pole position was merely as good as it was going to get for the first half of the season ahead.

Despite his pole position Button never became a race contender after he was beaten to the first corner by Fernando Alonso and then, on graining soft tyres, swiftly surrendered second to Räikkönen. Worse was to come in the latter stages with a fiery engine failure within sight of the chequered flag, when he pulled up short of the line, sacrificing a points finish in order to avoid an engine change grid penalty for the next race. The first three races of the campaign had left defending champion Alonso with a 14-point lead over his Renault teammate, and had left us with the growing sense that this was not going to be the epic season that ITV needed.

Chapter 16

ENGLAND LOSE... JENSON WINS

Back at ITV production headquarters on the South Bank, however, the potential of the Formula One season was not dominating thoughts. After the demise of *World of Sport*, numerous attempts at restructuring and the debacle of the ITV digital failure, the rump of ITV Sport was essentially a football production office, and top of the agenda in spring 2006 were the World Cup finals in Germany, just a couple of months away.

Although I was more than happy to immerse myself in Formula One, and hide behind the barricades of a completely separate production operation, the invitations for a possible involvement in the World Cup coverage were becoming more insistent. On my return I was invited by Mark Sharman to come to the South Bank to discuss things, with, of course, no obligation on either side. However, I walked straight into a gathering of World Cup editors and producers and was warmly greeted as 'the newest member of the team'.

I could have reacted like Nigel Mansell at the Science Museum launch 12 years earlier and conducted vigorous contract negotiations in these most inappropriate of surroundings, but basically it was too late; I had been stitched up and had to get on with it.

The irritation was that, for this summer at least, the appealing prospect of being able to concentrate on just one sport had to be put on hold, and it was back to the flat-out multi-sport schedule that I had hoped to have left behind in the *Grandstand* days. But on the positive side, the Football World Cup was one of the few major global events I had yet to work on, so it would go a long way to completing my career CV. In any case I was merely helping out my new employers in a big one-off head-to-head battle with the BBC.

But then came the official World Cup press launch at which I was announced as ITV's main presenter and, in particular, presenter for ITV's showpiece England games. It was only then that the ridiculous nature of the appointment became apparent. I was a football fan in the most routine sense, but I had no recent experience of live football presentation or any great appetite ever to get involved in what I had always seen as a crowded, indulgent corner of the sports broadcasting world. Furthermore my reluctant arrival was now clearly going to be at the expense of others on the team.

One was Jim Rosenthal, who had left the ITV Formula One team with the gracious observation that 'I will always be a motor racing fan but I am a football man at heart.' Now he was being shunted down the ITV football order by someone whose priorities were precisely the opposite.

The other was Gabby Logan, who had been installed by Brian Barwick as the successor to Desmond Lynam as main network football presenter. However, the new management clearly did not have the same enthusiasm for her style or talent, but instead of being direct and honest about the situation they had set about diluting her role in a spineless kind of way. Gabby was often left in a deserted studio getting the programme on and off the air while her studio guests would conduct their own match discussion in a different touchline location. It looked ridiculous and I was very aware that my arrival demeaned her position still further.

But the decision was taken, the ITV line-up was public and all I could do was underline to the ITV management that my priority was, and always would be, the Formula One coverage, and as far as I was concerned the World Cup would be an isolated extra commitment. The hard work of the next few months were set to involve intensive football research alongside getting to grips with the early days of my grand prix contract. Then there were the sheer logistics of handling a World Cup in Germany as well as the continuation of the Formula One season through Europe and North America.

In reality, though, I was more than happy to let the World Cup take care of itself, because I was about to have far too much fun with the start of Formula One in Europe. For example, it was good to be back at Imola for what was going to be the last San Marino Grand Prix. The big talking point was whether this was going to be the last season for Michael Schumacher, and he stoked up the debate by giving Ferrari their first win of the campaign. His 85th career victory came after qualifying on pole with Jenson Button alongside. Button seemed set for a podium until a couple of disastrous pit stops – including one in which he left with the fuel-hose attached – dropped him back to seventh. By the time we got to the Nürburgring two weeks later his ITV interviews had taken on that resigned air of desperate optimism with which we were all going to become so familiar. Michael Schumacher once again beat Alonso into second place at the grand prix of Europe, with Jenson a non-finisher.

This was the point of the season where I felt I had got to grips with the ITV way of doing things and I should have been looking forward to making a more positive contribution; but the World Cup was only a month away and the planning meetings were coming thick and fast. Three races would cut across the World Cup schedule. The plan was for me to present the British Grand Prix at Silverstone, then link up with the World Cup team in Germany ahead of presenting England's game with Trinidad and Tobago three days later in Nuremburg. Then it would be on to Munich for the Brazil–Australia game on the Sunday before heading to Cologne for Sweden against England. From there I would travel to Montreal to present the Canadian Grand Prix before coming back to Dortmund for a live second-round match. There would be another game somewhere else on the Thursday, after which I would go back across the Atlantic for the Indianapolis race. From that point on it was back to Germany for whatever ITV had in the quarter-final and semi-final, before the World Cup final itself in Berlin. All very exciting but not quite what I had signed up for.

But at least there was another distraction that had us looking way beyond the World Cup and way beyond the end of this Formula One season. We had all been aware of the talent and potential of Lewis Hamilton. He had shown it in every category he had contested so far, but now he was starting to demonstrate what he could do at the penultimate level. It was his first season in GP2, the feeder category for Formula One, and after a quiet start he had shown his brilliance in the third meeting of the season at the Nürburgring, dominating the race to such an extent he was even able to take a drive-through penalty without losing his race-long lead. He then came through from eighth on the grid to win the sprint race, and showed similar thrilling form in winning at Monaco.

Victory in such a fashion in the Principality was a very important showcase for Hamilton, but it was in the British Grand Prix support race at Silverstone that he impressed most of all. It would be nice to say that it was as a result of this race that the British public started to take notice, but that was not entirely the case. His drive in the feature race unfortunately coincided with the start of England's World Cup campaign and live coverage of their match was being broadcast on the Silverstone big screens.

Strangely, a large part of the British Grand Prix crowd who had just seen Alonso take pole position in qualifying (Coulthard 11th, Button 19th) decided to give the football their full attention and, I suppose, as ITV's number one World Cup presenter I should have taken a bit more interest in England's one–nil win over Paraguay. But out on the track something special was happening and Lewis Hamilton's stirring performance turned out to be the highlight of British Grand Prix weekend and a strong indication of exciting times ahead.

The following day a fifth win of the season saw Fernando Alonso extending his World Championship lead and, Hamilton apart, it was not a Silverstone weekend that would live long in the memory of the home fans. But from my point of view it was great to be back working at the British Grand Prix with all its wonderful memories of Mansell, Hunt and Hill and epic editions of *Grandstand*. It was something reassuringly familiar before heading to Germany on the Monday morning for something completely different.

Football had always been part of my life, but in a very different way to motorsport. I had played the game to a County level at school, was a regular at the Valley to watch Charlton Athletic, and had even become President of the North-West Kent Charlton Supporters' Club. But any impact the game had made on my television life was purely coincidental.

In my previous ITV career I had worked alongside the ultimate football broadcaster, Brian Moore, and even presented a couple of midweek games. At the BBC I wrote and presented *Football Focus* for a couple of years after Bob Wilson left for ITV and Gary Lineker was still getting to grips with the television business; but that was because I was the only one around to do it. I love the game, but from a television point of view I always felt it leaves you marooned in a studio conducting fairly predictable build-up and analysis, whereas motorsport and even golf have far greater editorial variety and potential, not to mention far nicer locations.

Also, within the BBC, with *Grandstand* being wound down, the football department and *Match of the Day* had become an impenetrable self-contained unit with its own style, its own specialist staff and presenters, and was doing a very distinctive and effective job; all that suited me fine, I was doing other things.

But now, by some curious programme policy, within six months of leaving the BBC to specialise exclusively on Formula

One I found myself going head-to-head with the BBC on the biggest football stage of all. In the opposite corner for the Corporation was Gary Lineker, 48 goals for England, who had now established himself, quite rightly, as the face of football on British television. For ITV there was me. And as I settled into the studio chair to present exclusive coverage of the second England game of the finals there were two thoughts in my mind: firstly, this is the first televised football match I have presented in 22 years; and secondly, roll on the Canadian Grand Prix.

But by doing the basics right I was able to get through it without alienating the audience too much. Mind you, the sheer size of the football audience tends to concentrate the mind. Over 20 million watched that Trinidad and Tobago game and a few days later the 22 million that tuned in for England against Sweden on ITV was the biggest single British TV football audience in five years.

Presenting football might not have been my thing, but an event on the scale of the World Cup is always a great thrill. The ITV operation was well organised and terrific fun to work on. Rather than being positioned in one location, as the BBC were in Berlin, we were ferried from one live match to the next in the former Status Quo tour bus. So late at night on the autobahn, with a few bottles of wine at the back of the coach, the conversation with the likes of Terry Venables and Sam Allardyce would be hugely entertaining. And it was not just football chat. Whether or not they were trying to make me feel at home, there was also a lot of discussion about Formula One and motorsport, with Ruud Gullit in particular showing himself to be a very knowledgeable fan.

Nuremberg, Cologne and Munich came and went, and then it was off to Montreal for proper sport. In the Canadian Grand Prix, Fernando Alonso maintained his dominance while Jenson Button continued his wretched season with another non-points finish, but I was really looking forward to my first visit to

Indianapolis the following weekend, even though I was going to get there via Frankfurt and Düsseldorf.

However, when I got back to Europe there was a message to contact Head of Sport Mark Sharman. Apparently ITV had terminated Gabby Logan's contract, and I was to remain in Germany to front the rest of the World Cup, with Angus Scott providing cover for the United States Grand Prix. It eased the travelling requirement of the next couple of weeks but the future with ITV was starting to look a bit more complicated. My problems, however, were nothing compared to Gabby's. She had been treated desperately badly. To diminish her role for so long and then get rid of her in the middle of a World Cup was insulting and insensitive. I am delighted that she was immediately picked up by the BBC, who gave her the proper opportunity to demonstrate what a fine broadcaster she is.

It made me more than a little wary of what lay ahead. I had agreed to join ITV to do a specific job, and this was now being disregarded with no reference to the signed contract. Money was not an issue – I'm not sure what Gary Lineker was getting, but I was doing the World Cup for nothing. Also, with Gabby gone and Jim Rosenthal not seeming to be flavour of the month, there was a worrying possibility that my new-found role as football presenter might have to be extended beyond the end of the World Cup.

Talking of which, England went out of the competition a day after I landed back in Germany, and the tournament would end with the usual ITV capitulation to the BBC in terms of ratings. Due to an administrative cock-up ITV did not even have a studio in the stadium for the final in Berlin, so we all had to troop back to London. The BBC inherited a strong audience from the Men's Singles final at Wimbledon and ended up with 17.5 million; we failed to do quite as well off the back of a rerun of *On the Buses* and ended up getting beaten six to one. I was looking forward to returning to the motor racing.

Magny-Cours is generally considered to be the middle of

nowhere by Formula One fans on a tight schedule trying to get to the French Grand Prix, but for me the drive south of Paris through Sancerre country was the perfect way to recover from the pressure and hype of the World Cup. It was also refreshing to be back with a team totally absorbed in the season and seemingly immune to the twists and turns of ITV politics.

However, the season was still not producing the kind of action that would take the nation's minds off the failure of their football team. Michael Schumacher had won in Indianapolis and then repeated the victory in France, and was 19 points behind Alonso in the Championship race. Jenson Button's season was falling apart. A non-finish in America was followed by an engine failure in France, but he was still available for his Saturday interview and, in public at least, never lost his belief that somehow it was all going to come right.

A fortnight later at the German Grand Prix at Hockenheim it seemed that his optimism was justified: a second-row position in qualifying was converted into a solid fourth-place finish; the team had made progress and Button's big hope was that they could continue that progress the following weekend in Hungary. In Germany, Schumacher had claimed his third straight win and was now just 11 points behind in the Championship. The World Cup was well in the past, and as I took the hire car in leisurely fashion to Budapest via Salzburg and Vienna this was starting to feel like the best job in the world again.

Since first staging the Hungarian Grand Prix in 1986, the Hungaroring had become an established challenge on the Formula One calendar without picking up a shred of Formula One glamour or sophistication; but give me passion over perfection any day. The circuit is built around a natural bowl, and a large part of the layout can be seen from an excellent viewpoint at the back of the paddock, a surprisingly rare feature.

It has a reputation for producing some dour racing, but it's also seen some significant Formula One history over the previous 20 years. In ITV's first year of coverage they were denied a fantastic story when Damon Hill, from the wrong end of the grid, very nearly gave Jordan their first victory; and five years before that, in 1992, Hungary was where Nigel Mansell clinched his dominant World Championship.

So Hungary could produce headlines, but in 2006 no one could imagine the kind of story we would be telling on Sunday afternoon. It was an edgy weekend. In Championship terms Schumacher was putting the pressure on Alonso, and the reigning World Champion was showing the strain. Both drivers picked up qualifying penalties and were back down the grid. Jenson Button should have been able to profit but all his Hockenheim optimism blew up with his engine on Saturday morning, and the ten-place penalty for the engine change left him back in 14th; no chance. When we talked to Jenson in the build-up to the race you could see, for the first time, the brave optimistic facade starting to crack. The frustration of another false dawn was starting to get to him.

In the circumstances it did not seem the ideal weekend to bring Jenson's teammate Anthony Davidson into the commentary box; the Honda test driver was covering for Martin Brundle, who would always take the Hungary weekend off. But for Honda, Renault, Ferrari and ITV it was shaping up to be a very strange few days.

The weather added to the confusion. Hungary is meant to be hot, but dull overcast skies throughout the weekend eventually produced a downpour a matter of minutes before we came on air. The pit-lane offered precious little shelter. We welcomed ITV viewers from underneath a narrow, dripping canopy, just outside the scrutineering bay. Then communications packed up and we stumbled through the first ten minutes of the programme with intermittent talkback and sound and no monitor. When, eventually, it calmed down, a soaked Mark Blundell turned to me and said, 'I bet Brundle is lying on a Spanish beach somewhere laughing his bloody head off.'

But then the race started to unfold, Alonso forcing his way

through the mixed-up field to take a thrilling lead by lap 20. Button, like Alonso on intermediate Michelins, was using all his smooth skills to make similar progress. The safety car brought the field back together and Button, in second, was now within striking distance of Alonso, the two drivers having started 14th and 15th respectively. It was great stuff from Jenson, but in his 114th grand prix he was surely going to come up short again – Alonso had it in the bag.

However, after his refuelling stop on lap 51 a wheel nut failed and Alonso was pitched into the turn two barriers: Button had the lead ahead of Michael Schumacher. Jenson was a picture of calm, Schumacher was fighting the failing tyres on his Ferrari and on lap 67 he crashed out trying too hard to defend his position from Nick Heidfeld.

Button was now just three laps from an astonishing breakthrough victory and suddenly Honda's Anthony Davidson was exactly the right man to have in the commentary box. At first he gave a cool if tense assessment of the team's tactics and the drivers' thought processes, but then he took on a style that reminded me of the way our BBC commentator Gary Herbert had handled the two big Olympic rowing finals in 2000 and 2004: in the last 500 metres Gary had abandoned all attempt at description and analysis in favour of yelling 'Come on boys... come on boys' into the microphone. Gary was spot-on in letting the emotions dominate, and so too was Anthony in the way in which he helped lead the celebrations for Jenson, even if he couldn't resist: 'I can't believe he's done it, I can't believe I'm here commentating on it... Martin Brundle where are you, what have you done?'

The last half-hour of the programme was such a contrast to the build-up. The sun came out, no talkback or monitors were required because all you did was follow the celebrations, the tears of John Button, the hugs of the Honda mechanics, and the genuine feeling right across the paddock that this was the most celebrated victory of the season. It was certainly popular with ITV. British success is not essential to the coverage but it is certainly an important ingredient and ITV had covered 65 races since last being able to interview a British winner, David Coulthard at Melbourne in 2003.

The win put Jenson on another level of self-belief and confidence. I like to flatter myself that my ill-judged comments at the Autosport Awards had given him the extra motivation he required, but I knew that Jenson would enjoy having proved me so wrong. Sure enough, at the 2006 awards at the Grosvenor Jenson came on to the stage with a large plate of steak and kidney humble pie and I was happy to scoff the lot while he milked the applause for being voted British Competition Driver of the Year.

There was also something else for ITV to celebrate as a result of Jenson's Hungarian heroics, the team being awarded the BAFTA for Best Sports Programme of the Year, although experience has long-since shown me that this award is actually for 'having the good fortune to be at the most exciting sports event of the year and not cocking it up'. But try telling that to Anthony Davidson; to him television must have seemed ridiculously easy... turn up... yell into a microphone... win a BAFTA.

Chapter 17

HAMILTON DRIVES THE HEADLINES

Fernando Alonso would take the title in 2006 and Jenson, with his new-found self-belief, would end the season with a solid and promising sequence of results. He stuck to his commitment of giving us an honest interview at every grand prix, and it built into a sequence revealing the frustrations of a man who knew he should be further up the grid but never had the car to get him there. He came across as a mature team-man with a work ethic that deserved to take him to the top step of the podium on a far more regular basis. Now that he was a race-winner we shared his optimism for 2007.

But the second half of 2006 had also seen the arrival at the highest level of Lewis Hamilton. His winning GP2 drives at Monaco and Silverstone had firmly established his potential, but it was his drive through the field from 18th to second in the sprint race in Turkey that left the Formula One paddock glued to the monitors and applauding in admiration; even Lewis was swift to nominate the drive as his finest so far in a racing car. He clinched the title on Italian Grand Prix weekend at Monza. The McLaren apprenticeship was complete; he appeared to be ready for a Formula One drive.

Nothing, of course, was being taken for granted – there is no formal career structure for grand prix drivers – but McLaren's Martin Whitmarsh had suggested that winning the GP2 title was an essential qualification. Now in the build-up to the Italian Grand Prix itself, with his title safely secured, he was being allowed to have a high-profile presence in the McLaren garage. He was almost being paraded in front of the cameras and was showing a genuine boyish wonder at the glamorous, sophisticated surroundings. It was surprising to learn that he had spent so little time in this environment, and even more amazing to reflect that he was only six months away from being the new star of it all, and only a year away from being at the centre of a vicious whirlpool of Formula One politics.

A couple of weeks later Lewis got the formal call from McLaren and was duly installed as the teammate of World Champion Fernando Alonso for the 2007 season. It was an important new element for the British television coverage, although, of course, at 22 years old Lewis would surely only be playing a bit-part role as he adapted to the demands of his first World Championship season.

It was just the sort of story that I was looking forward to in my second season as ITV presenter, although that season was not turning out to be the total immersion in Formula One that I wanted. Gabby Logan was gone, Jim Rosenthal was not being considered, so ITV approached me with the scenario they had said would never happen: would I present the midweek Champions League coverage alongside my Formula One commitment?

In fairness, in contrast to the World Cup they were offering a modest payment, but there would be no fresh negotiations or rewriting of the contract because the agreement was that this was a stopgap arrangement as ITV set about finding a new football presenter as a matter of urgency.

Over the next few months presenters like Eamonn Holmes, Jeff Stelling and Adrian Chiles were all apparently approached, and either negotiations broke down or they were considered unsuitable. So I got into the new routine of enjoying the Tuesday-night company of Andy Townsend and other assorted Champions League guests, but I was not a fan of the schedule that went with it.

It meant that there was always a bit of a Sunday-night dash to get from wherever the grand prix was taking place to the

Monday-night rendezvous, possibly somewhere else in Europe, ahead of the Champions League game; and when the grand prix was outside Europe life was even more complicated. On one occasion I left the Japanese Grand Prix at Fuji, headed into Tokyo, stayed overnight, got the morning flight to Heathrow, connected up to Manchester, hosted the Tuesday-night Manchester United game at Old Trafford, got the first flight in the morning to Heathrow, picked up the connection to Shanghai and was back with the team on Thursday afternoon to start the build-up to the grand prix of China. Madness!

Further complications were to come toward the end of 2006 when, in a surprise move, Michael Grade the Chairman of the BBC left the Corporation to become Executive Chairman of ITV. It seemed like good news until, in a macho flexing of corporate muscle, Grade inspired ITV to clinch the rights to the FA Cup and England football from under the noses of the rather dozy BBC negotiators.

Even at the time of the announcement there were not unrestrained celebrations within ITV. It was obvious that the deal had been done at the peak of the rights market, and it left ITV with a sports rights portfolio that, Formula One aside, was dominated to an unhealthy degree by just one sport.

It also meant that unless ITV could track down a new football presenter before the start of the 2008/09 season I would find myself presenting the biggest line-up of live football on terrestrial television, just a couple of years after signing a contract to concentrate exclusively on Formula One.

All that was for other people to sort out; I was happy to share in the heightened anticipation for a fascinating 2007 Formula One season. For Lewis Hamilton it was a winter of hard work, spending just about every day in McLaren headquarters for all the extra physical and technical preparation that his new role required. At the same time his public profile had grown out of all proportion for a driver who had yet to contest a Formula One race.

McLaren were aware of both the pitfalls and potential of

their new driver's popularity; it contained huge marketing possibilities and the ability to drive the sport to a whole new audience. They approached it with their usual neurotic thoroughness combined with a certain amount of confusion – one part of the organisation wanting to exploit the situation to the full, the other wanting to shield their new driver from every element of the media.

My suggestion to ITV was to get Lewis in front of the camera at every opportunity, certainly at every race. If a vibrant new personality had come along who was going to bring new viewers to the coverage, those new viewers had to be served. There was potential for the next couple of seasons to provide the same kind of boost for British audiences that we had ten years earlier with Damon Hill, and before that with Nigel Mansell. The ITV production team did not seem quite as convinced as myself that Lewis needed to be such a headline ingredient, but their feeling was that in the unlikely event that I could convince McLaren to make Lewis regularly available then we should go for it.

The initial reaction from both McLaren management and the marketing department was predictably defensive. Access to Lewis, certainly in the first half of the season, would be limited simply to his contractual responsibilities; there would be no exceptions to that, even for the British broadcaster. Their caution was understandable, and my assurances that we were not out to twist his words or trap him into indiscretions could not convince them otherwise.

A better opportunity came in January 2007 when I flew with Ron Dennis in the private McLaren jet in order to host the launch of the new team in Valencia. It was a chance to talk to him about the particular problems in introducing his rookie driver to the demands and scrutiny that lay ahead. I was able to persuade him that doing a regular low-key interview at every race was a useful way of learning how to handle the media, and preferable to being confined to facing the ITV cameras only once every couple of months when the pressure would be on to get a screaming headline, a personal revelation or a world exclusive. I was probably making it up as I went along, but Ron was happy to agree – albeit only if Lewis was willing to add this to his race weekend commitments.

Of course, Lewis needed no persuading at all. Behind the scenes as we prepared for the Valencia launch he was as wide-eyed about his surroundings as he had been in the Monza garage four months earlier. He regarded the attention of television, ITV in particular, to be part of the deal. But in the short term he was far more excited about being involved in his first high-profile Formula One team launch; he had watched coverage of them when he was younger, and this was right up there with the biggest.

The launch was not only unveiling the new car, and the most eagerly awaited new driver line-up – it was also announcing Vodafone as the new title sponsor for the team. Hamilton and Alonso would do laps of an improvised circuit around the Arts and Cultural Centre; no one knew exactly how many fans would turn out to watch, but in the end over 150,000 would line the streets of Valencia. Most were there to show their support for the double World Champion, but when I called Lewis Hamilton on to the stage the ovation served to underline that here was a driver who could take the sport to a new level. ITV were in the best position possible to be swept along by all the new enthusiasm... unless, of course, the 2007 season was going to serve up a huge anticlimax.

At least it was going to start in the right place, Melbourne being the perfect vibrant host city for the start of a Formula One World Championship; and at the end of the swing through Malaysia and Bahrain we would know a great deal more of what lay in store for the season.

We were getting some pretty strong clues in the first two days on the Albert Park circuit. Hamilton in his first day's work for McLaren was third in the Friday warm-up and then, the next day, qualified on row two, immediately behind Alonso who was on a lighter fuel load. In his first Saturday-afternoon appearance in front of the ITV cameras, Lewis gave us all the 'living the dream' stuff, and unlike just about everyone else on the grid seemed to have found the fun in Formula One. But when the rookie expressed his disappointment that he had failed to out-qualify his double World Champion team-mate on his Formula One debut it was the perfect cue for crusty old cynics like Brundle and Blundell to talk knowingly about patience and race experience and learning-curves, right until the lights went out on Sunday afternoon.

That was the moment that the season began and Formula One took off. Hamilton actually got a bit of a sluggish start, found himself potentially boxed in behind Kubica and instinctively pulled off the kind of move that you don't even consider in the first 300 yards of your Formula One career. It saw him dart across the track, sweep around the outside of Kubica, and the momentum of the move took him round the outside of Alonso as well. Räikkönen was away and would not be caught, but Hamilton, who would later be briefly in the lead on his first grand prix, had made a statement in that opening skirmish that would define the season.

There were no quotes to back it up but the assumption in the press was that Alonso would have been distinctly unimpressed by Hamilton's performance and, behind the scenes, would have to reassert his authority within the team; Hamilton's good-humoured innocence about it all must have made Alonso even more irritated.

Buried down the page in all the Melbourne reports and reaction and growing Hamilton excitement was the fact that McLaren had challenged the legality of the floor on the Ferrari. As the teams headed on to Malaysia this was interpreted simply as another bit of Formula One mischief-making; its true significance would only emerge later in the season.

There was always the possibility, maybe the probability, that Hamilton's stunning debut was merely an adrenalin-fuelled example of beginner's good fortune – Nico Rosberg had got a similar reaction after his impressive debut in Bahrain a year earlier. Except that Hamilton improved on his Melbourne performance at Kuala Lumpur three weeks later. This time, once again qualifying behind Alonso with a heavier fuel load on row two, he stormed past the Ferraris of Räikkönen and Massa to tuck into second place within the first two corners; it was a McLaren one–two to the finish, Hamilton being the perfect support for Alonso.

Then in Bahrain came the final confirmation that we had a very special season unfolding. Hamilton at last beat Alonso in qualifying. Massa had pole and converted that into a race win, but Hamilton in second never allowed him to relax. Now with three races gone and the Championship heading into Europe we allowed ourselves a verdict on Britain's newest and youngest Formula One driver, and the result was beyond any predictions. With a mixture of aggression and maturity he'd had three finishes, three podiums, and was tied with Räikkönen and Alonso for the World Championship lead. All his interviews still insisted he was just a young guy having an amazing amount of fun... and there was every reason to believe him.

He returned home to Stevenage for the first time since his Formula One debut to discover, in his own words, that 'life had changed'. Paparazzi were camped outside the house, his face had moved from the inside sports pages to the front pages of every newspaper, and he adorned the cover of just about every motorsport magazine. The effect on ITV had been extraordinary as well. The audience for the Malaysian Grand Prix was up 30% on the previous year, the audience for the highlights rerun of the Bahrain Grand Prix had more than doubled compared to 2006. It was the start of the so-called 'Hamilton effect' that would, in months to come, be seen in lengthening queues at kart tracks and increased sales of all kinds of motorsport games and gaming.

The growing attention on the sport was, of course, very welcome for a British broadcaster, but over the months to come ITV, and probably myself in particular, were accused of becoming obsessed with Hamilton, so that television coverage simply revolved around his prospects and performance. There was never an obsession and hopefully I never lost sight of editorial balance, but I would certainly plead guilty to arguing for Hamilton to be the dominant story, and enjoying the fact that he was driving the audience so strongly.

In this respect I had the advantage of not being an exclusively Formula One man, but a broadcaster who had experience of a whole range of major events. They were all very different in their demands and their appeal, but the one thing they had in common was that they were all being broadcast to a British audience. To my mind this always dictated the tone of the broadcast, especially if the audience had been swelled by viewers keen to see Faldo win at Augusta or Redgrave win in a rowing boat or Hamilton making history in a McLaren. Certainly if our audience was global you should expect to hear more from Nick Heidfeld and Jarno Trulli, but the British story was Hamilton; ITV had the access, and after all those years standing on the sidelines politely applauding the relentless genius of Michael Schumacher, they were determined to deliver the story as comprehensively as possible.

One thing that I did feel uncomfortable about was that our attention had switched rather brutally away from Jenson Button, who had been our loyal, round-by-round British interviewee throughout the 2006 season. Hungary apart it had been a litany of false hopes and failed expectations, and Jenson welcomed Hamilton as the man who would take all the media pressure away and allow him to work out his problems with the badly handling Honda in private. Throughout this period he was generous and classy, but you did sense that the afterglow of Hungary had gone and that the plaudits being piled on his compatriot merely increased his own frustration.

The Championship arrived not only in Europe but at Fernando Alonso's home event, the Spanish Grand Prix at the Circuit de Catalunya, just outside Barcelona. For the World Champion it was the ideal location to establish his superiority over his teammate. Lewis claimed there was no particular edge or tension to the weekend, but we could feel it, and around McLaren it was the unspoken subplot to the Spanish Grand Prix.

Within the team there was almost a sense of relief when Alonso qualified on the front row and Hamilton on row two; harmony was guaranteed and a sense of order prevailed. But then, in the race, Alonso tried to muscle his way past pole-man Felipe Massa at the first corner, the Spaniard was forced off, and Hamilton was resolute in making sure that his teammate rejoined the race behind him. Massa won the race from Hamilton, and Alonso had to be content with third.

For Lewis it was his third consecutive second place and it meant that at 22 years and 126 days he had become the youngest driver in history to lead the Formula One World Championship, taking over the honour from his team's founder Bruce McLaren. Hamilton led Alonso by two points and the fight was on, not only within the McLaren ranks but also at Ferrari, where Felipe Massa, with his second win of the season, had the edge over his more illustrious teammate Kimi Räikkönen.

A fantastic season was unfolding, and there was a buzz and an adrenalin rush about the ITV operation that was not quite there during 2006. From my own point of view Mark Blundell was a pleasure to work with. His wealth of experience was combined with a fine sense of humour that more than compensated for his notable failure to master the grammatical detail of the English language. He would really have flourished as part of a chorus instead of having a solo role, for example being alongside the likes of David Coulthard or Eddie Jordan in the BBC format; however, for reasons either of budget or timing this was rarely possible.

But I was enjoying his company and I was also even starting to like the busy combination of Formula One and Champions League football. When your working week involves travelling to Athens in order to present live coverage of Liverpool in the Champions League final, unwinding late into the night with some of the greats in the game, then the next morning getting a flight connection to Nice and driving along the Corniche in order to present the Monaco Grand Prix, you feel your career might be coming together. When the first commitment at the grand prix is to present a poolside charity fashion show with some of the world's great supermodels, and Prince Albert in the front row, end of discussion – you've cracked it.

Lewis, however, sidestepped most of the glamorous invitations, including the fashion show (although he would be there the next year as a model). It might have been his first Monaco Grand Prix but the World Championship leader had the credentials to win in the Principality just as he had done in previous years in GP2. It was an all-McLaren front row, with Alonso on pole. That order continued into the race; for the team it was the perfect grand prix on a circuit where overtaking was almost impossible. All that was needed was the team to ensure that their eager, highly competitive drivers, both of whom were capable of winning the race, did not take each other off.

Lewis had qualified with a heavier fuel load but was not allowed to run the extra distance in the race that would have allowed him to threaten Alonso. Then in the closing stages Lewis got the inevitable instruction to turn the engine down and keep the gap at five seconds. For the first time in his fledgling career he was being asked not to race and his reaction was one of rookie indignation. It needed soothing words from Ron Dennis to make him appreciate the bigger picture.

The British press, however, could not be placated and were full of conspiracy theories, and there was a huge overreaction from the FIA, who instigated an investigation into McLaren's possible use of illegal team orders. In the end common sense prevailed and the explanation that the team were simply trying to safeguard a one–two finish was accepted. But Alonso now had a share of the World Championship lead, and for Hamilton it seemed to be an end of the carefree innocence with which he had approached the start of the season.

This was reinforced, on arrival in Montreal for the Canadian Grand Prix, when Alonso gave quotes that hinted at the 'preferential treatment' that he felt Lewis was getting within the team. The McLaren response was to fuel both drivers equally in qualifying and Hamilton took his first Formula One pole position in style. It was a huge breakthrough, and it would signal the start of a week in North America that would take Hamilton's reputation to a new level.

From pole position he failed to make the best of starts but held off Heidfeld and got a close-up view of Alonso losing it at the first corner. Hamilton led, and from that point on the race was his to lose. But the race will not be remembered for his pace or maturity or his emotions in the moment of victory. The enduring image of the Canadian Grand Prix will be of the apocalyptic high-speed accident that, it seemed, Robert Kubica could not have possibly survived.

When his airborne BMW destroyed itself against the concrete wall on the approach to the hairpin, the inverted tub containing the motionless figure of Kubica then scraping a further 200 yards down the track, Mark Blundell was the only one of us gathered around the TV monitor who showed a shred of optimism. He had somehow survived a similar impact in a CART race at Rio in 1996 but had always acknowledged that his survival was miraculous. The fact that Kubica would emerge from the wreckage of Montreal with no major injury at all was not a miracle, but a tribute to the safety progress the sport had made since Ayrton Senna's death in 1994.

The progress has been so significant that some say the sport has become sanitised, and even the great safety campaigner Sir Jackie Stewart has been heard to suggest that although the danger and the serious risk of injury to the driver should never be increased, the penalty for bad driving or making a mistake should be made more severe. Wide run-off areas and gravel traps that can be driven through enable drivers to keep safe but should penalise their race prospects, ensuring that

Formula One remains the precise driving challenge that it is meant to be.

But that afternoon in Montreal we were all grateful for Hans devices, high cockpit surrounds, impact-proof carbon fibre and whatever other safety-nets the sport felt able to provide. Robert Kubica had survived and his good friend Lewis Hamilton was now able to fully celebrate his first Formula One victory.

The celebration was emotional but had to be low-key, because we were in the middle of back-to-back races, with Indianapolis following Montreal; and now the unthinkable had entered the equation, could Lewis possibly win the World Championship itself?

Everyone seemed to go to Indianapolis via a stopover in New York, and I was probably the last person that Lewis expected to see at the New York Yankees baseball game on the Tuesday evening. But it was business as usual by Thursday morning. For Lewis it was the first visit to Indianapolis, and it was mine as well. The legendary 'brickyard' circuit was at the top of my list of world sporting locations that I was desperate to see, even though it was with the sophistication of Formula One instead of the raucous world of oval racing. Meeting Mario Andretti had fired my appetite for all things Indianapolis, as well as hearing the stories and memories of Colin Chapman and Jackie Stewart.

Formula One was trying to rebuild its reputation in North America after the tyre fiasco of 2005. In 2007 this was helped by the victory of Dario Franchitti in the Indy 500, which made the American press ready to greet the new British superhero. However, the main story they wanted to write, and the opinion they wanted to hear from Lewis, was how did he compare himself in terms of image, career and sporting impact to Tiger Woods?

It was one of those comparisons that was so obvious and so seemingly meaningless that it had never come up in any of our pre-race conversations, despite these conversations becoming more and more wide-ranging. Indeed, the topic of colour and race had never come up because Lewis, and most other people, seemed to regard it as irrelevant. It was impossible, however, to ignore the similarities in the respective stories of Tiger and Lewis.

Both were identified early on as precocious talents, both had high-profile coverage from a very early age, both had strong and devoted support from their fathers (although Anthony Hamilton and Earl Woods were very different characters), both had the potential to fundamentally change the profile of their sports, and all that was aside from their colour.

I don't suppose there are many sports broadcasters who have had the opportunity to interview both at length and I must confess most of my exchanges with Tiger have been in controlled circumstances surrounded by public relations executives and press officers with clipboards and stopwatches. But in 1999 I was able to talk to him for about 45 minutes in informal surroundings in a clubhouse room at Wentworth. It was roughly the interview environment we were enjoying at each grand prix with Lewis, and Tiger was roughly the same age.

It was a pleasant enough exchange, and he wanted to talk about the vagaries of the West Course and the style and tone of the BBC golf coverage. But everything came at you through a veneer of suspicion and media coaching; the guard was never relaxed, the content was never surprising, and eventually in his career – especially after the implosion of his personal life – the shutters would come down completely.

Lewis, by contrast, wanted to open up on just about any topic with spontaneity and humour and, if required, a great deal of original thought. This ingredient was the significant contrast with Tiger, and to my mind made him more capable of having a positive long-term effect on his sport. But Lewis had yet to fully experience the suffocating scrutiny and constant media circus that surrounded Tiger. As far as Lewis was concerned there was no downside at all to winning races and leading the Formula One World Championship, and that attitude was all very refreshing to the Indianapolis press corps.

Fernando Alonso, however, was struggling to maintain his

positive attitude and sense of humour and delivered more press quotes on the unfair treatment he felt he was getting at McLaren. In the race he appeared to make the point more directly to his team, pulling to one side to seemingly gesture at the pit wall as he pursued the leader Hamilton down the straight.

It was a weekend of total frustration for Alonso, and one that fully endorsed the World Championship credentials of his teammate. Alonso was quicker through qualifying except when it counted at the end of the final session. At times he was faster in the race, but Hamilton had track position and defended it with the same calmness and authority that he had shown the previous Sunday in Montreal.

It was back-to-back race victories for Hamilton, who now had a ten-point World Championship lead. His achievement dominated the newspapers in Britain and inspired big headlines around the world. In the aftermath of the victory, in what was now peak viewing time in the UK, the grandees of the sport were offering their views on this phenomenon that was breathing new life into Formula One. The most memorable insight came from a breathless and excited Ron Dennis, who tried to describe Lewis as a kind of product of the era of computer games and virtual reality. 'With Lewis,' he said, 'his competitive instinct, his reaction time, his vision and his dexterity all come from hours spent alone in his bedroom with his Playboy...'

Lewis himself was struggling to absorb what he had achieved on this transatlantic trip. I needed to find him after all the press conferences had been finished to check one small bit of housekeeping for ITV. In the next few days we would be broadcasting trailers for ITV's upcoming coverage of the Goodwood Festival of Speed; I needed to check whether he was going to be there, and whether we could mention him in the voice-over. 'I'm not too sure of the schedule,' he said, 'I'm keen to go, but the plan is to have a quiet picnic with the family, somewhere up the hill.'

Even leading the World Championship he had no understanding of exactly how his life had changed.

Chapter 18

A GLORIOUS SEASON
FALLS APART

It did not take long for Lewis, and ourselves, to fully appreciate the impact of his achievements in North America. A crowd of 20,000 turned up for the pre-British Grand Prix test at Silverstone, only to be frustrated by Hamilton's absence. A few weeks later another 20,000 would wait in the rain in front of Goodwood House for the appearance of their new hero at the Festival of Speed.

But this period also confirmed that the second half of the season was not going to be the stuff of dreams that Lewis had enjoyed so far.

At the French Grand Prix at Magny-Cours Hamilton had qualified on the front row and would finish on the podium. But on his way to third place he had been passed by Kimi Räikkönen, the first time he had been overtaken in anger in his Formula One career.

None of this diminished the attention and expectation surrounding him in British Grand Prix week. A year earlier his GP2 victory was largely ignored as England opened their World Cup campaign on the big screens at Silverstone; now Hamilton's image dominated, not only the big screens but the billboards, the front pages and the back pages. For him, celebrity, fame and the oppressive scrutiny that comes with it had arrived, and you sensed that the last flickering moments of privacy were highly valued.

As part of that British Grand Prix week we joined Lewis at a Vodafone-sponsored appearance at the Daytona kart track in Milton Keynes. This was one of the tracks where he had learnt his craft as a youngster and there were about 200 young protégés awaiting an audience and a demonstration of a super-quick karting lap.

He would be arriving by helicopter (of course!), and we knew that we would only have one chance to properly mike him up for the subsequent dialogue with the young drivers, and that was before he left the landing area. This we duly did, and then Lewis donned his highly recognisable Senna yellow helmet, reacquainted himself with a 250cc kart, and headed out for half a dozen very impressive laps.

It was only when we played the tape back that it became obvious that Lewis had forgotten he was wearing the microphone and mistakenly considered these few minutes out on the track as his only complete privacy of the day. The soundtrack was full of expletive-laden excitement and delight; the perfect illustration that for a few laps he was away from the technology and the pressure and the politics, and especially away from the pit-to-car radio, and was back at his racing roots and loving it. None of this material was ever allowed into the public arena, but at ITV it told us a great deal and we enjoyed it immensely.

In a slightly more professional way he brought exactly the same exhilaration to Saturday qualifying at Silverstone. The airfield circuit was primed for its most exultant British Grand Prix weekend since Mansell-mania, and Hamilton's qualifying performance delivered everything required. Alonso had been quickest through Q1 and Q2; Hamilton was fastest when it mattered most, with a pole-position lap of total commitment and thrilling drama.

The race next day had everything in terms of excitement, but not quite the story that Silverstone had hoped for. Hamilton, leading but under pressure from Kimi Räikkönen, showed a little too much eagerness on his first pit stop; he twitched forward in anticipation of the removal of the lollipop and the pit-crew did well to salvage his race at all. Räikkönen would win for the second consecutive grand prix, underlining his title credentials, but Hamilton was third, to make it through the halfway point of the season with nine straight podium finishes and a 12-point World Championship lead.

As far as the 100,000 crowd was concerned he left Silverstone with his reputation intact, and the World Championship within reach, but we left Silverstone with the thought that certainly the season, and maybe the sport, was at a turning point.

Rumours had started to circulate after the French Grand Prix concerning accusations from Ferrari against McLaren of illegal possession of Ferrari documents that apparently had been taken to a High Street copy-shop in Surrey for duplicating. The accusations revolved around the disaffected Ferrari engineer Nigel Stepney and the McLaren chief designer Mike Coughlan. A court-ordered search of Coughlan's house had reportedly revealed computer discs and 780 pages of documentation relating to the Ferrari 2007. Stepney had been dismissed four days before the British Grand Prix and Coughlan had been suspended by McLaren.

This was the start of 'Spygate', a scandal that would almost tear the sport apart. Such a fundamental breach of the Sporting Code could lead to massive fines, exclusion from the teams' Championship and possibly, according to Max Mosley, the exclusion of Hamilton and Alonso from the drivers' Championship.

It was a hard topic to raise during the euphoria that surrounded that British Grand Prix weekend, and at ITV it is no shame that we tended to avoid the prospect of deflating the audience by explaining that despite his heroic start and his 12-point World Championship lead, our new young star could be disqualified from the whole lot in a few weeks time.

The honourable exception to this was pit-lane reporter Ted Kravitz, who from the earliest opportunity did his best to insist that this story was the biggest of the season, and maybe the most important the sport had ever seen. His sense of foreboding was unintentionally endorsed by McLaren boss Ron Dennis, who, at the upbeat launch of the new McLaren brand centre, had almost broken down when questioned about the wildly circulating rumours.

Whatever was going on it was clear that the optimistic mood that followed Indianapolis had now been replaced by a feeling that the Championship had become a whole lot more complicated. An outstanding sporting achievement was on the point of being swamped by politics and suspicion. The rookie had to become ruthless, McLaren had to fight for survival. Through Germany, Hungary, Monza and Spa it was going to be fascinating to watch, especially from our privileged position in the television compound.

A rain-hit grand prix of Europe at the Nürburgring gave a hint of the kind of chaos that lay ahead in the rest of the season. Qualifying had seen Hamilton's first big accident, going off at 150mph after a mechanical failure. He would start from tenth on the grid in a rebuilt car, but the heavy rain that came during the race meant that just about any result was still possible – in fact one of the early leaders was Manfred Winkelhock in the Midland!

Lewis's race included early contact, a puncture and, along with many other drivers, a trip to the gravel trap. However, he had kept his engine running and was lifted back on to the asphalt by the trackside crane, leading to more accusations of favouritism and opportunism.

It was clear to us that Alonso, especially, was obsessed with what he saw as the preferential treatment that Hamilton was getting. Not only that but he still saw ITV as the official mouthpiece of Team Hamilton and would only give the interviews and co-operation he was obliged to provide by contract.

Ferrari also had the same sort of persecuted attitude when it came to co-operation with ITV, which meant that editorial balance was becoming more and more difficult to achieve. I was seen as Hamilton-obsessed, especially among the traditional Formula One audience; I could live with that because the back pages and the viewing figures still showed that his exploits had captured the imagination of the wider public.

But the grand prix of Europe had punctured at least one part of the Hamilton dream. A bad tactical decision meant that he was unable to benefit from all the race confusion, and not only was he off the podium for the first time in his Formula One career, but, back in ninth place, he failed to add to his points total, and race winner Fernando Alonso was now just three behind with the next stop the Hungarian Grand Prix.

Once again the assumption was that nothing ever happens at the Hungarian Grand Prix. The drama of the previous year when Jenson Button won from 14th on the grid was surely not going to be repeated. So once again Martin Brundle took the weekend off and Damon Hill joined the commentary team for this 11th round of the Championship.

Behind the scenes 'Spygate' rumbled on, although there were signs that the potential furore might be petering out. The FIA World Motor Sports Council had met at the end of July, and with Mike Coughlan in possession of the Ferrari documents there was no alternative to finding McLaren guilty. But there was also no evidence that the information had been used at all, let alone to any advantage, therefore McLaren escaped punishment. Ferrari were furious and FIA president Max Mosley referred the matter to the Court of Appeal. Against this background the weekend at the Hungaroring got under way.

In the build-up to qualifying we made much of the animosity between Ferrari and McLaren and the frosty split that seemed to be developing between the two halves of the McLaren garage. But nothing could prepare us for the events of the last two minutes of qualifying.

Hamilton was on provisional pole ahead of his teammate, and with just over two minutes remaining Alonso came into the pits. In commentary Damon Hill was quick to highlight the mental battle that was now raging between the two drivers: pole position would be a vital psychological boost.

With one minute 50 seconds left, Hamilton came into the pits and queued behind Alonso. There was a delay, the lollipop was raised to release Alonso five seconds later. There was another delay of seven seconds before Alonso at last left the pit-box.

James Allen in the commentary box immediately spotted the significance of what had happened. 'I think he deliberately did that... I know it's a big thing to say about a two-time World Champion... he knew Hamilton was queuing behind him, and he knew how critical it was... and if Hamilton misses the chance to do a qualifying lap, there will be some stern words within that team. That is an extraordinary bit of gamesmanship.'

If Alonso deserves credit for anything it was his mental arithmetic. Hamilton duly missed the chance for a final qualifying lap by precisely the margin that Alonso had delayed him in the pits. It was clear that there were angry words on the McLaren pit wall, and later on it was also apparent that much of that anger was being broadcast from Hamilton's cockpit.

McLaren's chief press officer Ellen Kolby seemed also to have thought that Hungary was bound to be a quiet one and was watching it all unfold at home on television; how they could have done with her calm, good humour over the next few hours!

The damage-limitation process had started well enough, with Ron Dennis brushing aside Ted Kravitz and explaining that the press conference would answer all the questions after the team debrief. So it was half an hour later that a chaotic question and answer session got under way, Ron Dennis in one part of the brand centre, Martin Whitmarsh in another; Lewis Hamilton was behind a firmly closed door in a nearby anteroom.

The explanation that had been arrived at was, as you would expect, convoluted. It was all down to the calculations in the fuel-burn phase for which Alonso apparently had priority. There was no intention from Alonso to delay Lewis in the pit-lane, he was merely waiting for a gap in the traffic. Lewis, for his part, had seemingly failed to follow the team plan a little earlier by allowing Alonso through for an extra lap in the fuel-burning phase.

At that point Alonso and the team were called to the stewards' room to explain their actions, whereupon Lewis emerged from the side room and innocently contradicted everything that had been said at the post-race press conference. Basically, he gave the impression he'd been shafted.

By this time we were off the air, having analysed these controversial events as best we could. Damon Hill saw Alonso's actions as evidence of complete civil war within the McLaren ranks; Mark Blundell felt that the FIA had no option but to impose a grid penalty on Alonso for impeding in the pit-lane.

And that was where we now were, outside the race stewards' building waiting to see what action the FIA stewards would take. The five o'clock Saturday-night arrangement for our cosy chat with Hamilton had come and gone, and anyway had been completely overtaken by events.

So it was in a growing throng of around 200 press and TV crews that we waited outside the rather ramshackle whitewashed building that housed the race stewards and arguing McLaren personnel, until well into the evening. There was much talk of the tirade of abuse that Hamilton had supposedly directed at Ron Dennis; equally there was much discussion of Dennis 'holding' Alonso in the pit-lane in order to 'teach Hamilton a lesson' for disobeying team orders. And then there was Alonso delaying his exit still further after the removal of the lollipop, therefore imposing his own extra penalty on Hamilton. Wherever you looked there was guilt, lack of judgement, small-minded self-interest and a contempt for the sport. This was not just the turning point of the season, it was also the lowest point of what should have been a very special year.

Alonso was the first to emerge from the stewards' room, leaving swiftly via the back door and prompting a near stampede from the waiting press whose numbers had now been swelled by spectators, race fans and the merely curious. In the resulting cavalry charge a Japanese sound-recordist fell and broke his thigh. It was mayhem, and an angry Alonso was disappearing into the distance. He was saying nothing, the stewards having found against him. However, it would be just before midnight when the official announcement came that Alonso had been moved five places back down the grid and McLaren were to be excluded from registering any Constructors' Championship points in the race.

Ron Dennis and the McLaren team management were next to emerge; they were as angry as Alonso and also saying nothing. They disappeared into the recesses of the brand centre amid much slamming of doors.

We had already set up a camera and lights in a corner of the first floor of the McLaren HQ in preparation for the scheduled five o'clock interview with Lewis. The prospect of this had been long-since forgotten and abandoned, but the presence of the kit gave us the chance to regroup in quiet surroundings while a couple of hundred press still waited in the dark of the paddock, the other side of the sliding glass doors.

We were discussing the events of the evening and how the story should be told at the start of Sunday's live coverage when in strolled a relaxed but apologetic Lewis Hamilton. 'I'm sorry guys, I'm obviously a bit late for the interview, but I'm ready now... where do I sit?'

To say we were somewhat taken aback would be an understatement. Around us the Formula One press and the world's broadcasters were hunting for any crumb of a quote, any glimmer of a reaction to the controversial events of the evening, and now here was the man at the centre of the storm clipping our microphone on to the front of his race-jacket.

He explained that he was happy to talk about any aspect of the day's events, there were no topics that were off-limits. Not only that, but there were no McLaren staff with him, no press officers, no public relations personnel. Lewis sat back with a smile on his face; he was ready to unload.

He accepted only a small amount of blame for the day's events and talked with disarming frankness about what he saw as the breakdown of his highly prized relationship with Ron Dennis. He spoke for the first time about his failure to achieve any kind of partnership with Fernando Alonso; there was no communication and Alonso had barely talked to him in months.

Then came the wide-eyed naivety. All he wanted to do was race. All he wanted to do was express himself behind the wheel of a racing car. He just wanted to have fun and had no time for the politics that were suffocating the sport. Twenty minutes later he stood up, smiles and handshakes all round; we wished him well for the next day, and he was gone, via the back door.

We ran the entire interview the next day in two parts, and it formed the bulk of the build-up to the race. The first impression was that his views had been revealing and refreshing. The reality, I'm sure, was the opposite. He talked about his scorn and impatience with Formula One politics, but this was a political interview of which Ayrton Senna at his most provocative would have been proud. This was Hamilton claiming the high ground and positioning himself within the team. The rookie had become the street-fighter. The interview might have been full of smiling bemusement but clearly underneath it all was a resentment that had possibly been brewing ever since those team orders at Monaco.

From pole position Lewis won the Hungarian Grand Prix in dominant style and stretched his World Championship lead to seven points over Alonso. From back in the UK, Ellen Kolby had watched the events of the weekend unfold with some trepidation but contacted us to say that even though she probably would not have let the Hamilton interview happen, it told her more about the inner workings of McLaren than any memo or team briefing.

It probably showed her that this was a team tearing itself apart. The weekend had been a tactical shambles and a PR nightmare. Hamilton might have left Hungary with a smug smile and maximum points but the new star had lost his sparkle and started to make critics and enemies. He and Alonso were one and two in the Championship and McLaren, despite their Hungary penalty, were still leading the Constructors battle; there was still much glory up for grabs if only a semblance of unity could be restored.

But there was also 'Spygate' on the horizon, and it would emerge that among all the accusations and angry words that had been exchanged in the Hungaroring paddock, Alonso had threatened to reveal the contents of internal emails that would incriminate McLaren to a potentially ruinous degree. It was a form of blackmail that would further increase the tension and suspicion within the team and give strong encouragement to those pointing the accusing finger.

Chapter 19

LOSING THE PLOT
AT SPA

In Turkey at the end of August, a third win for Fel ipe Massa indicated that the Championship battle was going to be hard-fought, possibly going all the way to the final round in Brazil; any one of five drivers were still in with a chance of taking the title. The Italian Grand Prix gave McLaren a morale-boosting one–two, Alonso from Hamilton whose lead was down to just three points as the team headed into a critical and demanding week.

Prior to the weekend's Belgian Grand Prix at Spa the McLaren team had to appear before the World Motor Sport Council in Paris for the reconvened hearing into the 'Spygate' scandal and everything that surrounded it. Ron Dennis, to his credit, had wasted no time in going straight to Max Mosley with the details of Alonso's threats, and this, of course, changed the whole nature of the hearing; it was inevitable that some kind of penalty would be imposed.

Even so there was a sense of shock in the Spa paddock when the news came through that the team had been totally excluded from that year's Constructors' Championship and fined $100 million, far and away a record fine in any sport. I suppose from McLaren's point of view it could have been worse; they were still in business, they were still racing, and their two drivers had been cleared to battle on for the World Drivers' Championship. But there was also a feeling that any sport that could impose an internal fine of $100 million and have it routinely accepted had rather lost touch with the real world.

Most of what happened that weekend further convinced me that Formula One was now living in the realms of fantasy. It was great to be back at Spa, but the famous circuit could only produce a processional finish with a Räikkönen/Massa one–two for Ferrari and Alonso and Hamilton taking the next two places for McLaren. The build-up was dominated by the McLaren punishment. There was a stiff, posed handshake between Max Mosley and Ron Dennis in front of the McLaren brand centre, and then Mosley headed into the top paddock at Spa where he gave ITV an interview in which he claimed McLaren had 'polluted the Championship' and that 'the cancer of cheating' had to be eradicated and the best way to do this would be to exclude both their drivers from the Championship.

About 100 yards away, and down a flight of stone steps into the bottom paddock, a furious Ron Dennis heard the interview go out on the monitors in the brand centre. He rang the ITV production office and demanded the right of reply, and he wanted to put it on air straight away. I heard at least one end of the exchange down my earpiece as I was linking into a 90-second report on the previous day's qualifying session.

So, a minute and a half to get from the top paddock to the McLaren HQ with a camera, sound gear and all the attendant equipment, and sound cool, composed and organised at the other end. Twenty seconds to go and we had to punch our way through a ten-deep crowd of press and onlookers outside the brand centre, and I think the crew were still punching when I did a live introduction to Ron and asked for his reaction to what we had been hearing from Max Mosley.

Ron Dennis is a decent man, and I am convinced that he, and most of his team, had found themselves caught up in a whirlwind of events that seemed to be none of their doing. Ron gave a calm but quite impassioned defence of his own sporting ethics and the honourable manner in which the team had tried to conduct themselves, illustrated by the readiness with which the Alonso evidence had been volunteered. To call anyone a cheat is just about the worst thing you can do in sport, and Ron, correctly, made sure the record was put straight.

For my part it was off to a commercial break and then try to reverse out of the very irritated crowd of foreign broadcasters surging toward the McLaren boss and get to our next location. I was attempting to do this when I felt a tug on my shirt; I ignored it but it became more insistent. I managed to turn round and there was Bernie Ecclestone.

'Did you manage to interview Max?' he asked.

I replied that we had, and he said, 'You've just got Ron, and was he upset?' I replied that he was.

'Great fun, isn't it?' he chuckled, and walked off, making more mischief on his mobile phone.

There was, however, a moment of harsh reality on that Spa weekend and it came with the news on the Saturday evening that the 1995 World Rally Champion Colin McRae had lost his life, along with three others, in a helicopter crash near his home in Scotland. I had been with Colin at the Festival of Speed just a few weeks earlier. He had driven me down a quagmire of a rally stage but still managed to be entertaining and impressive.

We had talked in particular about the early days of covering the British Championship when we would use him as a filmed cutaway in the crowd when his father was in action. He was quiet and unassuming then, and he was exactly the same when he was World Champion. What a motorsport talent, and what a contrast with the $100 million fines and quarrelling grandees of Formula One.

Chapter 20

SO CLOSE IN
SHANGHAI

Three rounds remained for the sport to regain its dignity and sense of priorities. The first of these was the Japanese Grand Prix. The previous year ITV had been trying to save money when Japan and China came round, so we were watching it all from the London studio. Now I was not only about to get my first experience of Formula One in Japan, but was also at the location that had helped fire my enthusiasm for the sport over 30 years earlier.

The Japanese Grand Prix was returning to a rebuilt Fuji circuit that would always evoke memories of James Hunt clinching the title in 1976. It also gave us the same weather that helped deny Niki Lauda victory at the end of that epic season: mist, fog and rain for qualifying, and a more consistent downpour for race-day itself.

It proved to be a weekend of mature mastery from Hamilton. He qualified on pole then showed a champion's concentration and composure in taking victory next day. With Alonso crashing out and Räikkönen only managing third, it meant that Hamilton had a strong chance of winning the title the following weekend in Shanghai.

The race at Fuji had started under the safety car and the only perceived flaw in Hamilton's performance came in the manner in which he led the field around behind Bernd Mayländer's Mercedes. Video that had been posted on YouTube showed him jinking to the right and suddenly slowing in contravention of the regulations. Did this prompt young Sebastian Vettel's embarrassing collision with Mark Webber? Once again the stewards would be fully occupied in the run-up to the Chinese Grand Prix.

I would be fully occupied as well. ITV Sport were now well into the 2007/08 Champions League season and there were no signs of my reluctant flirtation with football presentation coming to an end. Mark Sharman, the Head of Sport, was continuously aware of my desire to return to concentrating 100% on Formula One as per the original deal. Apparently the earlier approaches made to both Eamonn Holmes and Jeff Stelling had each led to nothing.

But now, encouragingly, the BBC's *Match of the Day Two* presenter Adrian Chiles was talking openly in the press of his attempts to put a deal together to become, as he called it, 'Top Dog' on ITV Football, and with ITV Director of Programmes Peter Fincham in his fanclub such a deal seemed more than likely. The suggestion, however, was that I might still need to hold the fort until the end of the season. And this particular week 'holding the fort' meant that round trip from Fuji to Shanghai via the Tuesday-night Champions League match at Old Trafford. An early deal with Adrian Chiles would be welcome indeed.

The newspapers that I had brought back with me from the UK gave moderate coverage to United's win over Roma but a lot of coverage to Hamilton's potential title-winning weekend. The tabloids especially were not so much anticipating the triumph as the prospect of dirty dealings behind the scenes. The FIA, we were told, would find a way to penalise Hamilton for his performance behind the Fuji safety car and so extend the title battle to Brazil and maybe deny Hamilton the Championship altogether.

As it turned out even Formula One could not be that devious, and after a couple of hours waiting jet-lagged in the Shanghai paddock the news came through that no further action was going to be taken and Lewis was free to race for the title. It left ITV, for the first time in its 11 years in the sport, preparing for a race that could end with a British Formula One World Champion.

The ITV production team, and indeed the ITV audience, must have imagined this prospect on many occasions. They would have envisaged it taking place in the fervour of Monza or Brazil or even in a downpour in Fuji, but it looked as if we were going to have to make do with the soulless concrete acreage of the vast, newly built Shanghai circuit, which seemed barely 20% full even on race day.

The fact that the venue was devoid of atmosphere and any sense of occasion at least meant that Lewis was perfectly insulated from the huge expectation back in the UK, reflected in a six million early morning TV audience, and he duly performed with the composure of the previous weekend. He took pole position, albeit with a low fuel load, from Räikkönen, Massa and Alonso, who vented his frustration with some force in the McLaren garage.

Once we had put the Sunday race programme on the air, trying (but probably failing) to be balanced and sensible about the historic prospect that lay ahead, Mark Blundell and myself headed for one of the small lakeside pavilions at the back of the paddock that served as the McLaren team headquarters. There were only a few people in the rather spartan room, including Anthony Hamilton, sitting alone, his attention fixed on the TV screen and leaning forward with the kind of body language that discouraged any attempt at conversation.

I had built up a lot of respect for Anthony during the course of the season, and apparently we had sought his opinion on far too many occasions according to our critics, but I defy anyone not to wonder what it must be like to be the father of a son who was about to become World Champion in his first Formula One season. What could possibly be going through his mind? It was impossible to tell; his expression was unchanged and his stony silence just added to the tension.

But Lewis was relaxed and in command. The race had begun in the wet, virtually the whole field were on intermediates and

Hamilton established a five- or six-second cushion to Räikkönen. Then the circuit began to dry, and the leader began to struggle. His tyres were deteriorating at an alarming rate and back in the paddock his father leant forward still further, fists clenched.

Räikkönen went past, Hamilton stayed out. Anthony broke his silence, questioning what was going on. When Lewis was eventually called in his rear tyres were completely shot; he turned into the pit-lane but the back of the car got away from him and, almost in slow-motion, the car became beached in the gravel trap, the only grand prix pit-lane gravel trap in the world. Unlike the Nürburgring there would be no miracle rescue, no crane to lift him Scalextric-style back into the action. Seconds earlier he had seemingly been coasting to the World Championship title, but now there was only frustration, disbelief and desolation.

It's strange how, at times like this, experiences from other sporting moments tend to resonate. In 1995 I had stood with John Daly alongside the St Andrews clubhouse ready to congratulate him as the new Open Champion. As we watched the monitor together his only challenger, Costantino Rocca, rolled an impossible putt through the undulations short of the 18th green and into the bottom of the cup; play-off. Daly showed no emotion he just turned away from me and headed to the practice ground to ready himself for the extra holes that would give him the title convincingly.

Similarly, at that moment in Shanghai there was no flicker of emotion from Anthony Hamilton. He just stood up, looked straight ahead and strode to the garage; in the gravel trap Hamilton got out of his stricken car, kept his helmet on and also headed to the McLaren pit. The season went on, there was work still to do and surely the job would be completed in São Paulo in two weeks' time.

As for ourselves we tried to put a positive spin on what had been a huge disappointment; but Räikkönen had won the race from Alonso and Massa, and perhaps the drive of the day had come from the youthful Sebastian Vettel, getting his best-ever finish in fourth for Toro Rosso. Hamilton would have only a four-point lead to take into the last round of the Championship.

And maybe from a ruthless ITV point of view it was not all bad. The previous night we had gathered in a Shanghai sports bar with a few Antipodean colleagues to watch England score a sensational and rather unexpected Rugby World Cup quarter-final victory over Australia. The following weekend England defeated the host nation France in the semi-final. So on Saturday 20 October England would face South Africa in the World Cup final in Paris, live and exclusive on ITV. On Sunday 21 October, in the late afternoon UK time, Lewis Hamilton would attempt to clinch the Formula One World Championship at the climax of one of the most momentous seasons in history, live and exclusive on ITV. From the disappointment of Shanghai we were emerging with what was easily the best weekend of exclusive sport the network had ever had.

Chapter 21

THE WORLD CHAMPIONSHIP WAIT GOES ON

The two weeks between China and Brazil were everything that you would imagine: a blur of trailers and promos and hype. Even so, it rather surprised me that ITV were not willing to schedule any extra advance programming to coax what would surely be a huge new audience toward the weekend celebrations.

Instead there was a Saturday link between myself in the pit -lane in Brazil and Jim Rosenthal in Paris, a weird situation. Jim with all his Formula One experience who had never seen a British driver threaten the World title and myself with 15 years' of Six Nations and Heineken Cup experience who would love to be there when England won the World Cup.

ITV got the huge audiences it anticipated and deserved, but, of course, it cannot control the results, and I watched on a press centre laptop as England went down 15–6 to South Africa in Paris; the first part of ITV's big double-header, and there was no history yet. It was all down to Lewis.

And that was the obvious message of our pre-race build-up, which did not require much more than to just become immersed in the crackling atmosphere. This was the place to decide a World Championship. All Shanghai had offered was a concrete desert and a gravel trap in the pit-lane, but São Paulo had everything, from the threatening mood outside the Carlos Pace circuit to the crowds who were packing the banking and stands from eight o'clock in the morning and who were, at times, almost drowning the cars with their chanting and singing.

And the noise cranked up even further when Massa took

pole position ahead of Hamilton. It should have been no great problem for Lewis, fifth or better was all he required to take the title. It still should not have been a great problem when he made his worst start of the season, slow off the line; he locked up defending his position from Alonso and then was eighth at the end of the first lap; now this *was* a problem.

Slowly he managed to claw his way back, but then came the biggest crisis of all as, for no reason that has properly been explained, his gearbox selected neutral and Hamilton briefly coasted to a halt as the team on the pit wall coached him through the restart procedure. It destroyed his race, it destroyed his Championship, and I find it strange that it has not been analysed and agonised over in the months since. Instead it has been dismissed, at the end of a very conspiratorial season, with those very 'un-Formula One' kinds of explanation... bad luck... coincidence... sod's law.

The best that Hamilton could manage was seventh. Räikkönen won the race to take the title at the end of the closest Championship battle the sport had ever seen. For his form over the final stretch of the season and his six race wins – two more than any other driver – Kimi Räikkönen certainly deserved the title.

There was no real sense of anticlimax that evening. Lewis had handled the events of the whole fortnight with a great deal of dignity and had a handshake for everyone in the McLaren garage and promised it would be a title celebration next season.

Everyone in ITV and the media felt the same. The season had been an epic mix of tense action, personality clashes, politics and controversy. Through it all ITV's overall audience had gone up 40%, with 12 million watching the climax in Brazil. Now, with Alonso moving to Renault, Ferrari still strong with Räikkönen and Massa, and innovations to come, such as a night race in Singapore, the sport seemed to be capturing the imagination once again, and ITV at last seemed set for a significant return on their investment.

The close season formalities included the BBC Sports Personality of the Year, where Lewis lost out to Joe Calzaghe, and the Autosport Awards, which were televised for the first time for ITV. The programme relived the stories and action of the year and culminated in an emotional Lewis Hamilton receiving the main award from Ayrton Senna's sister Viviane. She had made a surprise entrance from backstage, kissed Lewis, who seemed totally overcome when she told him in her exquisite Brazilian accent that he was fantastic and his talent reminded her so much of Ayrton.

It was all very moving and was an effective reflection of the season, but two days later the Head of Sport at ITV told us he was very disappointed in the programme, having promised the Programme Controller something that was more like the Soap Awards!

For a lot of people in Formula One, the supposed 'close' season is in fact the toughest time of the year, with long hours to be worked in order to get a new car launched and tested. For me, it tends to be the awards season, and as well as the regular fixture of the Autosport Awards, in February 2008 came the invitation to help present the prestigious Laureus World Sports Awards. If the night at the Grosvenor had fallen short of Soap Awards expectations, then the Laureus Awards were a Soap Opera from beginning to end.

First of all, because the Sunday-night awards were being taken by other international broadcasters I had to get the formality of clearance from ITV to be involved; no problem, as long as it did not interfere with my involvement in the FA Cup semi-final replay at Anfield on the Tuesday. A week from the event I realised that the awards, in St Petersburg in Russia, were not on the Sunday night but on Monday night. There was no scheduled flight that could reliably get me back for the match that evening, or even for the mandatory Tuesday-morning production meeting in Liverpool. The organisers had the answer: they were sure the illustrious guest list would mean that there were a number of private jets leaving that night – they would make sure I had a seat on one of them.

It was a great event to be involved in, the Laureus Academy bringing an astonishing array of legendary sporting figures to the St Petersburg Opera House, from Mark Spitz and Nadia Comăneci to Shane Warne and Franz Beckenbauer, and using the whole event as a showcase for the magnificent charity projects that they were involved in worldwide. My co-host was Oscar-winning actor Cuba Gooding Jr, who made up for his lack of sporting knowledge with a disconcertingly exuberant approach.

As I stood respectfully in the wings listening to the closing bars of the Russian national anthem played by the orchestra of the Bolshoi ballet and looking at the stony face of Vladimir Putin sitting in the front row, it did occur to me that this was seriously bigger than the Autosport Awards. Then as Cuba and I joined each other centre stage he attempted to high-five me, which we had neither discussed nor rehearsed; it was a shambles, but soon forgotten when Cuba pointed at the front row, exclaimed 'Yo, Pootin' to the Russian President and got the show under way.

The embarrassment did not stop there, because Cuba also had an uncomfortable relationship with the autocue, insisting on using it even when it was behind him. It meant that every link had the audience laughing, no matter how serious the content.

Lewis Hamilton was in the audience in order to collect the World Breakthrough award for his 2007 World Championship and had been excited when he heard Cuba Gooding was presenting. He said, 'The man is an absolute legend', so although I was down to interview all the award winners I suggested to Cuba that Lewis would enjoy it far more if he did the interview. Cuba thought it was a great idea, 'Yeah... love the guy,' he said. So when I announced Lewis as the winner, there was a 30-second clip of VT on the big screens, during which Cuba strolled across to me to confirm that he was doing the interview and then, rather worryingly said, 'He's British, isn't he...?'

It was a relief when the whole show came to an end, especially as I had blagged a seat on a Lear jet heading back to Farnborough; however, it was nearing 10:30pm, the temperature outside was -10°, there was a blizzard, and the airfield was closing in an hour's time. Then we were told that because Vladimir Putin was staying on to meet the award winners there was a security lockdown, and no one could leave the building for half an hour. The situation was desperate.

Anthony Hamilton was also needing to get on the same flight, and together we smuggled ourselves past a couple of no entry signs into the Opera House kitchen, where we managed to follow a garbage container through the security cordon and out of the back door. From there we hailed a cab and sped through the backstreets of St Petersburg to the snowbound airfield, like something out of a Humphrey Bogart film.

As we settled into our seats in the mahogany-inlaid cabin, the pilot came to tell us that there was another passenger on his way, but the car driver had phoned through to say he was at least 20 minutes away; the pilot was convinced that if we did not take off in the next ten minutes we would not get out that night. Apparently I had to decide.

I took a large gin and tonic from the stewardess and thought about the situation, the FA Cup replay at Anfield and my ITV future. 'Let's go,' I said, with impressive authority. The pilot headed to the flight deck and the stewardess got out her clipboard, drew a line across the page and said, 'OK, we lock the doors... so no Mr Capello.' Suddenly it seemed my ITV future could be back in the melting pot – I had just abandoned the England team manager in Russia...

Back in the UK I grabbed a couple of hours' sleep, headed for the M6 and turned up at the ITV production meeting as if I was on a routine kind of schedule. Somehow, that evening I put the right words on Reading's Cup replay success over Liverpool and around midnight pointed the Range Rover south down the M6 and allowed myself a smile at the manner in which, logistically,

I'd somehow got away with it. I pulled into North Staffs services for a tank of diesel, a cappuccino and a BLT and resumed my journey. Two miles down the road the dashboard lit up and the car shuddered to a halt. I'd filled the thing with unleaded, and spent the rest of a freezing, foggy night on the hard shoulder. Fabio Capello was avenged.

Chapter 22

ITV PANIC – THE BBC
ARE BACK

With adventures like that the close season was mercifully brief, and I was really looking forward to my third year with ITV F1. With such strong story lines developing it was the perfect opportunity for the broadcast team, including Head of Sport Mark Sharman, to work out how to fine-tune some of the more tired elements of the coverage.

I had had two seasons to have a good look round and come up with a few ideas of my own, which largely centred around strengthening the live element of the race build-up, beefing up the news content and trying, if it was at all possible, to get rid of those phone-in quizzes, which might have been making money but were treating us and the audience like imbeciles. We had a couple of pre-season meetings and there would be a new approach, almost amounting to a relaunch of ITV's coverage, straight after the first three races of the season.

This was because the season began with the loop of Australia, Malaysia and Bahrain, Albert Park in Melbourne once again providing the perfect environment to launch a year of enormous potential. This was especially true for McLaren, although the fact that Hamilton and his new teammate Heikki Kovalainen carried numbers 22 and 23 was a humiliating reminder of the previous year's exclusion from the Constructors' Championship.

Rule changes for the new season included a ban on electronic control units and driver aids, which in theory would put more emphasis on the talents of the man in the cockpit. Whether that was the reason for an incident-packed race was not entirely clear, but only seven of the 22 starters were still running at the end of a race run in 37° heat.

But for Hamilton it was a faultless start to the season. He qualified in pole position and then kept his composure through a series of safety car outings to win from Nick Heidfeld and Nico Rosberg; Alonso was fourth and new Champion Räikkönen picked up just a solitary point in eighth.

In every respect the season had started where the old one left off, even down to Jenson Button going out on the first lap after a poor qualifying session. Jenson, to his credit, was still managing to hang on to his optimism and good humour, but it was becoming more of a struggle.

The ITV team assembled in Melbourne that Sunday night, excited at the prospect of what lay ahead in the season. Hamilton's win had once again been greeted with big headlines back home, it was clear that the 40% audience growth of the previous year had every chance of going higher, and there were a lot of ideas being thrown around as to how we should respond with an even sharper production. No one was in a great hurry to head to the even more oppressive heat of Malaysia, so we all went our separate ways for three days, and agreed to meet in the carpark bar around the corner from the hotel in Kuala Lumpur next Thursday evening.

Some headed to the beaches of Queensland, others visited Thailand for a couple of days; such gaps in the Formula One schedule were rarely available, and every opportunity was eagerly taken. There was not even a Champions League match at Anfield for me to cross the globe for, so I took time to enjoy the delights of Melbourne before a Thursday-afternoon flight to Malaysia.

Before leaving for the airport I took a morning run around Albert Park, which was slowly being turned back into the quiet green oasis that many Melbourne residents would prefer it to remain. I ran what I could of the grand prix circuit, dodging forklift trucks and piles of scaffolding; Formula One was being dismantled and was moving on, which was something of a metaphor for what was to happen next.

It was about one o'clock in the afternoon, I had packed and was preparing to check out when the phone rang. It was the ITV Head of Sport Mark Sharman ringing very late at night from the UK; he sounded tired and stressed, and maybe he'd taken a drink or two; in the circumstances he had every right.

'I'm ringing with some very bad news, the worst news,' he said and then paused.

It was one of those pauses that has your mind racing. Was it family, friends? I thought of the rest of the crew flying into Malaysia, maybe there had been some kind of accident.

It was almost a relief when he said 'I'm sorry to have to tell you that Formula One is going to the BBC, not only that but the BBC are taking over at the end of the season.' My instinct was to laugh, largely because despite his doom-laden voice the world had not ended, and anyway the whole notion seemed ludicrous. ITV still had three years to run on its contract, the audience was booming, and the BBC had spent the previous ten years distancing itself from motorsport in general and Formula One in particular.

But the explanation when it came was cold and brutal. At ITV, overall advertising revenue had taken a dive as the recession drew closer, and in terms of sports rights the company had to prioritise its targets. The number one objective it seemed was to put in a high enough bid to retain the Champions League and the rest of the somewhat bloated football portfolio. In order to pay for the bid something had to go. Formula One.

At a high-level meeting on the South Bank the decision was taken to exercise a break clause in the Formula One contract, and step aside from the sport at the end of 2008, allowing Bernie Ecclestone to take it immediately to the market. It was not clear whether the same meeting spent any time at all discussing the heightened popularity of the coverage, the exciting potential it was enjoying, or the production quality and prestige it brought to ITV Sport, and the essential extra breadth it brought to its advertiser reach. Sell it!

For me it was all reminiscent of that summer of 1984 when the accountants wandered around the television compound at Sunningdale effectively pulling the plugs on the ITV golf coverage on the eve of a golden era for the British and European sport; short-term savings followed by long-term regrets.

Whatever ITV's motives, flawed or not, Ecclestone apparently could not conceal his enthusiasm for the opportunity. He imposed a penalty payment on ITV and within hours sent his assistant round to ITV headquarters to collect the cheque and deliver the paperwork.

In the meantime the BBC received a call from the F1 boss and suddenly realised they *were* motor racing fans after all. Even though the BBC was the only logical terrestrial destination for the newly available rights, within hours Ecclestone had talked them into a massive £200 million five-year deal. By the next morning in the UK the BBC Sport website had announced the news, with Director of Sports Rights Dominic Coles proclaiming, 'The biggest motorsporting [sic] event in the world is returning home after 12 years.' It was Dominic who had taken great pleasure in telling me on my BBC departure three years earlier that Formula One was now so artificial it could barely be considered a sport, and was impossible to defend from the environmental point of view.

But now he was warming to the theme of his new and clearly favourite acquisition: 'F1 is a crown jewel of sports broadcasting, so to bring the rights back to their traditional home from 2009 is tremendously exciting.' The BBC website also talked rather curiously about how ITV had jettisoned the sport because 'viewing figures are not that impressive... they're not that great', and then went on: 'The BBC is saying the ripple effect of Lewis Hamilton is amazing, wonderful, millions are tuning in and the Brazilian Grand Prix was the most watched sports event of last year.'

Mark Sharman apologised and said he was getting the next flight out to Kuala Lumpur and that he would be in the paddock at the Sakhir circuit to talk to the ITV team and try to work out what happens now. I was flying on to Malaysia alone, and I'm not a great one for mobile phones and the Internet, so I had no idea of how everyone else was reacting to this bombshell.

As I indicated, it had echoes of the manner in which ITV got out of golf, but more than anything else, for me, it recalled that day in 1995 when we got the news that the Formula One rights had moved from BBC to ITV. Back then I sat on a flight to Lisbon full of anger and a sense of betrayal; strangely, on this occasion it was almost a sense of euphoria that another career crossroads had been reached. There was concern for those a bit younger than me on the team who, despite their talent and dedication, would be faced with real difficulty as a result of this random decision. This also felt like further confirmation of the ludicrous nature of the business we worked in.

And all of that was reflected in the strangely high-spirited evening that followed as the ITV team assembled in Kuala Lumpur. As you can imagine, there was much rubbishing of the ITV management and decision-makers, and also bewilderment at the long-term logic of the situation. No one talked much about where they would be working in a year's time; the serious jockeying for position would come later. Instead most of the conversation that night as we sat around on plastic chairs plucking cold cans from an oil drum, revolved around the BBC's sudden reinvention of itself as the motherland of motorsport, and the astonishing rights figure it had paid when it seemed to be the only available bidder.

Mark Sharman arrived on the first possible flight to address the troops, a gesture that was appreciated but was pretty futile. He spent 15 minutes distancing himself from any involvement in the decision but was keen to point out that, whatever our efforts, Champions League football was always going to be more important to ITV than Formula One.

With morale suitably boosted, the meeting broke up. We needed to concentrate on the immediate future, which was the three days of the Malaysian Grand Prix. Back home, however, the deal was big news and the British press got straight to the heart of the upheaval with their speculation that not only would the BBC bring back its iconic Fleetwood Mac theme music, but Murray Walker could be returning as well. For me, the most telling reaction came from Lewis Hamilton, when he was asked by BBC Radio Five's David Croft for his feelings about Formula One television coverage 'coming home': he simply looked confused and replied that he'd only ever really known Formula One to be on ITV.

In the days that followed at the Sepang International Circuit, Mark Sharman had gone from his failed group-hug to an attempt at one-to-one reassurance. I was taken aside to be told that I had no worries, any deals to hire other presenters were now off, and I would see out the remaining three years of my contract as ITV's main football presenter. The news was a great comfort. Apparently Martin Brundle and Mark Blundell were told that their future lay in working on the British Touring Car Championship. I'm not sure they saw it as a great step forward.

As ever in these situations those at the sharp end of the production, in front of the camera and behind the mike, could look after themselves; within hours of the announcement of the news, phone calls were being made and agents were busy. It was those who were putting in the hard graft and long hours in the ITV production team who were most vulnerable; promises that they might be 'absorbed' in other areas of ITV programming and production merely increased the anxiety and sense of betrayal.

These VT editors, producers and production assistants had dedicated themselves to the gruelling schedule and exacting standards that delivered the finest Formula One coverage the sport had ever seen, and the best service British viewers had ever enjoyed. They had moved the coverage light years forward from where the BBC left it in 1996, and their commitment, scheduling and production style would set the template for everything that would come after. They had collected a BAFTA in 2006 and were nominated for another one in 2007, and yet were being told by the ITV management that they were getting in the way of more money being spent on football. They were also reading in the British press that ITV F1 was rubbish; who wants to watch a race with commercial breaks? – bring back Murray.

For them, no word came from the ITV management – no support, no gratitude, no praise, and seemingly no recognition of the careers that were derailed. I would not have blamed a single one of them if they had pulled the plugs on the Malaysian Grand Prix, locked the door of the VT truck and said Phuket, let's head for the beach.

Instead the conversations in the back of the production truck and in the hotel bar were completely the opposite. There you heard a collective resolve to put in the hours and the imagination to make the coverage of this last season quite simply the best ever. The production team also knew that they would have to do it against a background of limited resources, budget cuts and a management who were more intent on a quiet exit than a big finish.

A couple of months after this various members of the F1 production team were invited by ITV to a pre-BAFTA awards reception in London. There, along with the rest of the ITV nominees, we were congratulated and wished luck for the awards announcement by Michael Grade and other members of the management, who made no reference to the non-existent future the sport and the team had on the network.

A short time later Neil Duncanson of North One collected the BAFTA on behalf of ITV F1, their coverage of the Canadian Grand Prix giving them the award for best sports programme for an unprecedented second year. This was even though prime-time scheduling restrictions had forced us off the air without any driver interviews or reaction! At the dinner that followed we were on an adjacent table to the ITV management, from whom there was still no meaningful communication. This would have been the perfect time for an informal discussion on the contract decision, an appreciation of the efforts and the achievements of the team, even a simple congratulation; but there was nothing.

In the end it was left to Harry Hill to get up from the management table, wander over with a bottle of champagne in his hand and tell the team he felt embarrassed at the way they were being treated; he had admired the ITV F1 coverage and thought it had been a shabby decision to pull the plug. It was a classy thing for him to do, it was appreciated, but the team deserved more from the evening than just a TV burp.

Meanwhile, within a few weeks the initial euphoria seemed to have disappeared at the BBC as well. We received a call from a very senior producer at the BBC asking if we would mind giving them a rough ballpark figure on what our production costs had been (aside from the rights costs) for putting a full season of Formula One on the screen. Such a friendly informal exchange of information was commonplace, despite the public posturing. When he was told there would not be much change out of £8 or £9 million there was silence, then 'Oh shit…', and the line went dead.

The BBC had bought Formula One in the same way a Monopoly player buys Mayfair. A combination of circumstances meant they had accidentally landed on a big property, and they were the only buyer in the market. This should have been the time for negotiation, for deal-making, especially with the recession gathering pace and question marks over the licence fee. It should also have been the time for putting guarantees of access and coverage in place. Instead the BBC had said 'Yes we'll have it' at the top price, in a sense of panic before the dice was thrown again. The implications were made clear three years later when the BBC and their unsustainable deal had put the whole future of F1 on UK terrestrial television in severe jeopardy.

But none of this should really concern the programme-makers themselves, and for myself and the rest of the ITV team there was a final season of Formula One to be played out – what happened after that could wait. In Malaysia Ferrari had come right back to form, Massa and Räikkönen locking out the front row and Räikkönen taking the race win from Robert Kubica in the BMW. A fifth-place finish for Hamilton meant that his fast start to the season had come to an abrupt halt, but he still led the Championship.

For ITV the two weeks before the Bahrain Grand Prix were supposedly a chance to return home and absorb the new directions that all our careers were going to have to take. On the middle weekend Ted Kravitz was due to go to a wedding, so I agreed to deputise for him, presenting the start of the British Touring Car Championship season at Brands Hatch. In the hands of Ted and Louise Goodman the programme had become a slick live afternoon on ITV 4 that gave coverage not only to the three Touring Car races but also the full support programme as well; it had become an invaluable showcase for British motorsport.

I was looking forward to getting back together with the man who was making it all happen, Alan Gow, who two years earlier had been made Chairman of the Motor Sports Association, the governing body of motorsport in the UK, and would go on to become the Touring Car Commissioner of the FIA. This would effectively make him the boss of Touring Car racing worldwide, which, in turn, was a ringing endorsement of the current prestige of the British Championship.

So he was now a serious motorsport figure, but he was also a good friend from the early pioneering days of the BTCC on *Grandstand*, so on arrival at Brands Hatch that Sunday morning the first stop was going to be the TOCA motorhome for a quick catch-up on all the news and gossip that might be around. But that morning it was more than just gossip; it was there in black and white across about half a dozen pages of the *News of the World*. The headline 'F1 BOSS HAS SICK NAZI ORGY WITH HOOKERS' really took care of the need to read the rest of the story, but it was compelling, humiliating stuff.

The verdict around the paddock that day was a unanimous one: Mosley was finished, and the question most asked was could 'Spygate' possibly be an element in all of this, or was it just coincidence? That has never been answered, so we suppose not. What we do know now is that Mosley was not finished. He contested the allegations (especially the Nazi element) with an avenging zeal and within three years it was the *News of The World* that was finished.

It is hard not to have respect for Mosley's self-belief and his persuasive talents in an argument. He may have won, but the collateral damage was huge, not only in his private life but also to the prestige and standing of the sport that had had its fill of negative headlines through 2007. We spent the afternoon, however, amid the raw competitive spirit of the BTCC, and the energy and the ambition of the support race drivers. For those in Formula Renault and the 15- or 16-year-olds in Ginetta Juniors, there was but one goal: to reach the top, the ultimate, Formula One. You really wondered what strange world they were getting themselves into; and that weekend the BBC must have been wondering what they were getting themselves back into as well.

It was no great surprise that Mosley was missing from the Bahrain paddock the following weekend. The Bahrain royal family had said he would not be welcome anyway, and Mercedes, Honda, BMW and Toyota all distanced themselves from the FIA President in formal statements. Aggravating the atmosphere, McLaren, at the instigation of Mosley, had been moved to the bottom end of the pit-lane, to the kind of 'naughty step' next to Force India. Here they were meant to further reflect on what Mosley felt was their true status as a team, having been excluded from the 2007 Championship. As if in acknowledgement of this, Hamilton had one of his worst races since coming into Formula One. He messed up the start and then was to blame for a collision with Alonso that left him finishing well adrift in 13th. Up front there was a Ferrari one–two; Massa won the race but Räikkönen led the Championship.

Ferrari continued to set the pace through Barcelona and

Turkey, but Hamilton was with them on the podium on both occasions. In Turkey he proudly announced his drive to second ahead of Räikkönen as his best-ever drive in Formula One. It was outstanding, but it was as if Hamilton was publicly trying to psych himself up for a renewed Championship push. He was without a win since Melbourne but his challenge had barely faltered – the McLaren driver was still only seven points off Räikkönen's lead.

At Monaco Max Mosley was back in the paddock. It was a low-key return, but behind the scenes he was putting himself forward as the protector of the sport from the predatory commercial interests that, he said, were gathering. Most of them seemed to be assembling around the catwalk in the Amber Lounge gardens, where Sonia Irvine was staging her charity fashion show. The drivers modelled some lurid outfits and I hosted the lavish production with Petra Ecclestone, who was setting out on a new fashion and media career. The whole thing was an education.

Hamilton had satisfied himself with his performance in Turkey, but on the streets of the Principality he impressed everyone with a Monaco win that put him back on top of the Championship table. In wet conditions it was a beautifully judged performance, despite the appearances of the safety car and the changes of strategy that were required. Hamilton described it as another highlight of his career and for the last few laps said he was just thinking about Ayrton Senna and his winning performance around the famous streets. There was a strong feeling coming away from Monaco that the sport had taken over once again from all the nonsense in the paddock and the committee rooms, and ITV's last season could still be the best.

It was certainly a season that was strong on unpredictability. Hamilton had left Monaco with a three-point Championship lead, but by the time we got to Silverstone six weeks later that lead had not only disappeared but the British driver was back down to fourth behind Massa, Kubica and Räikkönen. In

Canada he had failed to react to a red light at the end of the pit-lane and took out Räikkönen, who was waiting to rejoin the track. That gave him a ten-place grid penalty for the next race at Magny-Cours, where his over-exuberant attempts to battle through the field merely drew another penalty; no points scored in Canada or France. It all meant that Silverstone had the feeling of a pivotal race in his Championship challenge, and the British Grand Prix had the potential of a memorable occasion.

In 2008 Friday practice was not such a TV battleground as it is today. There was no competition for the coverage and there seemed no need to go live with any of the action. So it was a day for research, programme planning and feature production, and, if you planned it right, it could be a pretty relaxing day as well.

That particular Friday morning at Silverstone seemed to have all the right ingredients, and the paddock was full of familiar faces; it had all the makings of a low-key, sociable start to the weekend.

I was having breakfast in the BMW team headquarters when one of Bernie Ecclestone's assistants from Formula One Management sought me out. 'Mr Ecclestone wants to see you as soon as possible,' he said, half indicating that the rest of my breakfast would have to be forfeited.

Bernie's bus stands like a gleaming grey sentry at the head of the Formula One paddock, unwelcoming and all-seeing; behind its hissing smoked-glass doors deals are done, plots are hatched and egos are crushed. It was rare for a television crew to be invited, or even commanded, into the inner sanctum, but here was Bernie telling me to bring my crew here in half an hour's time because he had a big announcement to make. He wanted to do it in an interview with myself and we would distribute it to the world broadcasters.

I allowed myself a brief moment to wonder if this was the Ecclestone retirement announcement, or maybe there were more Max Mosley revelations; perhaps there was more 'Spygate' evidence emerging and McLaren were going to be thrown out of the Championship. Then he said: 'I'm fed up with this place, I've run out of patience. I'm going to announce that the British Grand Prix is going to Donington.'

There should be so many reasons for disliking Bernie Ecclestone but I find it impossible. He may be the ringmaster of one of the greatest shows on earth but he constantly gives the impression that he does not take any of it too seriously. When the crew arrived and set up their equipment, we were all ready to go with the announcement and the interview when the sound engineer wondered whether Bernie's microphone was straight. 'If it is, its the only bloody thing here that is straight,' said the boss of Formula One. We were recording – it's in the archives!

That statement was no kind of revelation, but the Donington announcement spread like wildfire around the Silverstone paddock and generated a mood of angry defiance from the Silverstone club and the members of the British Racing Drivers Club. Donington apparently had promised a £100 million investment programme, significant improvements to the access and infrastructure around the circuit, all of which was to be funded by a highly speculative debenture system of advance bookings and ticket sales. It was all very reminiscent of 1999 when Ecclestone had done an ill-fated British Grand Prix deal with Brands Hatch in order to put pressure on Silverstone.

Damon Hill, as President of the BRDC and all-round voice of reason, gave the first of many live interviews that weekend, explaining how the Donington sums just did not add up and there were certain boundaries of business and common sense that they would never allow Silverstone to breach, so farewell British Grand Prix and good luck Donington.

With three years of hindsight Bernie can look back at the events of that weekend with some satisfaction. Whether he planned it that way or not, Silverstone, shaken out of its complacency, now boasts state-of-the-art facilities, (although not state-of-the-art car-parking) and the future of the British Grand Prix is guaranteed at a circuit that can still proudly call itself 'the home of British motorsport'. But at the same time Donington, a circuit with equal claims to be part of the heritage of motor racing, was brought to its knees and almost destroyed. If it had gone, it would have been a victim of Ecclestone's cunning, connivance and ruthless business approach, but it is an approach that makes him the hero of the paddock and all those in Formula One who stand to profit from his efforts.

In everything that was said and all the interviews that were given that weekend, Ecclestone did nothing to dispel the fear that if Donington failed to get it right the event would never be allowed to return to Silverstone, and the British Grand Prix would be off the calendar – a statement that certainly concentrated the minds of the UK's proud new TV rights holders. As a result there were so many reasons why the British Grand Prix of 2008 just had to be a classic.

It was the race where Hamilton restored both his reputation and his title challenge. He could only qualify fourth, to the disappointment of the Saturday crowd, but had the perfect set-up for Sunday's wet conditions. His team made bold decisions on brakes and tyres and Hamilton behind the wheel delivered a victory margin of 68 seconds over Nick Heidfeld, lapping everyone outside the top three. We left Silverstone with a three-way tie for the Drivers' Championship – Hamilton, Massa and Räikkönen – and the knowledge that we had seen one of the all-time great wet-weather performances. Some Silverstone fans, with deliberate irony, even compared it to Ayrton Senna in the 1993 grand prix of Europe... the only F1 race of the modern era to have taken place at Donington. So far.

A win in the next race at Hockenheim gave Hamilton the Championship lead, but it was a win that came with a further reminder of how the sport was moving into a strange technological era. Hamilton had to fight his way back through the field after a bad tactical call by the team. That call, it seems, did not come from the pit wall but from the McLaren boffins sitting in front of computer screens at the team's headquarters in Woking. That evening we had an airport lounge discussion about the events of the day, Ted Kravitz and James Allen seemingly happy to see Formula One immerse itself in the computer age; I was the dinosaur arguing for the preservation of improvisation, daring and driver input before the sport became a gadget show.

I only had to wait six weeks for a rain shower at Spa to cause perfect chaos in the Belgian Grand Prix and emphasise my point. It was the sort of chaos that would cause furrowed brows and much rebooting of computers in Woking. The rain started to fall three laps from the end of what had been a fairly routine race. Hamilton was hunting down the leader Räikkönen, knowing that only these wet conditions would give him a chance of victory. Cars were spinning, cars were slamming into the barrier, and Hamilton was forced outside the limits of the track at the Bus Stop chicane just as he was overtaking Räikkönen.

Down the straight he immediately gave the place back in accordance with the rules, and then attacked and went past Räikkönen at La Source. The team, feeling somewhat neurotic after all the pain of 'Spygate', checked with race director Charlie Whiting that Hamilton's series of moves were legal. Hamilton took the chequered flag but at the end of the race was penalised 25 seconds by the race stewards and dropped down to third.

There were arguments on both sides, but to me the rigid interpretation of the rules in the carnage that was going on all around the circuit was unrealistic and silly. Also, to announce that McLaren's appeal against the decision would be heard in Paris a fortnight later, two days before the Singapore Grand Prix, also made the sport look very foolish. But other people seemed to see far more sinister goings-on.

Sections of the British press in particular saw the post-race events as clear evidence that the sport was fixed, and were even able to quote Niki Lauda, who reckoned the Spa stewards had made the worst decision in the history of Formula One, and it did seem the sport had somehow become biased in favour of Ferrari. The headlines proclaimed that FIA now stood for Ferrari International Assistance. Hopefully we avoided such slanderous suggestions in our hastily re-edited highlights package that evening in Belgium, but we did know that a lot of extra adrenalin had been pumped into the title battle, and this had stoked things up very nicely for ITV's last couple of months of Formula One.

Chapter 23

A CHAMPION
AT LAST

Race day at Monza, the Italian Grand Prix began with an early-morning reflective moment as the more long-serving members of the Formula One fraternity gathered on the grid to honour the 30th anniversary of the race that gave the title to Mario Andretti, but took the life of his Lotus teammate Ronnie Peterson.

Three years later when I was lucky enough to sit down with Mario at his home in Pennsylvania, the memories were still vivid of that fateful few hours. He recalled how Sid Watkins had suggested that he held back from going to the crash site at the end of the straight but he went anyway, and found Ronnie, with terrible injuries to his legs; he was shocked but conscious, and Mario felt reassured. The following day the newly crowned World Champion, driving himself to the hospital, stopped at a toll booth on the autostrada, and the attendant said, 'Haven't you heard? Ronnie's dead, it's just come up on the news.'

Everyone standing on the Monza grid on that Sunday morning in 2008 had their own memories and feelings about the events of 1978; for me it underlined how the speed of communication in the sport and the world had changed – Mario got the news on a motorway, I learnt of Peterson's death from an evening paper placard at Liverpool Street; but it also represented 30 years since my first-ever weekend with a television crew in a Formula One pit-lane.

The Italian Grand Prix in 2008, having started with a look back 30 years, also gave us a glimpse into what a large part of the next 30 years might hold with the first victory for Sebastian Vettel. He became the youngest winner in the history of Formula One, at just 21 years and 73 days. Hamilton, with tyre problems, was back in seventh but his main Championship rival Felipe Massa was only sixth, so no great damage was done, although Hamilton's Championship lead was now down to a single point.

Much was made at Monza, not only of this being the first win of an obvious future World Champion, but of it also being the first win by a supposed underdog team, Toro Rosso, born out of the ashes of Minardi. The reality was that a well-supported customer team of Red Bull had won a grand prix, benefitting from its access to the most advanced technology in the sport, an army of research personnel and a £500 million budget. We had certainly seen the future at Monza. The arrival of Vettel was exciting, but we had definitely not seen the return of the inspired, adventuring entrepreneur. Formula One was even more the domain of the corporate giants.

I was also aware that we were only four races away from Formula One becoming once again the domain of BBC Television. Monza was the last European race before their new contract began and it struck me as strange that there had so far been no significant BBC presence in the paddock. Even for those who had worked on the sport ten years earlier it was essential to take every opportunity to become familiar with the new personalities and the completely new motor racing environment they were entering. However, that would have to be done at the considerably more expensive long-haul venues that completed the 2008 calendar.

I do not recall seeing any of the future BBC team at Singapore either, but the first-ever Formula One night race would have been a spectacular start to their education. 'A great weekend for Renault and a proud weekend for Formula One' is how race winner Fernando Alonso described the Singapore Grand Prix; but with the benefit of hindsight, the opposite is true.

There were those who left Singapore with an uneasy feeling

at the coincidental manner in which Renault's return to winning form had been achieved. There was the poor qualifying session, the nonsensical gamble on a light fuel load, and then the mysterious crash of Alonso's teammate Nelson Piquet Jr that brought the safety car out at the absolutely optimum time; a million-to-one shot had seemingly come off, and on what was a particularly high-profile race for the team's sponsors.

It was a year later that a disgruntled Piquet made sure the full story of 'Crashgate' came out, a scandal that was probably more damaging to the reputation and prestige of the sport than 'Spygate' the year before. The thought that a driver could be instructed to deliberately crash a car in the middle of a Formula One Grand Prix prompted outrage and disgust and saw the once proud Flavio Briatore thrown out of the sport.

Singapore did not deserve its innovative night-time grand prix to be remembered in this way. The logistical and technological achievement in closing streets, reorganising downtown Singapore and providing daylight-standard lighting was astonishing, and all so that European television viewers could watch the coverage at a more civilised hour.

But Singapore was proud of what it had achieved and when the track was ready and the lights came on for the first-ever race at the Marina circuit you would have thought it was bound to be a great moment; Singapore was ready but unluckily Bernie Ecclestone was not. Eighteen shiny new race-prepared Fiat 500s had been brought in for the first actual race under the lights but unfortunately Bernie had forgotten to book any drivers. On the Saturday morning he explained this to me and wondered if I and any of my 'chums' from ITV would fancy a drive, and he'd fill the rest of the grid with 'blokes' from the press room. In the end the press, in particular those who were not working too hard, filled the bulk of the grid. This was despite the fact that the season's biggest contingent of ex-World Champions, including Rosberg, Häkkinen and Fittipaldi, were present at the circuit that weekend.

It was another depressing example of Formula One arrogance and complacency, and you had to feel sorry for the Singapore organisers. After all their investment and originality, Formula One had rewarded them with a bunch of journalists in Fiat 500s for their opening race, and a 'fix' for the main feature. It failed even to have a huge effect on the title battle, although with Massa out of the points Hamilton's third place meant that he led by seven as we moved on to Japan and China.

It was enough of a lead to crank up all the excitement and anticipation that this time Lewis might actually nail down the title. Three races to go, the run-in to glory started in earnest at the Fuji circuit, but ITV decided that an FA cup-tie at Havant and Waterlooville was a greater priority for me. Any protest was pointless because it would just prompt the depressing reminder that in two months' time football would be my full-time future.

But at least it gave Martin Brundle his one opportunity to move out of the commentary box and into the role of main presenter, and when I joined up with him later that week in Shanghai he was still buzzing from the experience, which I found strange but quite gratifying. He described it as the biggest adrenalin rush since he climbed out of a Formula One car and it was an interesting perspective on the presenter's role.

I've always regarded the role as being that of a kind of conductor of the orchestra, the navigator of the ship, although definitely not the captain. You have to be able to steer the programme through its many junctions and landmarks, and because of the commercial breaks there are far more of those on ITV than BBC. Like a conductor you need to be able to orchestrate the contributions of the guests and pundits, which is mostly percussion and brass in Formula One, and (this might seem glaringly obvious) you need to listen to what they are saying.

This is harder than it seems because you also have to pay careful attention to the constant instructions from the editor, director and PA that are coming down what seems like a bad, crackly phone line into your earpiece, the same earpiece through which you are also meant to be listening to your pit-lane guest. On several live occasions I knew the guest was talking because I could see his lips moving, but I was praying that he did not either stop or come out with an amazing revelation or, heaven forbid, ask me a question, because for ten seconds I would be absorbing a vital instruction from the producer and if I did not get it right the programme would surely fall off the air.

The perfect environment in which to conduct this role is in a darkened room with a cold towel on the forehead; the second best is in a purpose-built air-conditioned studio with a high-definition monitor, autocue and state-of-the-art communications, plus sandwiches and coffee. The worst environment, bordering on the impossible, is in a Formula One pit-lane, hassled by a jobsworth, drowned out by a McLaren, run over by a Renault, with only an intermittent feed of the programme and sporadic communications. Oh, and by the way, could you see your way clear to injecting a bit of originality and personality into the thing as well?

This was the leap into the unknown that got the adrenalin pumping for Martin Brundle, and watching in the early morning from my hotel in Havant he handled it all annoyingly well, especially as he was then still required to head to the commentary box where he had to be fresh and up-to-date with all the stories and possibilities for the race ahead.

Martin, quite correctly, was among the first to be offered a place on the new BBC team, and one of the first to go public with his acceptance. Out of all the sports I have worked on and all the broadcasters I have worked with, few have embraced the challenge and opportunities of the job with quite the relish of Martin. The feature ideas spin off him, and his technical analysis – especially in partnership with the brilliant video production skills of ITV's Kevin Chapman – have rightly won a succession of awards. All the control he had in the cockpit he likes to bring to the commentary box, and it did not surprise me when, a couple of years down the line, he had a successful season as the main commentator on the BBC coverage.

In Japan he had to present, commentate and then analyse a very disappointing, error-strewn day for Hamilton that saw him start on pole position but finish only 12th. His character and determination came through, however, in Shanghai, with a race win that helped to erase the memory of the manner in which his title challenge had unravelled at the grand prix of China the year before.

It was in the vast empty acreage of the Shanghai paddock that the new BBC team turned up in significant numbers for the first time. It was good to see my former colleague Mark Wilkin and welcome Jake Humphrey to this, his first serious look behind the scenes at a Formula One grand prix. Jake and I shared the same agent and I had known for some time that he was going to take on the BBC F1 presenter's role. I thought it was an excellent, brave decision, although inevitably many regarded him as just 'the bloke off kids' telly', but he was ready to put in the hours of preparation to win over the hardcore of Formula One; in particular he had that enthusiasm and sense of wonder about the sport which after 30 years and the recent batterings of 'Spygate' and 'Crashgate' I was finding increasingly hard to muster.

Because of this I never considered myself a candidate for the BBC job. I did have one rather obtuse lunch with the man who had been installed as BBC Head of Formula One, my former *Sportsnight* producer Niall Sloane (more of him later). We seemed to talk of everything except what was going to be happening in 2009, but I did take the opportunity to plant a few names of people behind the scenes who, in my experience, would help give the BBC a flying start. That was also the gist of my conversation in China with Mark Wilkin, who despite his apparent late arrival on the 2008 scene seemed to be prepared and confident and, in my opinion, was the best BBC appointment of all.

So we were very conscious of the BBC team waiting in the wings; Martin Brundle also spent much of the weekend introducing himself to his new colleagues. But for ITV it was not over just yet. There was one more grand prix to come, probably the last in my time of front-line involvement. It could bring us a British World Champion at last, but no one could imagine we would sign off with one of the greatest Formula One stories of all time.

Hamilton had a seven-point lead over Felipe Massa in the Drivers' Championship heading to the Brazilian Grand Prix at Interlagos. The simple mathematics were that if Hamilton finished no worse than fifth, the title would be his, irrespective of what Massa did in the race. A large part of the British press, it seemed, were celebrating early, on the assumption that this was such a routine requirement for Hamilton that there was no way he could fail.

In fact the challenge facing Hamilton was anything but routine; it is sometimes an achievement simply finishing a grand prix, let alone one with this kind of agenda and pressure. Eddie Jordan rather ungallantly proposed that Hamilton could settle things by taking Massa out in the style of Senna against Prost; it was also suggested that Hamilton had not made a huge number of friends down the grid in the course of the season and there would be some who might be looking to ease Massa toward the title.

And then there was the psychology behind claiming a 'mere' fifth place: do you go aggressive with all the risks involved, or do you go defensive and make yourself equally vulnerable? It all seemed so easy, but this was the Formula One equivalent of the four-foot putt to win the Open, or the penalty kick to keep England in the World Cup, or the single run required for a century at Lord's; the more time you have to think about it, the harder it becomes.

It was probably just as well that Lewis was not given much time to dwell on things in the build-up to the race; he would have been forced to recall his erratic performance in similar circumstances at São Paulo the previous year, and his ill-judged lunge on the opening lap which had cost him any chance of victory in the Japanese Grand Prix a month earlier.

And from the ITV point of view it was just as well we did not have time to brood on things and could concentrate on making our last grand prix a very special sporting occasion for the huge audience. This involved, I'm embarrassed to say, being persuaded to perform alongside Lewis in recording a kind of farewell ITV rap, the kind of thing that would be far better suited to Jake Humphrey in years to come, as the uncomfortable look on Lewis's face amply testified.

Behind the scenes we were determined to mark the occasion in a more traditional fashion and on the Friday night booked the entire ITV team into a very convivial restaurant in the centre of São Paulo that was a regular haunt of the Formula One fraternity. Everyone, from riggers to commentators, was in the party. The steaks arrived, the wine and Caipirinha flowed, and the bill started to mount up.

Needless to say, the evening had not been prompted by a message from our bosses to 'go out and enjoy yourselves and thanks for all your hard work'; in fact I am not sure we had a message from ITV management at all. I'm sure we could have smuggled a bit of the tab past them, but not the kind of bill that was being compiled. With some trepidation James Allen and I called the waiter over and told him we needed to settle up. He smiled and said, 'Nothing to pay, it's all been taken care of by the gentleman in the corner', and he pointed to Ron Dennis, who was deep in conversation with Martin Whitmarsh. A classy gesture, which was hugely appreciated by the whole team and in no way influenced our coverage two days later.

On race day, Hamilton, with the help of his father, tried to immerse himself in a bubble of normality. There was clearly a plan. Hamilton had qualified fourth with Massa on pole, but Hamilton was probably carrying a heavier fuel load and had intimated that if he finished the race where he started, that would be just fine.

The atmosphere was unbelievably tense, and also oppressively humid. Ten minutes before the scheduled start came a heavy rain shower and there was a delay and a scramble to the pits to switch to intermediates. When the race started Hamilton was able to preserve his fourth position but David Coulthard was hit by Nico Rosberg, and his final grand prix before retirement (and a position as a BBC pundit) ended early.

Hamilton was caution personified, taking an age to get past the Force India of Fisichella after the first round of pit-stops. In fourth place he was on schedule for the title, but with Sebastian Vettel pushing hard behind he could afford absolutely no mistakes; up ahead, Felipe Massa with a string of fastest laps appeared to be a certainty for race victory.

As the laps were ticked off the anxiety grew. Interlagos is one of the most atmospheric circuits, based around a Brands Hatch-like bowl, and the crowd is the most fervent, knowledgeable and joyously vocal of the season. They had been making their noise since eight o'clock in the morning in anticipation of crowning a Brazilian world champion. With eight laps to go that was still a possibility, but something needed to happen to Hamilton.

Interlagos is the place to persuade you that Formula One, especially working in Formula One television, is by no means glamorous. The paddock is scruffy and cramped, and with those last few laps to go Mark Blundell, the other three members of our ITV crew and I were sitting around a white plastic table doing our best to follow the drama on the small pole-mounted television monitor. Ominously the picture was getting sharper because the skies were getting darker.

What happened as the drizzle began to turn into heavy rain has now been analysed and argued over for more than three years. James Allen and Martin Brundle had to make instant judgements and calculations on behalf of ITV viewers, and they got it right where so many – including Ferrari and

BBC Radio – were left confused. It was ITV's last four laps of Formula One coverage and thanks to James and Martin it was perhaps their best.

Hamilton and Vettel, battling for fourth place, both came in for their tyre changes on lap 66. Up until this point Lewis reckoned he was comfortable and just looking to preserve his Championship-winning position. That was all to change when Robert Kubica, trying to un-lap himself, forced Hamilton wide, Vettel got through, and suddenly with two laps remaining Hamilton was out of the top five and Massa was heading not only to victory but also to the World Championship title. The ITV group, drenched by the rain, had abandoned the white plastic table in the paddock and had taken refuge under the only available shelter, the awning of the Ferrari garage; just like the audience back home we could not believe the title was slipping away in this manner; surely there was no way back? But Mark Blundell spotted the opportunity at just about the same time as Martin Brundle.

McLaren were urging Hamilton to 'get past Vettel... you have to get past Vettel', when in fact the real target, and the escape route to the world title, was Timo Glock. The Toyota driver had stayed out on dry-weather tyres, had got himself up to fourth, and was now just trying to hang on through the final lap as he lost virtually all grip.

The overtaking moves that took first Vettel and then, crucially, Hamilton past Glock on the run to the final corner were hardly spectacular, and from Glock's point of view they were impossible to resist, but Formula One had never seen a more thrilling, glorious climax to the World Championship season. Lewis Hamilton had won the ultimate prize.

At this point we had about 25 minutes to off-air, we were deep into Sunday-evening prime time, and despite an exultant 11 million audience who were just coming to terms with what they had seen, as far as ITV were concerned the story had been told and they did not want us hanging around. So ITV's final moments of live Formula One coverage became a celebratory blur. After Mark Blundell had so sympathetically broken the news to the Ferrari computer boffins that their man was not World Champion, we headed out into the pandemonium of the pit-lane.

Lewis had been well past the chequered flag and well into his wind-down lap before he had it confirmed that he was World Champion, and many others were still trying to work out the astonishing events of the last couple of laps. We had to get the reactions fast, and Ted Kravitz ploughed through sharp elbows and a microphone-wielding mob to get the first thoughts of the new King of Formula One. Up on the podium Felipe Massa was being applauded as winner of the Brazilian Grand Prix, but a bigger issue had been resolved, and it was astonishing that Formula One had created no ceremony, no celebration or press conference to acknowledge the winning of the title.

In the pit-lane the rain was now hammering down. Ron Dennis was soaked through, so too Martin Whitmarsh. All that was ignored, because their exultant emotions were born out of all the crises, accusations and penalties of the previous two years, as well as their pride in a World Champion, the youngest in history, who had been part of McLaren since his childhood.

In the midst of all this it was right to pay tribute to the dignity of Felipe Massa, paraded as race-winner but not as World Champion. The manner in which he, and his father, absorbed the most cruel of disappointments was an object lesson to all those in Formula One and at the highest level of sport.

And then it was the task of taking ITV F1 off the air for the final time, at least in terms of live coverage, and the message was obvious: after nine years with the network, on the last corner of the last race of the last season, we had finally got a British World Champion.

This was the second time I had paid off a network's coverage of Formula One (I tried to resist taking it personally). Nine years earlier at the end of the Japanese Grand Prix I shook the hand of Nigel Mansell and walked out into the grey dawn of a White City Sunday morning; Formula One was going to ITV. Now, I walked out of the back of the paddock and down the hill through the rainy darkness of the São Paulo infield; Formula One was going back to the BBC.

At the television compound they were already winding in cables and dragging monitors off racks. There were thanks all round and the odd handshake, and then came the battle through the interminable São Paulo traffic to a much-delayed flight back to London that took in an unscheduled three-hour stop in Madrid; and that was it, my glamorous involvement with the coverage of Formula One was over. The only consolation was that the BBC, deep into their preparations for the 2009 season, would have been watching Brazil and wondering 'Will we ever get a better story than that?'

Football commitments back home had prevented me taking part in any more of the exuberant McLaren post-race celebrations, not that I was entirely in the mood, but that was more than made up for by being asked to act as Master of Ceremonies for some of the events surrounding Lewis's homecoming a few days later.

First there was a breakfast reception at Claridges in which, within a few hours of getting off the plane from São Paulo, he had to explain and enthuse over the particular features of a certain newly launched mobile phone. Then I went ahead of him to the McLaren Technology Centre at Woking where the entire workforce had gathered in the futuristic reception area, flanked by the cars that marked the company's progress through the sport, and occasional dominance of Formula One. The latest car to join the hall of fame, the McLaren Mercedes MP4 23, the car that had produced the team's first World Champion in eight years, was just about to make its entrance.

Lewis had climbed into his overalls at the front gate, and now, in spectacular celebratory style, blasted the car round the narrow path that formed the edge of the lake in front of the

Technology Centre. If he had got it wrong it would have been the picture of the year, but he got it absolutely right, and a few seconds later the glass doors had hissed open and the reception area was full of tyre smoke, the smell of burning rubber and the sound of tumultuous applause.

It was an occasion that really served to emphasise that even though Formula One is huge business, it remains at heart a team effort, represented not only by the race crew and the gurus on the pit wall but by the office staff, accountants and research personnel back home. Get them all together in the reception area in their red for victory tee-shirts and they number the best part of a thousand. In most other companies they would have nothing more than an end of year balance sheet to celebrate, but at McLaren they had a World Champion with a big smile and a big thank you for each one of them. It was all the embodiment of team effort and team celebration.

There was something similar but not quite as heartfelt a couple of hours later when I introduced the new World Champion on to the stage at Vodafone headquarters at Newbury. For the team's biggest and most energetic sponsors this was success by association, but it was an education to watch how Lewis had precisely the right message for the assembled workforce and endless patience with all the demands still being made of him in his exhausting schedule.

But then again he was a World Champion with a glorious future ahead of him; we were ITV with one more small highlights programme left to record before our race was run. Martin Brundle and I got together to record our links for this one morning in December at Silverstone, followed by a quick lunch at the Green Man in Syresham. After that it was a handshake in the car park, I wished him all the best with the BBC, and that was it. I headed off to be a full-time football presenter.

It was certainly the end of an era, but nothing in terms of emotion or significance compared to what was happening, at exactly the same time, a mile down the road at the Honda factory in Brackley. There Jenson Button was meeting the factory staff in what was a poignant contrast to the exultant reception for Lewis at Woking. At Brackley, Jenson Button and everyone else was trying to come to terms with the bombshell news that Honda were pulling out of Formula One. Potentially the team was no more, and Jenson was no longer a Formula One driver.

Chapter 24

ANOTHER NEW
BEGINNING

For ITV there was one mildly satisfying footnote to everything that had happened in 2008. Having won a BAFTA for our coverage the previous two years, ITV were nominated yet again, this time for our coverage of the Brazilian Grand Prix. It was a fairly meaningless nomination because the programme was up against the epic coverage that the BBC had given to the Beijing Olympics; the coverage had already, quite correctly, seen Chris Hoy sweep Lewis Hamilton aside in the voting for BBC Sports Personality of the Year.

One Sunday evening the following April, I had driven back from Thruxton after an exhausting but satisfying day hosting the British Touring Championship for ITV 4. All the preparation and then seven hours of live coverage always takes its toll, and I stretched out in front of the television and started watching *Heartbeat* with a large glass of white wine.

At that moment one of the neighbours rang and said 'Congratulations! I assume you're watching the BAFTAs...?' I switched over and there was Neil Duncanson receiving a third BAFTA on behalf of ITV Formula One. Although I was one of the names on the trophy my first thought was that the award had been clinched by the outstanding commentary of James Allen and Martin Brundle; my second thought was for the massed ranks of the far more deserving BBC Olympic team, who were present in large numbers in the auditorium ready for the celebration, now, no doubt, outraged by the result. My third reaction was that it just summed up how bloody stupid the whole business was, so I poured another large white wine and went back to watching *Heartbeat*.

By this time, anyway, the BBC Formula One team were well into the season and well into their stride. They had been gifted a fantastic story but were delivering it with skill and energy and (it has to be said with the help of airtime, budget and facilities) were rapidly moving the coverage on from where ITV had left it.

Jenson Button was an also-ran when ITV bowed out at the end of the 2008 season. He had amassed a total of only three World Championship points and had been outperformed by his teammate Rubens Barrichello. But only two years earlier, before Lewis had arrived on the scene, Jenson had been a race-winner and the focus of British interest. It was impossible to think that all that smooth driving style, maturity and new-found fitness and dedication was going to bring him so little.

At Honda a lot of work had gone into preparation for the new season, and they were optimistic that with Ross Brawn at the helm they could make a highly competitive interpretation of the sweeping 2009 rule changes. But the Honda bosses could not see past the balance sheet, which is why in December they had pulled the plug. The team was doomed and Jenson seemed to be cast adrift. However, the close season transformation became one of the most astonishing stories that Formula One has ever produced.

As potential suitors shied away, Mercedes were persuaded to support the team, which was to be renamed Brawn, and never was a single name so totally going to dominate a season.

From trailing around at the back of the field as Honda in Brazil, the same team were unbeatable as Brawn in Melbourne in March. The brilliant Ross Brawn, with his imaginative interpretation of the rule changes, had given the relaunched team such an astonishing advantage it was now down to Jenson to get as many wins and points in the bank before the rest caught up in the summer.

He did it with the cool assurance that we knew had become

his trademark as his Formula One career had progressed, and it was reassuring that perhaps the most technically gifted driver in the field was, at last, being rewarded. But at the same time it identified something irritating and unsettling about Formula One as a supposed sporting contest.

World Championships exist to identify the greatest performers in sport; in their purest form they have been able to easily single out Usain Bolt as the fastest man in the world; after that it gets a bit complicated. Federer, Nadal and Djokovic battle it out to be recognised as the greatest tennis player on any particular weekend, while in golf the recent major championships have named only who has found luck and who has found form. That, I suppose, is the imperfection and the beauty of sport.

But the Formula One World Championship is supposed to tell us who is the greatest driver in the world – except that, probably, the World Rally Championship is far more efficient in this respect. The Formula One World Champion is almost inevitably a good driver (sometimes a great one), in what is demonstrably the best car of that season.

In the winter of 2008/09 Jenson had not gone from the back of the grid to the front in terms of driving ability, but his car had gone from being an also-ran to a world-beater, which is why Jenson ended the 2009 season as World Champion. It is the inherent, unsatisfactory nature of Formula One as a driving contest, and we should not think any the less of Jenson's achievement because of it.

One of the quotes that made the biggest impression on me when I started to work in Formula One was James Hunt saying in 1978, after Mario Andretti had won the title, 'You could have put any driver on the grid in that Lotus 79 and they would have won the title.' He was probably right, but to me the sport lost a bit of its mystique that day.

It was also true the following year when Jody Scheckter won the title in the outstanding Ferrari, and in 1980 when Alan Jones was unbeatable in the Williams FW07. Then when Nigel

Mansell took the title in record-breaking fashion in another Williams in 1992 it was clear that Formula One had become a technological and engineering exercise, with the driver just required to become a solid and reliable component hoping that he was in the right seat at the right time.

When I talked to each of these drivers in detail for the Sky *Legends* series over the last year they all conceded that maybe their World Championship season had not been their greatest driving season, but each saw their World Championship titles as reward for past endeavour and sacrifice.

So to identify the best driver in Formula One maybe you have to go back down the grid, into the midfield, to find a driver who is scoring occasional points but punching above his weight and outperforming the limitations of his car. That for many years had been Jenson Button, and he had been paid back handsomely in 2009, but to my mind what came after that, especially getting the better of Hamilton for long periods at McLaren, has been Jenson at his absolute best.

So the BBC got an astonishing story in their first year back on the circuit; they handled it well, and the audience grew. David Coulthard and Eddie Jordan became a lively pit-lane double act and the team made excellent use of all the new technology available, especially the post-race red-button interactive facility that gave the opportunity for increased reaction and analysis, aimed at the more diehard Formula One fans.

My own ITV contract had me seeing out the back-end of the football deal and especially gave me the chance to work with a greater commitment on the ITV 4 coverage of the British Touring Car Championship and all the support race action that went with it. Through the hard work and belief of many people, especially producer Simon Parry, the coverage had evolved into a fully live seven-hour spread of race action that reflected the dynamic heart of British motorsport.

ITV might have run out of energy when it came to Formula One, but here on this television backwater, apparently without the interest or involvement of too many of the high-flying executives, it was making its peace with the British motorsport viewers. Typical of that was the final meeting of the 2009 season, which decided not only the Touring Car title but the majority of the support programme as well.

The dramatic and emotional manner in which Colin Turkington had taken the title was almost a match for what we had seen in São Paulo 12 months earlier, and alongside that the young chargers in the Ginettas, the more experienced racers in the Porsche Carrera Cup and the future Formula One challengers in Formula Renault, produced equally thrilling action across the whole afternoon in front of a huge Brands Hatch crowd. For me it was one of the most satisfying motorsport outside broadcasts that I had ever worked on, and I am delighted that the audiences and the ITV commitment seems to be growing still further.

So after all the upheaval of the Formula One switch, everyone seemed to be happy apart from the odd confused ITV executives who kept wondering why we had ever got rid of such a prestigious sporting property, and the growing number of angry voices from the deeper recesses of the BBC Sports department.

From my conversations with former colleagues there was increasing despondency at the manner in which budgets were being reduced and staff and facilities had been cut back in order to accommodate this new motorised monster that was dominating the schedules. There was resentment among the BBC Golf team that their once proud schedule of events had been hacked back by around 75%, and even the seemingly untouchable Masters at Augusta had surrendered half its live rights to Sky. The same story and the same opinions could be heard in other departments such as Racing, which feared it was heading for extinction.

In every case the finger was pointed, sometimes unfairly, at Formula One, which seemed to be demanding a disproportionate slice of the budget while serving only one specialised section of the sports audience.

This was all part of the uncomfortable transition that the BBC had no chance of avoiding, that required them to participate in an ever more competitive sports rights market while still trying to satisfy viewers who had grown up with the good old BBC delivering just about every major event on a free to air plate – 'After all, it's what we pay the licence fee for...!'

What the BBC had to do was plan and prioritise, and be ruthless and clear-sighted in the way they did it. To what degree should they battle for the big occasions compared to a commitment to grass roots or emerging sport? How closely do they analyse what is well catered for in other broadcast media and does not require the attention of the BBC? To what level should they use public money to engage in expensive rights-bidding in order to further line the already well-insulated coffers of the Premier League or Bernie Ecclestone?

In this context the manner of the BBC Formula One deal of 2008 remains a very expensive example of getting it wrong. The spontaneous smash and grab nature of it all had enabled the BBC to generate some triumphant headlines, but now the bills were starting to come in and the internal discontent was getting stronger.

And then the bloated nature of the deal became even more apparent when the licence fee was frozen and the BBC was faced with making cuts and redundancies across its entire production operation. The pressure increased on Mark Wilkin and the team to justify their existence with even more high-quality coverage, which they did, but they were also reliant on the sport continuing to produce the drama of the previous three years, and the potential dominance of Sebastian Vettel and Red Bull was looking threatening. Even with great racing and a growing audience, the BBC was clearly facing the kind of Formula One accountancy crisis that had seen off ITV in 2008.

Chapter 25

ANOTHER PARTING OF THE WAYS

In the meantime reckless behaviour and marginal business sense was not confined to the BBC. Over at ITV in the spring of 2010 I was into the last few months of my contract, which would conclude with presenting the World Cup in South Africa. I know everyone should get excited about working on a World Cup but this one looked a bit more of a chore. Although the previous World Cup in Germany had been great to work on with its travel and stadium presentation, it seemed that this time we would all be confined to a Johannesburg studio behind high security for the entire duration. But at least it looked like a big event to effectively close my career, and I was well into my research and preparation.

Early one Sunday morning towards the end of April I got a call from Head of Sport Niall Sloane, wondering if I had seen that morning's *Sunday People* (which of course I had not), and referring to an exclusive announcing that Adrian Chiles was joining ITV to present the relaunched *Breakfast* programme and was taking over ITV's football, including the World Cup in South Africa; and he said, very solemnly, that the story was true.

I can't honestly say I was that surprised. Adrian had been waiting in the wings for so long and I had been plugging the gap for so long, but the fact that he was now stepping in without any discussion and with three months left on my contract was a bit rich. But what annoyed me most of all was that despite being in the communications industry I was left to hear about it from the *Sunday People*.

Just a few weeks earlier I had been alongside Director of

Programmes Peter Fincham helping to launch the ITV World Cup coverage, but now despite repeated calls to his office it was three days before he came back to me with any kind of explanation or even a begrudging apology. In that time Adrian had been unveiled at an ITV press conference as ITV's new football presenter and, most importantly, as the exciting fresh face of ITV's new *Breakfast* programme that was apparently going to take the whole network into a dynamic modern era.

I am not a great one for bad language, but when Peter Fincham eventually rang me I'm afraid I did let rip for a few minutes. When things had calmed down I explained the circumstances by which I had been filling the ITV football chair for the previous two years in anticipation of the arrival of someone like Adrian, and I felt it was a good appointment of someone who was far more in tune with the ITV football audience. However, I pointed out my revised contract that took me through to the end of the World Cup in South Africa and I also expressed my reservations about his breakfast TV potential. I was then lectured by Peter Fincham about how he understood these things better than I, and had spotted his talent from way back. 'But let's not argue about that now,' he said; 'give me a ring in a year's time and you'll see I was right.'

I have been generous enough not to make that phone call and I was not keen either to end the conversation in the spirit of bonhomie that he was eager to generate. What had been obvious to me from the phone call was that he had no idea that my contract had been rewritten to formally include the 2010 World Cup, and that ITV were massively in breach of it.

The next couple of weeks were pure farce. I was told that Adrian had been working hard and wanted to take some time off before starting his ITV commitment so I would still be doing the remaining England internationals and the FA Cup Final as per my contract. 'Is this the contract that ends with the 2010 World Cup? I'm sorry, but I did my last ITV football the weekend before the *Sunday People* came out.'

The daft thing is that with a bit of communication the unpleasant side of the whole business could have been avoided. Adrian has turned out to be an excellent addition to the ITV Football team and, with certain arrangements in place, I would have been more than happy to ease his path into the role. But now lawyers were involved, injunctions were being prepared, and sensible thinking had ceased to exist, illustrated by the offer that ITV made to me, twice, to join the *Daybreak* presentation line-up by way of compensation!

The settlement, when it came, was at a level I cannot disclose, but I would have been very unhappy if I had been an ITV shareholder. The settlement also included the presenter's role at the 2011 Rugby World Cup, which was a far more appropriate conclusion to my 'non-motorsport' life in front of the camera.

It was in the spring of 2011 that the rumours grew suggesting that the future of Formula One on the BBC was becoming more and more uncertain. The freezing of the licence fee had meant that the internal savings and cost-cutting required were savage and across the board, and in that context the sport was seen as a very expensive luxury. At the same time it was suggested that Rupert Murdoch had strong ambitions to buy into Formula One, these being the days before the News Corp phone-tapping scandal had spiralled out of control. Those ambitions had to be shelved, but maybe they paved the way for the announcement that came in July.

In what seems to be the time-honoured tradition, the BBC team in the field were 'hung out to dry' by the timing of the bulletin. Just as we, three years earlier, had to absorb the announcement that ITV were pulling out as we were assembling in Kuala Lumpur for the Malaysian Grand Prix, the BBC team got the news as they gathered in the Hungaroring paddock. The BBC, although they were extending their contract for the sport through the next seven years, were stepping back from exclusive live coverage. Sky would be transmitting every race live, the BBC would do only ten live with extended highlights of the rest. For the first time subscription television had a foothold in Formula One, and for the first time the BBC were pulling back from a sport mid-contract.

This is the age of spontaneous reaction and instant communication, and in terms of tweets and social media, what came out of the Hungarian Grand Prix paddock and the rest of the Formula One community over the next few hours might even have surprised the BBC executives who were busy trying to persuade us that they had saved the sport for the nation.

Martin Brundle gave it a surly 'not impressed', which was an early indication that he was the number one candidate for the Sky F1 commentary box, while Jake Humphrey, who had become a tweeting cheerleader for all things BBC, tried to suggest 'it was only sport', which was a bit of a misjudgement of the mood of his audience.

To them it was a 'sell-out', and 'a betrayal'. They may have been passionate about Formula One, but the thought of paying extra to watch it – especially if the payment was to the 'discredited' Murdoch empire – was a 'scandal'. It was a reaction that overlooked the detail that via a variety of strands and outlets the Formula One audience was about to be served better than ever before.

The contentious element was not the passing of the rights, or even a portion of the rights, from one broadcaster to another, but for the live rights to be taken out of the free to air environment for the first time. It was a duplication of the position that ITV had found themselves in at the start of the 2008 season. In theory ITV could also have said 'We need to make savings but we also want to hang on to the sport', and done the same 50/50 deal incorporating Sky. In those circumstances it would have been a distinct possibility that the dramatic finale to the 2008 season would only have been seen live by a subscription audience.

But instead ITV, as far as I can understand, whether it was for reasons of honour or naivety, told Bernie Ecclestone they wanted to step aside in favour of any other broadcaster to whom he wished to offer the rights – presumably the BBC.

Three years later the BBC was eager to paint a scenario by which their compromise deal had not only guaranteed the BBC presence in the sport but had also made fantastic internal savings for the BBC. This ignored the fact that there would always be pressure inside Formula One to maintain a terrestrial live presence that would satisfy the high expectations of the sponsors; and it also ignored the fact that there was a substantial and realistic offer on the table from Channel 4 that would have kept the whole of the live sport on a free to air service.

The Concorde agreement that governs the internal administration of Formula One specifically states that television coverage should always be 'kept on free to air where possible'; the quality of the Channel 4 proposal, and the money attached to it, guaranteed that amid all the discussions during the summer of 2011, that total free to air option was always available. Indeed, Ecclestone apparently described the Channel 4 proposal as the best he had ever seen – it covered a wide range of programming and platforms and came from the network that had helped transform the coverage of cricket.

It was at this point in the process that the involvement of Sky was triggered, seemingly by the BBC. As a result the money on offer from their joint proposal soared beyond what Channel 4 could justify. The sport could posture all it liked about audience reach and production quality, but it was money they cared about, and Ecclestone had no problem selling the new compromise between terrestrial and subscription television down the pit-lane, and the only casualties were the hard-pressed Formula One viewers who engulfed the websites with their outrage.

Sky would have been there to pick up the pieces whatever happened, and any suggestion of aggressive, bullying tactics on their part would be seen to be unjustified. But if there was any indication of complicity on the part of the BBC in blocking another terrestrial bid, and they were willing to jettison 50% of the live rights just to maintain their presence in the sport, then the Twitterati and Formula One faithful on tight budgets had every right to cry 'foul'.

As it was, the BBC anticipated that by simply taking this one step back within the contract they would save enough money to guarantee the survival of BBC3, which is an illustration of just what a bloated monster the whole thing had become to the Corporation. The BBC announced that it was delighted that it had been able to preserve its presence in the sport but was careful not to suggest that it had been the only terrestrial option, nor even the best terrestrial option.

The irony is that almost by accident this is an excellent deal for the sport and a good one for the long-term television future of Formula One. What had been preserved was at least a fair percentage of the outstanding production quality of the BBC coverage, and the arrival of Sky had released to Formula One the kind of imagination, resources and airtime that had transformed the sports broadcasting landscape in the UK.

I do, of course, speak as one who, in a small way, was caught up in the Sky recruiting whirlwind that followed the July announcement, with the BBC equally frantically trying to plug the gaps that were appearing in their own ranks. Ted Kravitz, David Croft, Anthony Davidson and, most damagingly, Martin Brundle would move from the BBC across to Sky, and I was delighted to see Ben Edwards – who had been a brilliant commentator on the British Touring Car Championship, among many other things – at last get his chance in the BBC commentary box. On Five Live my old colleague James Allen got the call-up to prove once again that he was maybe the best of the lot.

It looked set to be quite a pit-lane rivalry between the two broadcast organisations and it would be a competitive edge that would surely keep both operations sharp and dynamic. I, however, was battle-weary from the last 15 years and had no great desire to get involved at the sharp end of that particular contest, but was delighted to be invited by Sky to boost their non-existent Formula One archive by interviewing, at length, as many surviving world champions as we could muster and anyone else who would qualify as a legend of Formula One.

This was the perfect job for an old cynic who was tending to view the sport with more affection for the past than enthusiasm for the future. It was my opinion that modern grand prix drivers were struggling to establish their personality and identity amid all the corporate responsibility and photo-opportunities, and a couple of hours in the company of Mario Andretti or Alan Jones just increased the feeling of nostalgia.

But now, along comes Sebastian Vettel, who threatens to dominate the sport in the manner of Michael Schumacher but is not going to suffocate the sport in the robotic style of the seven-times World Champion.

To me the perfect illustration of this came at the 2011 Autosport Awards that I was presenting for the 23rd straight year at the Grosvenor House Hotel. The previous year Sebastian had made a triumphant entrance into the Great Room after winning the title in 2010. That was in marked contrast to Schumacher, who declined to make an appearance at all despite an annual invitation and constant persuasion.

Now, in 2011 the date clashed with an important appointment Vettel had on German television, at which he was due to receive a major award. But without any undue coaxing from us he sent his apologies to the Germans and said he would much prefer to be at our 'fun' evening.

The Autosport Awards *are* fun, and are meant to be light-hearted wherever possible. But up on the stage it is also a long evening and can be a difficult ship to steer. On this occasion we also had to make sure we paid proper respect to the memory of Dan Wheldon, who had died in that horrendous IndyCar crash a few months earlier; we were especially mindful of the mood and were honoured that the Wheldon family were with us in the Great Room that night.

The one area that could produce the compulsory banter was

the nature of the new television deal and the rivalry that it represented. Christian Horner was the first to start it off with a few well-chosen barbs when he presented an early award. Martin Brundle carried it on in more forthright style, and Jake Humphrey mounted a rather po-faced defence of the BBC. Then Jenson Button, keen to give me another Autosport Awards bashing, also piled in on behalf of the Beeb, which was probably the right thing to do.

As the evening drew to a close, and I was dreading the arrival of another smart-arse on the stage, up came Sebastian Vettel to his deserved ovation. He, too, had some ill-informed views on the British television landscape, but he was witty, charming and happy to give his spontaneous insights on the events of the previous season. In a way he made a similar impact to Ayrton Senna on the same stage ten years earlier, but where Ayrton was all smouldering charisma, Sebastian, who had clearly enjoyed the evening so far, came across as a sort of inebriated best man at a wedding. He was difficult to get off the stage, but the audience loved it.

At the end of the awards, and particularly after an evening like this, I head up to the production crew in the gallery, cringing at the libellous statements that might have been made and the inappropriate jokes that might have been cracked. I was consoling myself with the thought that it's meant to be an informal, club-like evening and nothing goes beyond the four walls, when I was called over by an excited dinner-suited researcher who was crouched over a laptop.

'This is fantastic, congratulations,' he said. 'You're trending on Twitter.'

'What on earth does that mean?'

'Well, everyone who has been watching it are now sending messages, and the [Autosport] Awards are the most popular topic on Twitter!'

He went on to explain that for the first time the whole evening had been transmitted live on the Internet, and needless to say, within 12 hours all the juicy bits and clumsy exchanges had been clipped up and smeared all over Facebook and YouTube. It made for some uncomfortable exchanges when I met the Sky hierarchy a couple of days later, and it served to show that the whole communications industry was heading into the kind of waters that, for me, were likely to remain uncharted.

Chapter 26

SO WHAT DOES IT
ALL MEAN?

So in March 2012 the televising of Formula One entered a
new era. What that era promised depended on your point
of view. If you were a Sky Sports marketing executive you were
about to be brought closer than ever before to one of the greatest
spectacles on the planet; if you were a loyal fan not prepared
to pay beyond the BBC licence fee, then the sport – with the
complicity of the BBC itself – had sounded its own death knell
and certainly lost you as a viewer. Myself, I was content to take
a step back and survey the bewildering television journey the
sport had taken in this country.

A mere 34 years ago when I had watched Andretti take
the title there was no great competition for rights, and you
could wander into most Formula One grands prix with a film
camera and whatever broadcast agenda you cared to set. Bernie
Ecclestone, with his aggressive view of the commercial potential
of the sport, created the environment for that all to change.

At the BBC, Head of Sport Jonathan Martin, aided by the
chemistry of Murray Walker and James Hunt and the regular
format of the grand prix highlights programme, helped change
the television profile, even though *Grandstand*, while providing
a regular live showcase, gave the impression that it was never
totally committed.

That commitment came from ITV when it sensationally plundered
the rights in 1997 and helped the sport release the range of state-of-
the-art live broadcast technology that created the modern spectacle.
While they were doing that, helped by a strong, committed

broadcast schedule, the BBC had been taking the attitude that it was a discredited, over-commercialised, environmentally unjustifiable activity that would never interest them again.

Back they came, however, at the merest hint of an invitation in 2009, doing a deal that had broken the bank, but producing coverage that had been an outstanding progression even on ITV's award-winning efforts. And in 2012 they were still investing mind-boggling sums, simply to be a junior partner to Sky, and the two broadcasters combined were committing over 100 production personnel to the opening round in Melbourne.

The opening round in Argentina in 1978 had to battle for late-night highlights on BBC2 and any column inches at all in the Monday-morning papers. But in 2012 every main road into London was flanked by giant Sky billboards counting down to the start of the season, and it was impossible to miss the commercials and trailers promising high definition, Dolby surround sound, interactive opportunities, viewing options and programming platforms. The sport had moved from 30 minutes on BBC2 to its own dedicated channel for satellite viewers plus a strong mix of live action and highlights for the terrestrial audience. The broadcasting transformation was total; but had the sport actually changed?

The diehard fans (perhaps myself included) would argue that if anything it had less appeal. I have referred on a number of occasions already to the modern marketing and commercial straitjacket in which F1 racing finds itself, stifling spontaneity and leaving the sport struggling to establish personalities.

Modern Formula One technology is mind-blowing, and is sometimes an entertaining soap opera, but tends to focus the audience even more. The core audience will always be fascinated by the optimum route for exhaust gases, and the critical tenths of seconds that can be gained or lost. The reality is that despite the brilliant minds, staring at a battery of computer screens, those of us less technologically inclined see a sport still striving to find a way for one car, realistically, to be able to pass another.

Then there is the large part of the audience who will always watch the sport for the daring and danger, with a politically incorrect appetite for disaster. Paying the ultimate price will never be completely removed from the equation, but the sport now is as safe as it is ever going to be. But while applauding the amazing work that has been done around driver safety, it is a bit like professional boxing in head-guards, or uncontested scrums in rugby – it's the same sport, but then again it isn't.

There was still a fantastic anticipation ahead of the 2012 season, and it was amazing to watch from the sidelines as a major broadcaster started filling a blank sheet of paper and delivering one of the biggest new commitments in the history of broadcast sport. But conversely, while the sport was preparing itself for its most advanced coverage ever the documentary movie *Senna* was winning awards and captivating audiences with its portrayal of a season 18 years ago that was looking more and more like a golden age.

There is no sport in the last 50 years that has transformed itself so fundamentally – which is inevitable in a sport that has largely become an arena for designers and engineers. There is no other sport that delivers itself to the audience (at least the broadcast audience) in quite the sophisticated fashion of Formula One; but has the packaging overwhelmed the product, including the simple objective of identifying the best driver in the world?

Commercial ambitions have taken grand prix motor racing into territories with no great motorsport tradition, but with plenty of revenue potential. The drivers have been required to race in anodyne arenas in desert locations, hosted by dodgy regimes. Apart from GP2, there has seldom been an attempt to augment the show with any other track activity of value; rarely is there a support programme of prestige or relevance. As a result, when the Formula One cars fire up in Bahrain or Kuala Lumpur or Shanghai the pictures may go around the world, but the sound echoes off the concrete interiors of empty grandstands.

I can perfectly understand how the balance sheet has taken over Formula One and dominates everything within it. The situation is largely the same in every other form of professional sport. The sport maximises its income at every level from perimeter advertising to admission charges and, most productively, TV rights. At the same time it proclaims the need to cut costs, pointing mainly at the internal testing and development budgets of the teams.

But to my naive, layman's way of thinking there are so many ways to further maximise the value of Formula One.

For a start you have a race schedule that is now up to 20 grands prix a year, going back and forth across the globe taking in five continents. The approach seems to be that the more venues you have, the greater the profit. But it should be 'the more *races* you have the greater the profit'.

The typical grand prix weekend takes in two practice sessions on the Friday, vital to the teams; the diehard fans may love it but the casual spectator would feel a little short-changed. Television tries to show an interest, but it is meagre fare. Saturday has a further practice session and then qualifying, which can effectively be distilled down to 90 seconds of excitement at the end of the third session. The rest of the day is spent behind closed doors in debriefing, press conferences and sponsor duties. Race day has a further warm-up session and the race, and at most circuits little other activity on the track. Once again spectators can leave disillusioned, and it's very moderate stuff for television.

Here's an alternative.

First of all cut down the venues, cut down the cost. Rationalise the calendar.

Friday morning becomes a practice session, and then qualifying in the afternoon. Suddenly a Friday ticket means a lot more to the spectators and the whole day has far more value for television. If you really want to crank up the value and relevance, offer World Championship points for qualifying.

Saturday, a morning warm-up session and then a Formula One race in the afternoon, shorter distance but with World Championship points awarded – very much along the lines of what is already happening in GP2. The purpose would be to design a grand prix weekend where the engineers could show their craft, but also where the drivers could showcase their talents.

Then on Sunday the traditional grand prix.

The purists will protest at every level, but there are so many areas of compromise. If the precious grand prix cars cannot race twice in a weekend, stick the drivers in something else, a level playing-field of single makes. After all, we are trying to identify the best driver in the world.

The benefit for the sport would be a far stronger television product, which equals more expensive TV rights. There should also be bigger attendances and a far stronger atmosphere across the three days of a grand prix, and we would also see the drivers develop their identities and personalities in a far more dynamic racing environment. One essential of this format is that the heartland of the sport, the great venues like Spa, Monza, Monaco and Silverstone, have to be preserved on the schedule forever and not jeopardised by madcap sponsor-driven schemes to race past Buckingham Palace or round and round the Olympic stadium.

Every modern sport has had to adapt and almost reinvent itself to take advantage of the modern commercial environment, cricket being a prime example. It seems strange to me that Formula One, which is the most marketing-driven sport of all, is so slow to react and evolve. But what do I know? By following a policy of responding to the highest bidder and making the requirements of the television viewer and live spectator a pretty low priority, Formula One still sits proudly as the most successful global sporting event.

With the encouragement of KERS and DRS, the racing has come alive, and there is some thrilling young talent emerging who will make sure that the battle for the World Drivers' title maintains plenty of interest through the next ten years.

And the UK television package has never been stronger. It may be a bit more expensive but there is choice, variety and hours of airtime, with both the BBC and Sky at the top of their form in terms of both production and presentation. The BBC claim they are committed for the long term, but there is justification in being nervous about this guarantee; in five years they have gone from an organisation with no enthusiasm for motorsport in any of its forms, to one which now sacrifices its historic involvement in horse racing and live golf in order to have the funds to remain a junior partner in the coverage of Formula One. They claim that the future is assured because Formula One will always need high-profile terrestrial television, but if that is the case, why on earth did the BBC not drive a tougher, more sustainable deal in 2008? I am sure their commitment is genuine, especially if Bernie Ecclestone is imposing his customary penalty cause, but the impression you will have got from earlier pages of this book is that Formula One, especially the television landscape of Formula One, is ever-changing.

***

But the history and the legacy that goes with Formula One will never change, and it has been a thrill to be able to relive some of the great stories with the World Champions of the past, for the *Legends of Formula One* series on Sky.

For example, there was a real sense of privilege sitting down with Sir Jack Brabham, the oldest surviving Champion, and listening to the extraordinary account of the perils and sacrifices that were required to reach the top in the '50s and '60s. In particular his account of how he won the 1959 World Championship, by pushing his stricken car across the finish line at Sebring, made Lewis Hamilton's success at Interlagos in 2008 seem relatively low-key.

Sir Jack is not in the best of health. He requires dialysis

support and has fading hearing and eyesight, and the hour-long interview telling the story of his amazing career required a big effort on his part. We were at his home down the coast from Brisbane, four days away from the Australian Grand Prix in Melbourne.

Despite an invitation to go to Albert Park he clearly was not fit enough to make the journey.

'This is where I will be for the whole weekend,' he said, easing himself into a very comfortable armchair in front of the large plasma television screen. 'Formula One coverage these days is absolutely amazing, I love it.' He paused. 'If only they had had coverage like this in my day.'

Now that really would have been something.

INDEX

INDEX

Leabharlanna Poibli Chathair Bhaile Átha Cliath
Dublin City Public Libraries